BUTTER SIDE UP

Gray and Eleanor Campbell in Banff, 1942. (PHOTO BY PETER WHYTE)

BUTTER SIDE UP

by
Gray Campbell

Horsdal & Schubart

Horsdal & Schubart Publishers Ltd.
Victoria, BC, Canada

Front-cover photograph by Terry G. Farrant, Sidney, BC, 1994.
Back-cover photograph by Lloyd Knight, Lethbridge, Alberta, 1948.
All photographs in the text are from Gray and Eleanor Campbell's collection.
The original edition of *We Found Peace* was published in 1953 by Thomas Allen Limited, Toronto, Ontario.

This book is set in New Baskerville.

Printed and bound in Canada by Kromar Printing Ltd., Winnipeg.

Canadian Cataloguing in Publication Data

Campbell, Gray, 1912-
    Butter side up

    Includes index.
    ISBN 0-920663-32-X

    1. Campbell, Gray, 1912- 2. Gray's Publishing Ltd.—History. 3. Publishers—British Columbia—Biography. 4. British Columbia—Biography. 5. Ranchers—Alberta—Biography. 6. Alberta—Biography. I. Title.
FC3844.25.C35A3 1994   070.5'092   C94-910778-6
F1089.V3C35 1994

FOREWORD

I CALLED Gray Campbell "a national treasure" in *The Vancouver Sun*.

That was in the 1960s when I was book editor at the *Sun*, in the days when there was no book publishing in British Columbia, and perhaps I was trying to shame the elite of Toronto publishers, then the be all and end all of Canadian publishers. Today, this province is swarming with regional publishers. Many do it for the love of publishing, for a book is a precious and wondrous thing. They do it, surely, hoping to make money. and some do. Most, I suspect, do it out of a compulsion I still do not understand.

Gray Campbell led the way. He showed that with dedication and the faith he instilled in others and one hell of a lot of hard work intertwined with almost day-to-day frustrations he, the little guy, could publish regional books that big publishers scorned. But most important, he had an eye and a nose for a good story and if he found one, he would publish it, working out of his fir-shaded house in Deep Cove. He also had a wife, Eleanor, who, as the song goes, "... trusted him all his life."

But if he was born to be a publisher, a few things got in the way. He was a Mountie for seven years and then a bomber pilot during the war. Later, in an office job in Ontario, he realized that this was no life at all, packed family and possessions into an old car and headed west. Knowing nothing about ranching but with that inherent risk factor that all pilots and publishers must have, he bought a ranch in the Alberta foothills backed by his Veterans' Land Act grant. The Campbells were successful, and the government agency wanted to write them up to show their program was working. Eleanor said, "If it's worth a story to them, why don't you write it yourself?" He did: *Maclean's Magazine* bought it, and from that article came his best-selling book *We Found Peace*. And when they sold out and moved to softer climes on Vancouver Island it seemed right he'd try publishing.

Gray being Gray, with that smile in his eyes and voice, first published the book of a blind war veteran named John Windsor because he knew it was a good story. Authors, retired and otherwise, gave him advice. R.M. Patterson, a famous English gentleman and outdoorsman, came to him, perhaps recognizing the character of Gray or to give him a helping hand. That book, *Far Pastures*, is one I still pick up for pure delight. George Clutesi, an Indian artist, was unknown, but he had a story to tell. Gray climbed up on the roof of the Clutesi house, where George was working, to try to convince him that Gray's was interested in publishing his book.

Like any regional publisher, Gray had his tough times. Raising finances or credit. A printer who wanted his money now. A fractious author. Deadlines not met. The 101 problems the readers do not realize can happen when they pick up a book in the store. It is, at all times, a life fraught with perils. Like the 14th-century maps of the world with the mid-Atlantic lettered: "Dragons Dwelleth Here". Gray saw his share of them.

In his quiet voice, he said, "It was always a hustle to sell books and collect accounts in time to pay the printer first, then the authors, and then the operating contingencies," and there were many. What was left was his profit, and when I'd meet him for lunch with a new author, I'd order the cheapest item on the menu—curried rice with shrimp. And after every lunch and interview I'd think "He's still running on air."

Publishing is very sophisticated now. It is like comparing the binder with the self-propelled combine. Gray's operation was mostly himself and his family—his kids took to the road with carloads of books and sold them—and a whole big bunch of friends who realized the value of what he was doing. John Barclay, retired navy commander, worked for free.

Book reviewers were kind to him, not only because of the man but because he produced damn good books that otherwise would not see the light. A Gray's Publishing book had the trademark of excellence and value. But everything must end. He sold Gray's Publishing and has been giving out a ton of free advice and help to old friends and senior citizens in writing and marketing their books.

Gray was the daddy of regional publishing in BC, and now at 82 he is the granddaddy, and this book is probably his last hurrah! As a book editor for five years, an author for 22 years and a reader for all but six of my 69 years, I know what he has done, and, in all sincerity, I say, "I salute you, Gray."

Barry Broadfoot
Nanaimo, BC, 1994

For

Arabella and Adam
Marty and Marina
Ebin and Mira
Asia and Miles

CONTENTS

INTRODUCTION

THIS IS not an easy memoir to write for it is an attempt to do two things at once. At the same time as the older grandchildren were asking how our family arrived on Vancouver Island, a publishing friend was suggesting we attempt an update to our first book *We Found Peace* (1953), which they planned to add to the original book. I have, therefore, tried to please both and it has kept me out of mischief for at least a year. When I say that "we attempt" this project, I refer to my partner, Eleanor, who for 52 years has ridden the roller coaster of thrills and spills trying to keep me on course.

After many drafts on a typewriter, then wrestling with a borrowed computer, I handed the result over to our old, but young, friend Marlyn Horsdal, whose advice I have grown to respect.

Our adventures with Gray's Publishing would never have been possible without the enthusiasm and extraordinary help of the late Clair "Sainty" Rivers, Bill Duthie, Glen Hyatt, and Charlie and Dick Morriss who have handed on the torch to others. All through the experience of trying to get this together I have felt the spiritual presence of Flos Williams, Art Willis, George Pownall and a host of Good Samaritans who made it all possible.

Casting back for highlights after 82 years of an average career, I am forced to add that life is filled with imponderables. There must be at least one "what if" in everyone's life, whether you call it fate or divine guidance. I have been dealt a few dandies. If my room-mate in the Mountie barracks at Banff, Scotty Harrison, had not ordered me to get back into the old Hudson Terraplane because I was the driver, I would have taken one of the Doukhobor bullets that killed Sergeant Wallace and Scotty in 1935. If I had not been grounded in London with the 'flu in 1944, our crew would have been on the battle order when our Lancaster, "C for Charlie", failed to return from a raid on the Ruhr, its fate unknown.

There are twists and turns in life that appear without reason or warning, mundane, unpredictable but, as our Bomber Command squadron motto had it, *"Carpe Diem"*. Time and again we had to seize the day.

This, then, is our attempt to recall some of the highlights.

PART ONE

PART ONE

IN RETROSPECT—BACK TO THE BEGINNINGS

AFTER MY 80th birthday I took time to look more closely at our modest library. Over the years we had acquired an uneven collection of titles, the result of restless attempts at careers that sputtered from military service to book publishing. Through all this, and 50 years of marriage, had I missed any treasures collected along the way, not yet relished?

One morning, I scanned the shelves and ran a finger along the packed titles. My eye fell upon a clean, 1963 volume that opened the flood gates of memory. It was a valued treasure, *Henry Thoreau, American Rebel*, and had been sent to us nearly 30 years ago by the author. I had only skimmed it at the time for I felt familiar with Thoreau, having read Walden in my youth.

T. Morris Longstreth, the author, had been an old friend, and this was probably the last book he had written. By the time he had reached 86 years of age he had published 48 books and was still creating a monthly column for the *Christian Science Monitor*. This volume had reached us when we were settling on Vancouver Island, having left our cattle ranch in southern Alberta after 12 hard years. It was a year after I had accidentally taken a fling at book publishing in an attempt to help a blind war veteran. Caught up in the success of *Blind Date* by John Windsor, I had put Thoreau aside where it had rested comfortably except for the odd dusting.

My thoughts went back to our first encounter in the grey years between world wars. Just out of high school, with restless indecision, I had obtained my first job marking the New York board for the stockbroker firm of E.A. Pearce & Co., in Ottawa. The salary was a magnificent $60 per month when you could buy a pair of shoes for five dollars, a meal for 50¢ and a suit of clothes at Tip Top Tailors for $24!

I had just managed to master the codes and stock-market jargon when the greatest crash in North American history hit the New York Stock Exchange in October 1929, reverberated around the world and introduced the Great Depression. The ticker tape ran hours behind, unable to keep up with millions of shares traded. I watched the daily attendance of regular customers dry up.

One quiet little man continued to appear, standing at the back of the large room, staring at the screen but never taking an empty chair. He spoke only to one of the assistant managers and seemed mysteriously quite out of place. Several of us became curious and were told that he was an American author from Lake Placid who had recently written a history of the Royal Canadian Mounted Police. From my Boy Scout childhood to years in the militia I had admired the appearance and conduct of these redcoats in public.

I went to Hope's book store on Sparks Street, picked up a copy of *The Silent Force* and rushed home with it. For hours I was lost in the stories of adventure, bravery and achievement by these dedicated men, often alone in the wilderness on patrols by horse and dog team. For days my imagination allowed me to escape from the world of growing desperation and I went around almost in a dream state. I was 20 years of age, fit from rowing, skiing, boxing and handball. My world would never be the same again, and here was a chance to escape.

I went looking for the author, Mr. Longstreth, who, after overcoming his initial surprise, told me how to go about joining this world-famous outfit. I had been advised it would not be easy, for there were in the 1930s about three times as many applicants as serving members. If I decided to take the plunge, Mr. Longstreth offered to telephone the adjutant who handled recruiting at headquarters. He must have made many friends while he was writing the book and one of them was the adjutant, Vernon Kemp. I was interviewed, had the medical after completing the written examination, met the commissioner, Sir

James MacBrien, swore allegiance and signed up. I bade farewell to Pearce & Co., told family and friends, then went home to wait.

It seemed only a matter of hours before the telephone jangled and I was instructed to catch the next train west to Regina, where the Depot is established. On the way to the train I stopped at the boarding house where the shy little author was in temporary residence, to have him inscribe my precious copy of his book.

For seven years I endured my share of bumps, bruises and excitement from Banff to cowboy country on the Montana border. Morris followed me all the way, sharing his wisdom and experience. In 1939, with war clouds on the horizon, I purchased my discharge, took the last sailing of the *Aquitania* from New York before the convoys started and arrived in London mid-September. The Longstreth letters followed me for six years as a pilot in the Royal Air Force through training, marriage and a tour in Bomber Command. His letters were post-marked Washington, D.C., Concord, N.H. and Westtown, Pa. He would often include one of his columns from the *Christian Science Monitor*.

Our exchange naturally faltered in the last year of the war when I flew my Lancaster "C for Charlie" touring the Ruhr and visiting nervous naval bases with names like Kiel. But when I returned to Ottawa with an English wife and son we picked it up again. Now an old friend who had maintained a lively interest in me for most of my adult life, he no doubt received his share of my frustration and despair in the unsettled period of adjustment after six years of bitter conflict. While I longed for the freedom of southern Alberta, the chances of returning there in the R.C.M.P. were not encouraging. It was also a family decision, sparked by my wife, Eleanor, who had shared the war years with me from 1941, that I should try life without a uniform.

Unable to adjust to a business career, we took the bit in our teeth and headed west to go cattle ranching. Morris Longstreth never lost interest in our struggles, and our letters to him, together with a diary we kept, resulted in a book. When *We Found Peace* was published in 1953 he reacted enthusiastically and mentioned it in his column. Someone passing through Fort Macleod picked up a copy and a passage from it appeared in *The New York Times* book supplement—pretty heady stuff.

Then we moved to Vancouver Island and took off in several directions, which included 12 years of book publishing. All this came back when I had finished studying the Thoreau book,

On the Campbells' cattle ranch in southern Alberta.

In the heyday of Gray's Publishing. (PHOTO BY DANE CAMPBELL)

turning back to soak up the pearls of thought and digging out some of the last Longstreth letters, which had become shorter and pithier as his sight began to fail and our letters were read to him.

I placed his Thoreau book back on the shelf but I could not let the matter rest there. I opened an old trunk and searched through over half a century of memorabilia. I flipped the pages of scrapbooks full of clippings yellow with age. Finally I found it, a precious poem he had written and sent me in a letter back in the dirty thirties, probably during my romantic years in Banff. It had been published in *The New York Times*.

THE OLD FISHERMAN
Daily he comes there to the shrunken pool,
Made secret by its wind-guard of old pine,
To smoke his pipe and loiter by the cool
Sweet water, like Time's truant, with his line.
Even a child would know no fish are left,
For streams like men may fall on evil days,
Yet still he lingers where his joy ran swift
As a trout leaping .... Now the dusty rays
Of afternoon lie golden on the land
And the tall dark creeps nearer from the wood,
And there he stoops, the old rod in his hand,
For one last try before he goes, for good.
The line floats out ... though not to water flung
But far upon the days when he was young.

TML

In the fullness of time my old friend slipped away as quietly as his Old Fisherman but his memory, his thoughtfulness and generous friendship remain forever green. I never saw him again after that first encounter in 1932, nor did we ever exchange photographs, so I always visualize the soft-spoken, retiring little figure standing at the edge of the overcharged crowd in October 1929. Perhaps it is good to pause a moment now and then to reflect over the years.

*

Eleanor Russell Benson was born in South Africa where her father had worked for the British Civil Service from the time of the South African War. Her Danish mother had joined a family in Kimberley as governess. When little Eleanor was born her mother held her in her arms while the wagons rumbled by relentlessly, carrying the corpses of the victims in the dreaded 'flu epidemic of 1918.

Six years earlier I was born at home in Ottawa, at 177 Stewart Street in Sandy Hill, which today is the older part of the capital. In 1912 Stewart Street had not yet been paved and one crossed the road on a path of sand or ashes at the end of the block, particularly in spring or fall. The empty fields in Sandy Hill were being filled with fairly large, substantial homes.

When my parents were married, their families helped them build a large house next to 179 Stewart, the home of Mother's family. And in the process they connected the third floors of the residences with a covered passage so that Grandmother Gray could keep a Scottish-Presbyterian eye on her flock. She was a dignified, unbending but kindly disciplinarian who read her Bible every day and little else. Her grandchildren cannot remember ever seeing her smile.

There is a lovely family anecdote that illustrates the custom of the time, a hangover from the Victorian age. One Sunday, after church and the usual heavy dinner at noon, the household was somnolent. My father, Ebin Campbell, suggested to George Gray, Mother's brother, that they try a quiet game of billiards and the two conspirators crept quietly upstairs to the billiard room on the third floor of our house. It was out of bounds on Sunday.

They were playing a pleasantly concentrated, quiet game. Uncle George was just lining up a shot when Ebin thought he heard footsteps from the house adjoining and, behind George's back, slipped into a cupboard.

There was a rustle of silk and the tall, thin apparition of Grandmother Gray appeared at the entrance of the passage to 179. She stared, horrified, at Uncle George's back. Just as he was about to take his shot a stern voice cried indignantly, "George, how could you. What would Ebin think of you playing billiards on the Sabbath?" Uncle George froze, turned to face his mother, put his cue away and followed her to do penance in the parlour at 179.

Eleanor's family returned to England from South Africa and when she was four years of age her mother, Henrietta (Petersen) Benson, took our Eleanor to Denmark for about six months to get acquainted with her maternal grandparents. When she returned to her home in England, the child was fluent in Danish but had completely forgotten her English, and went through an uncomfortable period of adjustment. Then she enjoyed a marvellous English childhood, which included piano and dancing lessons, and Roundhay High School for girls where she came to the attention of her geography teacher and the headmistress who took her on wonderful camping trips and journeys to historical sites during the holidays.

While Eleanor was enjoying the enrichment of a classical English background, I was running into the Great Depression of the dirty thirties, escaping into the haven of the Mounties and then going into the Royal Air Force. Eleanor's dancing lessons took her to perform at a recital in the Albert Hall, London, and she began to consider making it a career. When her parents objected to her appearing on the stage she thought of teaching, until she realized she wasn't cut out for it. She graduated from Princess Christian College in Manchester and took a further course in London which qualified her for a position as nurse to the Shepherd children at Robin Hood's Bay in Yorkshire. And there we met.

After Hitler was defeated I joined the other veterans, returning home drained of energy. But I had growing responsibilities and a burning desire for peace.

* * *

PART TWO

PART TWO

WE FOUND PEACE

Chapter One

EVERYONE THOUGHT we were quite mad in 1946. It just
didn't make sense. I can understand now the lack of sympathy
among friends and relatives in Eastern Canada, their pity for the
young girl of 22 whom I had married in war-torn England
during 1941 and for the child she had borne. They did not care
how I wasted my life. But why should I be selfish enough to drag
Eleanor and three-year-old Dane into a doubtful future of
struggle and obviously bitter disappointment? The crazy uncertainty of it all! Hadn't my wife enough sense and control over my
restlessness to ensure her own security and future happiness?

We were then in Hamilton, Ontario, making last-minute plans
to trek West in our modern covered wagon. Eleanor, morally
convinced that her mission in life was to discover where I could
fit into the scheme of things, was daily becoming alive to the
promise of adventure. There must be a place, a condition of
living somewhere, that would untangle the jittery nerves and the
lost feeling of post-war uncertainty. In spite of pleadings and
dire forecasts we were cutting our ties, quitting the job with a
glowing future, and driving west in a 1939 Ford pulling a
second-hand trailer, to start again.

How could those who had not shared the war years interpret
our mood? Ours was a war-time marriage. There wasn't a thing
to recommend its future to a discriminating parent. Eleanor's
mother and father, bless them, saw only one logical reason for

the union. Their daughter was happy in her first love. And her mother got her teeth into the idea. For better or for worse, however bad it might be, and certainly she had no reason for great hopes, her lovely daughter should not rebound to a second choice. She had faced this fact with blind instinct even when, in discussing such a vague future as we faced, reason intruded through the fleeting, blissful days of courtship that were allowed us.

When we married in June of 1941 we simply wanted a chance to live together, with a desperate, hurried feeling that we were not to be cheated out of whatever marriage had to offer, in spite of war. There was no time to consider the future. You couldn't see further than the next few days or weeks. A leave that could be figured in hours, a haven of peace away from the bombing, a period of flying to the next leave. That was it. You could reason it to stretch on as long as mind and coordination of instinct and body for self-preservation could manage the miracle of keeping alive.

During 1941 I was flying "bits of wood and cardboard tenuously supporting twin engines, held together by cold water paste and glue", as one technical officer put it, at the R.A.F. College. While the cream of the class went on to Hampdens, Whitleys and Beaufighters, I remained behind on the staff to instruct, serving in the same flight where I had spent anxious weeks as a pupil. "Plenty of time to get on ops," the Flight Commander said. "The war won't end next week and we'll all get a crack at it."

You may want to know what was behind the person in Air Force uniform. There was very little of interest to fill out the character. He imagined himself important in the eyes of his contemporaries, who were all English. But in truth he was just another undistinguished Canadian with no more background than any stereotyped character—a spotty education, no deep roots, countless friends and seven careless years in the Royal Canadian Mounted Police, beginning at the age of 20. It is necessary to point this out because the police years afforded service in the West, in the Alberta short-grass, foothill and mountain country.

So he was 27 when the war started. But he had not grown up. He was an untested boy scout. The formative years were ahead. The war years.

The good people in England were wonderfully kind to, and tolerant of, the mad but dedicated crowd who arrived in England

during September of 1939. From early in the war Lady Frances
Ryder in London was doing an enormous job helping to keep us
out of mischief. She had some grand people helping her entertain and her house was always open to welcome the strangers
from across the seas. Officials in our legations would suggest we
drift around there to take tea. Our own L. B. Pearson at Canada
House gave us the word and on one occasion Lady Frances interviewed me. She arranged several charming invitations and on my
return to the dreary station I received letters asking me to week-
ends at country homes in Yorkshire.

Not until I had graduated from Cranwell did I accept. It was a
fateful day when I journeyed to Robin Hood's Bay. For there I
met Eleanor. In spite of the war, in spite of the fact I was
crowding 29 and thought I was safe—this was it! Tall, graceful,
athletic and accomplished, she brought fun to everything we did
together, from walking in the rain to sipping tea before the
coziest of fires. It was wonderful, but frightening because of the
war. I wanted to sneak out and send myself a wire recalling me to
duty. But I was weak and stayed on. I talked to Eleanor about
Canada and the days of peace. I tried to express my nostalgic
memories of the happy days in Alberta. Like all people in love
among new friends and kindly strangers we were confident that
no one knew our secret. But to Mr. and Mrs. Harold Shepherd,
our hosts, it must have been quite obvious.

Back at the College the foulest of winter weather washed out
flying and I wrote letters to Eleanor for ten days. Nothing
seemed quite the same. I sneaked back to Yorkshire for a week-
end, met her at Leith Rigg, then at the home of Leo Walmsley,
the Yorkshire author. We became engaged. On the next leave I
journeyed to her home to meet her mother, buying the ring first.
We were engaged for three months but it seemed like an
eternity.

It was a real war-time marriage, but neither the vicar nor
anyone else threw it at us. We were together two months, then
separated for seven. I faced the choice of being posted to Kenya
to instruct or going back to Canada. I couldn't take my wife to
Kenya. I couldn't get her to Canada either, but we didn't know
that and after running into sticky red tape I had a stroke of good
luck. While flying a kite from Halifax to Calgary I ran into L. B.
Pearson at the Chateau Laurier cafeteria. When I told him the
British were holding up Eleanor's passport he agreed that she was
now a Canadian and managed to reunite the Campbell family.

We lived together for a short time in Calgary. Then the station moved to Swift Current where we spent a year and we began collecting furniture for after the war. For the first time since our marriage, life had an even tenor. We began to have faith in the future. Dane was born at Swift Current in 1943 and we had the world by the tail. It was too good to last. There was a sudden posting back to England. The station broke up. Eleanor sold everything we had accumulated, packed and stored a few personal things and moved to Calgary to visit friends. I wangled leave from New Brunswick, flew back to Calgary but failed to see her settled. She managed to rent a one-room summer cottage just outside the city, hung on until the snow drove her out, then travelled east to Ottawa with baby and dog to stay with my sister. The personal treasures and the wedding gifts we had never opened were left stored in Calgary. Some day we hoped to be back.

This second period in England was joyless. Whereas the others were returning to families and friends, I seemed to be more astray than the first time. The original crowd had scattered far and wide. Then I joined the squadron.

It was a tails-up squadron, 576. About a third of the boys were Canucks. A few of us were married types with our wives at home. There was a certain security to life at the squadron. You had 32 trips to make. Okay, let's get it over. Get as many trips in as quickly as possible. Kiel, Hamburg, Cologne, Stuttgart, Leipzig, Bochum. Come on, Johnny, put me down for tonight, I'll find a spare gunner. Life on the squadron changed a lot of things. Sometimes life was grim; it was war and it was for keeps. A lot of the best crews simply disappeared. Sometimes there was fragmentary evidence. We picked our buddies carefully, tried not to get too friendly. It wasn't like the early days. If you relaxed you went large on the right rein. You couldn't stop to speculate or dream. Maybe you let yourself go in letters, but you wouldn't admit it. You hesitated to get too close with anyone but your own crew. Close friends had a nasty habit of leaving a big gap. And you treated replacement crews like outcasts.

I remember a new skipper arriving with his bunch to replace one of the best crews we had ever had. You hated to look his way because he reminded you of the loss and made you wonder just what had happened. It wasn't the poor guy's fault, but for weeks he was left outside the pale. Johnny Acheson spoke to him first and said to me: "Cam, this fellow is O.K." So we cultivated him, and indeed he was. We began to forget the other crew. When the skipper got word his wife had been delivered of a son we all helped him celebrate. We began to look for him in the mess, share our jokes and horseplay. Against our better judgment we accepted him.

Not many nights later we returned from a hot target. Johnny and I waited in the briefing room until about two in the morning. But he didn't show, and the Intelligence Officer sent us to bed. We couldn't sleep. Next morning we heard he had sent a signal from the channel—on fire, one member of the crew dead, trying to make Manston, an emergency field in the south. Just as he was limping in on final approach his kite fell apart.

They picked up enough remnants for seven coffins and had a big funeral down south. No one from the squadron was present but most of the relatives were, and we thought of the young skipper's widow with the baby. Back at the squadron we withdrew into our shells.

Some weeks later Johnny came into my room. "Remember the swell crew that got it at Manston, Cam? Listen to this. The rear gunner was married as well. Just the other day he walks into his home. His wife must have thought she was seeing a ghost. She had buried him with the rest, saw the coffin lowered with his name on it. He says the skipper gave them a chance to bail out over France, and he had. Doesn't know if anyone else did. The gunner beat his way back, didn't report anywhere until he saw his wife. Imagine the flap at the Air Ministry, re-rigging the records. It makes you wonder if any others got out, but I guess the skipper is a write-off."

After you had chalked up 20 trips and could see the end of the tour you might allow yourself to think vaguely of home. What would it be like? Would we pick up where we had left off? Could it ever be the same again? No one could find the answer. Toward the end, too, we had a wistful desire to keep on sticking together, we boys from Canada. But we didn't know that forces beyond our control would decree otherwise. We didn't even come home on the same ship after leaving the squadron, although we finished duty within days of each other. I think most of us were lost souls. We had left some part of ourselves behind in England.

Eleanor met me in Montreal. We had a shake-down cruise around the restaurants and night clubs. Dane was waiting in Ottawa, and Eleanor, in her great wisdom, had taken a cottage at a friendly lake for a month. In spite of careful briefing Dane was strange and shy with his father. But with Eleanor's wonderful cooking, fishing expeditions and games to excite a little boy, in no time he was calling me "Daddy", and a new life opened for us both. It was pure magic, but like all good illusions it couldn't last. I began to worry about a job, a place to live. The plans we had made in 1941 seemed very remote.

Eleanor and Gray at El Morocco in Montreal, July 16,1945.

Chapter Two

AFTER SIX years and better in the Royal Air Force how does one settle down? Can a person throw off the uniform, change to a suit of civvies, mix with the crowds and just forget? By putting away log books with several thousand hours of flying, can one erase the memories of those exciting years? There was the grim forced landing on a hill top in England. Shouldn't have walked away from that one, coming down through fog to four hundred feet. The trips over Germany entered in red ink, each laconic line opening the flood-gates of the mind to a story that still grips the innards. The times we went to Cologne and always picked up flak. We thought we had had it over Bochum. But we came through. Could we pick up the old life right where we had left off?

The home town seemed incredibly tiny and strange. Only Pappy, a navigator from the old squadron, was around. We were together as much as possible to swap yarns, always talking about the crews. The present seemed unreal; the past made sense. It was hard to mix with others or make friends with strangers who hadn't been there. Perhaps if I had returned to the R.C.M.P. the old uniform and routine might have been a fair exchange. With luck it might have taken us back to Alberta. But Eleanor had experienced enough of service life. We wanted a life of our own. And I had to prove to her, to the friends and relatives back in England, that she had married well. The offer of a position in a local firm had wonderful opportunities. The fact that I had no previous business experience did not seem to be a prohibiting factor. They would train me. It was a fine organization with a young outlook and a happy family atmosphere among employees.

Months of tuition followed at the factory, absorbing the business, studying at night, learning and practising and orienting. We rented a converted chicken coop at the edge of the city, bought a second-hand car and felt more bewildered in the strange environment. Eleanor spent her days on the outskirts with Dane while I was trying to pick up business methods in the city. Demonstrations, meetings, classes, days in the field with the trained men. Daily assurances that I was a bright boy destined to go on and up. Selling business systems.

When it was time to solo we were sent to Hamilton, Ontario. Here was the big opportunity for the right man, a tough competitive market. It seemed that all the industrial might of Canada was located there. But our first few months were plagued with finding a place to live. Had we been alone, just the two of us, it might have been easy. But we had Dane and a cocker spaniel. The dog wasn't such a problem but the child proved a terrible handicap. We paced the streets, advertised, chased all kinds of leads. Finally the Veterans' Administration sent us to a small hotel where we rented a single room over a beer parlour. The steady hum of voices below was soothing, but the smoke drifted upstairs through the rooms, hanging heavy like a London fog. It was difficult to sustain the buoyancy and optimism needed for the business of selling.

Finally in desperation we bought a trailer. Dane wouldn't have to be bottled up constantly and fed in restaurants. He was getting out of hand. We moved to a trailer camp and felt more independent. When we changed location to a summer cottage district by Lake Ontario where we could swim and play on the beach, Eleanor, Dane and the dog had their first break.

As their spirits rose, mine declined. Big business didn't show any interest in the new man. There were plenty of old-timers who had been around for years. In addition the chilling realization began to dawn that I never would be suited for the business. Perhaps we had two strikes against us because we were living in the past. We were not making enough new friends, and those we met were always being compared with the old ones, to their disadvantage.

From frustration I slid into a hopeless feeling of inferiority in everything I did. There seemed no escape and no point in struggling on. What was I fitted for in this rat race? There was no answer. What would I like to do? Ah, that was better. I would like to fly again. But Eleanor did not approve. It would take a change of environment, a drastic change, to pull out of this slump. There was a subconscious yearning to return to the West, preferably Alberta. Perhaps I could recapture out there the old feeling of buoyancy that always sustained me through ups and downs during the seven years in the police. How about returning to the R.C.M.P.? Eleanor was not too enthusiastic, but she was now ready to try anything that held a promise to restore the old spirit. So I wrote to the Commissioner. The Adjutant replied that they would offer me my old rank if I travelled with wife and family at my own expense to New Brunswick!

What were we struggling for, here and now, in Hamilton, Ontario? To make enough money in the next ten years so that we could live the way we wanted. It had always been our dream, from the first walk on the Yorkshire moors, to have a home in the country with horses to ride, dogs and children to train, to be able to live off the soil. But we had to have money.

We read a book entitled *Ten Acres and Independence*. We read pamphlets put out by the government for establishing veterans on the soil. We had considered this government plan while I was still on the squadron and hoped to profit by it later after we had become established. With this in view we had not used our War Service Gratuity for immediate needs. It was still there if we could qualify. But could we transfer it to the West where we both wanted to live? It was a faint hope. At this stage I was not sleeping well, and when thinking through the night, began to doubt myself capable of achieving the simplest plan. Always in the past after being slammed down for the count I had managed to bounce back on my feet. I remembered the bounces. But this time there was no fight left.

One night Eleanor woke up when I was lighting a third cigarette and shook me out of lethargy. "Let's do something about it right now," she said. "We can't go on like this. Chuck the job and start again. I won't argue even if you go back to flying. Start working on the next move. And for goodness sake don't start feeling sorry for yourself. I can't stand self-pity."

Some flying schools were located between town and the trailer. I did a few hours in Cubs, obtaining a limited commercial license

in Toronto. I also wrote to friends in Swift Current, Medicine
Hat and Banff. Those wonderful Westerners threw the ball right
back and left out the platitudes. Every reply carried the warmth
and expansiveness of the West together with the spirit that made
it great.

From Swift Current Edgar Burke wrote that his son and other
young men were interested in a flying school. They had a license
and were looking for an instructor. He figured I could fit in.
There would be charter work besides. It didn't read like a letter
from a retired business man, for it carried the enthusiasm of a
20-year-old.

Tip Volway wired us from Medicine Hat. About to leave for
Toronto on business, he sent us his time of arrival and a request
to meet him at the station.

Pete and Catharine Whyte wrote from Banff. Why wait ten
years to make enough money? Come out now before we all get
that old. By the time you make enough money to do what you
want it may be too late. They also sent R. H. Bennett's book, *The
Compleat Rancher*, directed to veterans who might be casting
around for an outdoor, active life.

Eleanor and I read that book, lived with it every waking
moment, memorized sections that argued in our favour. Here
was the answer, something concrete that crystallized our own
vague longing for independence, for a permanent, lifelong
pursuit in which we could be equal partners with a family.
Raising and improving a herd of beef cattle, building a home
from the land—for us, we felt, that was it. Though I still had
trouble sleeping my mind was afire with ideas. If you get hold of
a dream and chase it through hell and high water, you may not
complete its realization in the original but you will have a lot of
fun trying.

That was the decision we made. I also thought of the very real
partnership in such a dream—Eleanor and I, and later the
children, riding our own land, working our own cattle, taking off
our own crops. Doing everything together. We didn't stop to
think rationally or put down a bunch of figures on paper. That
might scare us. A powerful urge took hold. We would not
tolerate the arguments of logic. There wasn't time. We just had a
feeling about it—a crazy, excited feeling that we were going to
grab the world by the tail. And with our dream we compared our
present condition carried to the ultimate—my days spent in
offices and factories, Eleanor at home with the children, my

return in the evenings too tired and dull to discuss anything that had happened during the day, living separate lives, growing further apart. Was there any partnership in that? The sales manager had lectured me about joining clubs and organizations, cultivating business friends, living the business by day and night. It worked out that if you were making ten thousand a year you were expected to spend some eight thousand living up to the job—entertaining, joining, chasing. A hell of a life. On the other hand Mr. Bennett says on page . . . .

So I resigned from the firm, to be effective the end of September 1946. Tip arrived in Toronto and I drove him to the trailer on Lake Ontario. He had a shave, introduced us to a drink, reminisced about friends in the West, then got down to business. "When are you coming West? Sure you are. I talked over this flying business with the boys. No future in it. Now you two know the West. Your best bet is to start ranching. You are suited for it. Mack Higdon, Gene Burton, Harry Hargrave and the rest will give you lots of advice. Don't forget nearly all the old-timers started from scratch and you don't want to expect any different treatment. You know all your friends will be pulling for you. Come straight to our house if you land in the Hat. Use it for your headquarters. Now I want to say something to Eleanor and I don't want her to forget it. You have to be ready now, if things are slow starting to break for you, to see your husband in some hotel slinging beer or running a hamburger joint. But what the hell. The main thing is to get started, and if you are in that frame of mind you'll win. Are you game, Eleanor? I knew you would be. I'm just warning you, that's all."

Dear old Tip! He's gone now to another range. His passing was a great loss to Medicine Hat and countless friends throughout the country. Wherever he is you may be sure there is laughter and good fellowship. But memories are green in the West and a fellow like that lives on in the hearts of his friends.

Tip had given us the final shove. The die was cast. We hooked trailer to car, stocked up with food for the trip through the States and headed for the border with about $80 in cash and a million dollars' worth of enthusiasm.

Chapter Three

AS WE rolled along the highway, day after day, with our worldly belongings now pushing, now pulling and swaying behind the car in our little trailer, there was, for me, a definite feeling of suspension in time. Very unreal it was, as though we had stopped growing. Time stood still, and we were perched precariously between two periods in our life.

Normal persons might have worried about the future but we felt that once we reached Alberta we would be home. It wasn't rational, but after the years of travel and uncertainty we were dead sure that as soon as we crossed into that province we should be safe. It was the same feeling I had after leaving a target and heading the Lancaster for England. The navigator only had to sing out: "Over the channel, Skip!" and when I could see the searchlights along the coast of England I would know with absolute certainty that another operation was safely behind.

But with the time factor narrowing our chances, would we get to Alberta? We were travelling the most northern route, avoiding the cities and enjoying the lakes and woods that afforded remote camping spots. When we hit the prairies our pace quickened and we began eating up the miles. At one lonesome spot we stopped before a huge sign that pointed north to Canada and, in large letters, SWIFT CURRENT. Was fate calling us this way? I turned to Eleanor and we recalled the kind, enthusiastic letter from Edgar Burke. Would we turn here to begin our adventure? We

Starting west — September 1946.

remembered the friendly little city from 1942 when we were part of the R.A.F. Flying School that had moved there from Calgary. I was curious to investigate the flying set-up and talk things over with the Burkes. We remembered the other good citizens and also the fact there would be many missing faces. I rather favoured going that way. But Eleanor remarked that we both wanted to go ranching, that Alberta had been pulling us over the miles whereas it was only I who was interested in flying, and the idea did not seem down to earth compared to the glow we received just thinking of the promise in *The Compleat Rancher*. We used to quote passages from the book to each other during the long spells of driving and were continually re-reading chapters. So I put the car in gear and drove on, not, I may say, without some doubt as we drew away from that promising turning point.

We seemed to be heading into strange country after that until we came to Havre, Montana. I had known this town during my police days on border patrol, and as it was at the end of a long day of driving we decided to camp. Again we held council. Where would we go from here? I thought of Calgary, Lethbridge or Banff.

Eleanor objected. "It doesn't make sense, going to a city or a mountain resort. We want to go ranching. If we head for those places you will invariably start visiting old friends to talk things over and you may get side-tracked into a city job."

"That's all very well," I argued, "but shouldn't we talk this over with government officials who run the Veterans' Land Act first?"

"That's the last thing we should do," she reasoned. "Can you picture getting a good reception when the nearest thing to ranching we have is a talking knowledge of this book? That would spoil everything. How about the big ranchers you used to know? Would they be interested in hiring a couple as green as we are, with a little boy as well? We're going to need experience before tackling the Veterans' Land Act. Mr. Bennett advises going as a working hand on a ranch, and if you think *you* have a lot to learn consider me and the problems *I* face for a moment."

I began to doubt the wisdom of setting out with an ideal but no plan. Was Tip's warning about to confront us and would I finish the long journey slinging beer in a hotel or slapping hamburgers on buns while looking for that break?

The magic of green pastures that had pulled me out of a slump in Hamilton, the activity of getting ready, the anticipation of travelling had suddenly vanished here in Havre. We put Dane to bed in the trailer and walked along the main street. Nicely tanned cow men in big hats, jeans and riding boots were on the street, in hotels and driving large cars. They seemed like giants from the mysterious world of cow camps. We became excited again. I stopped one to ask if the old trail into Canada that took one to Medicine Hat was serviceable and still in use. "It's there all right, but with all the rain we've had I reckon you will need chains and lots of luck," he said.

Back in 1938 I had been stationed at Manyberries, real stock country. I had spent a memorable Christmas at the Bar N Bar ranch of Mack Higdon. Would Mack be there? I tried to remember the names of the cowboys. What would it be like arriving there, not as a member of the R.C.M.P. in the good old days but as another unsettled veteran with no job or prospects and with a wife and child as well? I tried to recall other patrols, other ranches. By Jove, I had it! Between Manyberries and Havre was the Federal Government range experimental station. Yes, and Harry Hargrave had been in charge. Just the man to give some direction to our wanderings. Better still, Eleanor had met him in Swift Current when he attended the Saskatchewan Stock Growers' Convention there during the war.

"Do you remember Harry Hargrave, El?"

"You mean the nice chap who visited us one evening with Barney Crocket? Of course I do."

"Well, unless he's been moved his outfit is just north of this place—the Manyberries range experimental station. Would it make sense if we drove up that far tomorrow? I must warn you that I feel we should continue west to Coutts and enter Canada on the good road. It's hard surface and we could make Lethbridge tomorrow. You'd have friends there while I looked around, but if you think we should go right for our target we could try this rough old trail to Harry's place."

"I think we should try to get to Harry's—you know how I feel about a city. Can we find out if he's still there?"

I tried the telephone and spoke to a man at the station. No, Harry was away but would return in a day or two. I gave my name and asked the chap to advise Harry I would be driving up from Havre to see him.

We started early and I found the trail by instinct. If Eleanor could get used to this, I thought, she would look at the other ranching districts as paradise. Mr. Bennett had described the foothills and mountain country, clear cool streams, cattle standing in lush, deep grass, evergreens and warm chinook winds. We were driving along a rutted trail on sun-baked alkali flats. No trees, fences broken wherever they showed and, miles apart, the odd, abandoned, broken-down dwelling. The centre of the trail was taken over by thick coils of rattlers and bull snakes. We drove over them with a bump and they didn't seem to notice.

Eleanor became alarmed. "Is this our country?" What grass cover there was seemed inadequate, a blade here, a blade there. No stock in sight. It was hot. I tried to tell her this was the famous short-grass country of large ranches and big herds. She wasn't interested and perhaps I wasn't very convincing.

After clearing Canadian Customs at Wild Horse, Alberta, we bumped and swayed until well into the afternoon when, like an oasis in the desert, we gazed at a belt of green trees. That must be the station. There would be people, water and possibly a reason for this stupid drive.

But when we arrived we found only strangers. Harry had not returned. We could camp near one of the houses and hook on to the lights. The little boy and the dog would be safe on the lawn but they had better watch out for snakes. The foreman would be along soon and if we required anything we could ask him. He lived in the nearest house. We went to bed that night wondering if this was just another camp stop or if we were close to the end of our journey. A lot would depend upon the interview next day.

In the morning I was out walking at six, trying to figure out a line of talk for Harry. A door slammed, and I turned to see a big fellow hurrying across the lawn in my direction. He sure looked familiar, and then I started to grin. It was Eddie Goodfellow. The big moose was miles from his own pasture. He used to run the bus and mail north of Medicine Hat to a place called Hilda where I had spent two lonesome winters. He stopped some yards from me, speechless with surprise, scratching his head. He held out his hand and started to pump mine. I thought I had grabbed a ham. Eddie was the foreman.

"For gosh sakes," he said, "what are you doing here?"

"I came out from Ontario to go ranching, Eddie. What are you doing?"

"I got married, left the farm and took this job."

"Well, I'm married too. My wife is in that trailer. We came to see Harry about finding a place."

"I heard there were visitors for Harry but never figured on you—for gosh sakes."

"Is Harry still a nice guy?"

"Just the best fellow in the world. Always the same."

"Think he can help us? Is he back yet?"

"He'll sure bust a gut trying. Came in late last night. You'd better look him up after breakfast. I've got to get the chores done."

"Okay, see you later." And off Eddie went, still shaking his head in wonder and grinning while I hurried back to the trailer to wake Eleanor.

If Harry wondered just why a tired-looking car and trailer with Ontario license plates had deposited an almost forgotten casual acquaintance on his doorstep, he gave no sign. Face to face with the first person who might put us on course, I became nervous and at a loss for words. It was important to sell ourselves and our sincerity to this man, our first contact in the West. Harry had a knowledge of ranches, ranching problems, developments and trends in the cattle business second to none. He had the power to send our illusions flying and our light-hearted expedition scurrying to the safety of another obscure city job.

These thoughts rushed through my mind as he smiled gravely and shook hands. I stammered that we had detoured this way to have a talk with him, but would be pushing on. If he could spare the time, would he listen to us? I guess he sensed that something was up, for he assured me he could find the time and insisted that having come to this remote spot we should not be in a hurry to rush on. I told him that what I had to say, and how he might react to it, had better take place before Eleanor. I told him it was terribly important to us, that Eleanor had just as vital an interest in the question as I had and begged him, before passing judgment, to hear us out first. Harry agreed to come around to the trailer for a meal that evening.

Eleanor remembers that we had hamburger for that fateful meal. I remember that she had the trailer looking as cozy and homey as possible. We squeezed ourselves around the tiny table with Dane sleeping soundly at the other end. During the meal we sketched in our travels from the Swift Current days, enquired about mutual friends.

The meal over, we waited for Eleanor to clear away. We tried to settle ourselves comfortably. I looked at Eleanor and she looked at me. Harry remained calm and relaxed. We simply could not get down to business. And then out it came like a torrent—a wild jumble of pent-up cause and effect, the decision, the drive and the vague yearning to go ranching, to get on our own. Somehow Harry grasped the idea. Fortunately he had read *The Compleat Rancher*, knew R. H. Bennett and his ranch. But he did not enter into our innocent and perhaps imbecile discussion as we tried to convince him of our purpose. We were definitely trying to sell ourselves to ourselves against secret fears. Nor did he interrupt us, as, in looking back on this desperate phase, I am certain he might have, to point out that no one else to his knowledge had ever gone into the business in our condition and at our age. But, bless him, he said nothing that could so easily have spooked such a jittery couple as we were then. We finally dried up without putting forth, I am sure, one sensible point.

Then Harry began to talk, quietly and sincerely. He described the difference between ranches—the large spreads in the short-grass country with their big acreage and small carrying capacity, the small units in the foothills that could carry a family and support a cow on less land. He pointed to big ranches that changed hands frequently where one found sudden wealth or quickly went under. Then he explained the home life of the foothills ranch, the permanency and the stability. He warned us that we would never make a lot of money on the latter but always a good living. He spoke wistfully of the security and family team-work on a ranch, the advantages of bringing up children, the deep satisfaction of working hard for oneself.

When we asked if he thought we could make it with insufficient funds and no experience, he pointed out that many others had started with less and the least we could do after coming this far was to try and find out if we had it in us. We tried to thank him and were assured he was delighted we had come to him for advice. He said we made him wish he were younger and that sometime tomorrow he would have a few suggestions to offer. After he left, Eleanor and I talked late into the night, remembering too late the things we might have said. Isn't that always the way it goes?

Next morning Harry returned to the trailer. He felt sure that if we held to our present mood we would eventually want to settle in the foothills. But he was also very sure that neither of us knew whether we could stand the life—being isolated, on our own, facing the problems and responsibility. How about a trial on one of the ranches? If he could place us with a good man, would we be willing to roll up our sleeves, work and learn, both of us? If we spent a winter cut off from all other interests in the short-grass country and emerged in the spring with the same enthusiasm, he believed we would then be in a position to sell ourselves to the Veterans' Land Act officials for backing. And probably we would then know what type of country and what kind of ranch we wanted. It made sense. Turning to Eleanor, Harry asked if she would mind spending a few days alone in the trailer while he look me on a little trip. Eleanor welcomed a chance to stop in one place long enough to catch up with washing and mending. Harry had to inspect some experimental bands of sheep and if I joined the party we might, on return, look in on some ranches.

The party included Professor A. H. Ewen of Saskatoon and Dr. Rasmussen of Lethbridge. They inspected sheep at Manyberries, Scandia and Lethbridge. Acres, corrals and barns of sheep, technical talk of sheep, noise and smell of sheep—until I thought they would give me insomnia and began to wonder where this was leading. When the inspection finished at Lethbridge I got the point. Harry was going to run Professor Ewen into the Porcupine Hills out of Macleod to look at ranches.

It was a lovely day, clear and sparkling, when we headed for the Hunter Brothers' layout where they ran purebred Herefords. Steve Hunter came along as guide. As we climbed into the hills Professor Ewen explained that he had spent the war in the army, had thought of the Veterans' Land Act and was interested in finding a ranch for investment purposes. He called this the promised land. I told him what Eleanor and I had in mind and picked up some advice I have never forgotten. "When you work around stock," the Professor said, "you will come across lots of jobs you won't like, and working with neighbours you will find many who can do the unpleasant chores better. Don't lean on them, make yourself learn and insist on doing these things yourself."

Toward the end of the day, after calling at some half-dozen places, Steve Hunter declared: "I tell you fellows, these ranches don't change hands very often. There is one other I can think of where an elderly couple talk of selling. They can't exactly make up their minds, but it's a swell little place to look at if you want to drive that far. I think I can find a trail over these Porkies that will cut down the miles. It's on the west side." I was in the back seat not caring one way or the other but Harry and Professor Ewen decided to make this their last call.

There wasn't much daylight left when we got there, but you could see at a glance it was the prettiest setting of them all. The land sloped south, and off in the distance you could see the first range of the Rockies. Harry and Professor Ewen remarked on the bunch grass, black loam and the slopes that were laid bare of snow by the warm chinook winds. They were obviously interested and waited around to speak with the owner. Professor Ewen told me the price was fair and he would write the owner later about a deal. It was dark as we dropped down to the valley floor with the towns of Lundbreck, Cowley and Pincher Creek winking their lights in friendly fashion. I sat quietly in the back seat full of envy for Professor Ewen, his knowledge and experience, his position that enabled him to look at ranches for purchase. Some day it might be our turn, but we had such a long way to go. I thought of Eleanor and Dane patiently waiting. If Eleanor could just see this country before settling down to an apprenticeship the sacrifice ahead would be easier to bear.

When we returned to Manyberries Harry got on the telephone. J. D. Gilchrist owned the Deer Creek Ranch of 32,000 acres, about 50 miles east. The married couple who worked there had just left. Joe was alone with one hired man. "I sent word you might be around for the job," said Harry. "Better leave in the morning."

Chapter Four

WE TOOK off early in the morning without the trailer, Eleanor map reading from a sketch of the route which Harry had made for us. There were few landmarks and no signs where the trails crossed as we worked east through badlands and deep coulees from one prairie flat to the next. At one junction Harry had marked on the sketch an old stove to indicate the turning point. When we found it we knew we were on course and wondered how many years it had been there and with what hope it had been transported into the country.

About noon we found the ranch house and saw Joe Gilchrist working in the corrals. He came up to prepare a meal and after we moved into the living room began to talk business. Joe explained that his family had a house in Milk River where the children were attending school. He had one man on the ranch who had been with him some years. He required a married couple as well, the wife to look after the house and meals, the husband to be chore boy and general ranch hand. As I began by explaining that Eleanor's cooking would more than make up for my lack of experience, Joe asked if I could milk a cow. I was afraid the truth might disqualify us and hastened to assure him I could. Eleanor glanced at me and I felt a tight little knot in my stomach. I hated myself for lying to Joe. He was a good guy and we took to him right from the start. When I confessed we were expecting another child and asked if it would make any difference, he said he had three of his own and was used to them.

The wages he offered were $75 a month for the two of us. He showed us the bedroom we would use over the kitchen and said we could have the run of the house. We explained why we wanted the experience and agreed to take the job. I told Joe we had to drive to Medicine Hat so that a doctor could give Eleanor a checkover and that we would return in a couple of days with the trailer. He showed us where to park it. As we got into the car to drive away Eleanor was feeling awful. The strangeness of everything, the large house, the meals to prepare, the job she had to face in her condition—it was a tough prospect. Joe must have sensed that she was on the verge of tears. "Don't worry about us around here," he said. "We're not hard to get along with."

So this was to be our new home for a bit, a step in the right direction. I was feeling relieved that it was working out more quickly than we had expected. We had the right kind of job without having to detour into the hotel or restaurant business. But I was windy on one point. I couldn't milk a cow. Perhaps some time in the next few days I could pick it up at the Government station and Joe would never know. Although she was as ignorant as myself Eleanor said milking was easy. All you needed was a little practice. Anyway, the obstacles were getting smaller and our courage was rising. We would meet our troubles when they came, and not before. As we drove along we counted our blessings as Eleanor's mother kept reminding us to do. However, just to prove it wasn't as easy as we thought and to hold out some tempting bait for a change of plans, fate hit us a couple of low blows. On the return to the station we had a flat tire about half way, some 15 or 20 miles south of the settlement at Manyberries. Shortly after changing to the spare we had another flat! I began walking for help and had just disappeared from sight when I met a truck heading for Manyberries. We picked up Eleanor, Dane and the tires, were driven to the garage and returned to our car by a kindly man who refused any payment for his services. Well after dark, and very tired, we reached the trailer.

There was no rest in the morning. We had to reach Medicine Hat and the doctor. I checked the tires and they were all standing up. The spare was good. If they would just hold up for this last dash we would soon be at the Deer Creek ranch and our troubles would be over for some time. The car could rest. We waved gaily to Eddie and his good wife who had been so kind to Eleanor, swung around the yard and started to pick up speed when the engine fell to pieces! It was almost the last straw. After taking us West the old motor apparently felt it had done its job.

What were we going to do now? I wondered if we should call off the bargain at the Deer Creek. We were a good 120 miles from the Hat. I couldn't buy another engine, and if the car was beyond repair what chance did we have of getting the trailer out of here? Harry had told me that if we didn't take the job at Joe's ranch he would be delighted to hire me. A stockman was leaving. The starting pay at the station was twice Joe's offer. Eleanor would not have to work and married quarters were provided. Nice little homes they were, too, with Eddie and Edna as neighbours. It was a chance to save money, to work regular hours. In time we could forget the risk of getting on our own or postpone it indefinitely as we settled into the steady routine. In her condition Eleanor would be safer here. Perhaps we should do the sensible thing and stop taking risks. All we had to do was move in and forget the car for the time. But a little voice said that if we really wanted to make things go our way, all this was not so important as learning how to run a ranch from a man like Joe.

Eddie came along, looked at the motor, did some tests, decided it was a write-off and took charge. He had a truck going to Medicine Hat which could tow me in. It wouldn't cost a penny.

"But Eddie," I said, "I can't get a new motor put in right away. We haven't got any of that green stuff left."

He just grinned and pointed out that the car wasn't any good to us here. If we towed it to the city at least I could sell it. "I have to go in anyway," he said. "I'll take my car and bring Eleanor and the youngster."

He directed the truck driver to haul the car to a garage he recommended. I met him there and listened to the mechanic confirm Eddie's fears. They could rush a job on a new engine. Eddie took me aside. How much money could I pay down? I had about $20 and the prospect of $75 a month at the Deer Creek. Eddie took me to the office, ordered a new motor, told them I would pay a little down and guarantee the rest in three months. He signed a note for me. Everyone was happy. In that town Eddie's word was gold.

He turned to me. "Now that's settled, is there anything else worrying you?" It had happened so quickly I hadn't had time to think. I tried to explain that we had some insurance and stocks but Eddie shook his head. "Leave your capital in storage. It's okay this way." And after making sure we had a place to stay he went about his business.

Eleanor, Dane and I walked to Tip Volway's store. We had a lot to tell him. But he had gone to the States where he had a horse racing. His two boys came up to give us a big welcome. Jack had been in the Air Force, and they told us their father had left instructions that if we called we were to be given the keys to the house. Philip drove us there, insisted on our taking the big bedroom, told us the kitchen was stocked with food and left us wondering what to do about it.

I picked up the telephone and called the clinic. Dr. Wilf Campbell, whom I had known since 1937 during my days in the police and who insisted that all Campbells are related, was surprised to hear we were in town. He saw Eleanor that afternoon and after the examination agreed to take the case if she could get in to see him every three months.

The second day in town we visited a number of old friends. The car was ready the day after that and we drove back to the station.

While helping Eddie with some welding on the trailer hitch I remembered that I hadn't found the time for milking practice. Eddie pointed out the chore boy, an elderly Scot, and when he started for the barn with milking pails I sauntered up and asked him if I could help. He was suspicious, but when I told him I just felt like doing something he pointed to one of four cows. "What side of the beast do I sit on?" I asked innocently.

"Go on! You're joshing, man," was his indignant answer. So I waited until he began milking and then tried to copy his technique.

I couldn't get any joy out of that cow at all. She didn't mind— at least she didn't kick—but I could get only a few drops at a time. Soon a crowd gathered, including some agriculture students from the university who demonstrated and explained before I retired, defeated. Eddie heard about it and convulsed himself laughing. Harry didn't let on that he knew. I felt it was a black mark against me and if Joe found out he would fire me in disgust. Eleanor thought it was very funny. After a final meal with Eddie and his wife we retired early for the drive to Joe's place next day.

Chapter Five

AT DEER Creek the first thing I did was to have a heart-to-heart talk with the top hand on the ranch, Harold Haugen. I apologized for being the kind of dude who would ask too many questions and make his work harder by my ignorance. I told him that I knew nothing about the job but that I sure was willing to learn. He thought that was fine and said my attitude made it much easier for him. Then he told me of the hired men they had in the past who knew it all. They would send one out on a job and he would break something, or have a runaway, and they couldn't get things done the way they wanted. He said it was easier all around if he showed me the jobs the way he did them and I could follow the same pattern.

We got away to a good start. Harold broke me into the milking gently, but just the same I had to learn the hard way that you cannot bully a cow, and have to come down patiently to her level of speed. Then he showed me how to harness the teams. When we started fencing I couldn't have had a better teacher, and Joe confided one day that Harold was the best man on fences he had ever had. Harold was a perfectionist at everything and proud of his trade. We got along fine.

Then we divided the chores. It was always a job to beat Harold out in the morning. He would start the pump engine for the water system, fill the large stock trough, clean the horse barn and jump on the jingle pony to wrangle the horses from their pasture, cutting out from the string whatever we needed for the day. I looked after the bulls, chicken house, cow barn and, fortunately, just one milk cow. As soon as I got on to the job of milking one cow and had recovered from the equivalent of writer's cramp Harold brought in a second fresh cow, and it was like learning all over again. At the other end of this milk business Joe was teaching Eleanor how to look after the cream separator and clean the milk pails. Eleanor's early-morning chores consisted of turning out a mass of hot cakes, eggs and bacon, which Joe considered the only breakfast fit to stay with a man during a morning's work on a ranch.

During those first weeks of apprenticeship something new had to be learned every day. Harnessing and driving teams, hoeing irrigation ditches, digging the large garden, hauling produce for the root cellar, shingling a roof, being blacksmith's helper at the forge, cleaning corrals and hauling manure, hauling and shovelling coal from the strip mine demanded long, hard hours of manual labour. We butchered a cow, and then a pig. I wasn't much help here and I didn't enjoy it at first. It reminded me of Professor Ewen's warning about unpleasant jobs and made me determined to learn.

After we had been almost two months on the ranch Harry dropped in unexpectedly, remained for a meal, and complimented Eleanor on her cooking. She was really doing well. It was a treat to watch Joe lap up her Yorkshire pudding. By this time we were one big happy family, my back and arm muscles were not screaming so loudly, and it was easier to hit the floor in the morning and scramble around doing chores. But oh how we loved that extra hour in bed Sunday morning!

Harry wanted to know how we liked ranching. We were just beginning to realize how little we knew about it. When he asked me how I liked cow punching, I recalled that so far I had not even spotted the big herd nor had I been trusted on a horse for more than one casual ride with Joe. I wondered if I would ever get a chance to do some cowboying. Then I shuddered as I remembered that one ride. Joe had taken me along to look for a stray bull. I dreaded the thought of separating from him for I might get lost and, moreover, if I did come across some cattle I was not sure that I could pick out a bull. Joe must have sensed my doubts for in his quiet way he said: "Surely you know what a bull looks like—he has horns."

One day he appeared with a second horse and called me over. "This is your pony," he announced. "I just bought him cheap. When you need a horse, ride this one. Get Harold to fix you up with a saddle and bridle and keep the same outfit."

As I led the horse away to the corral I called back: "What's his name, Joe?"

"Darned if I know—you give him one."

That night at supper Joe kidded me about my horse and asked what I called him. I decided to tag him Jughead for no reason at all.

When we did get away from the barns and buildings Harold and I would proceed by saddle horse, truck or team and wagon. Generally it was a fencing job. I began to learn how to brace corner posts, tighten wire, splice wire, dig and tamp post holes, use an axe and drive a good staple. The ranch lay on both sides of the Milk River and we had to fence across the river at various points. Just when one job became tiresome we were able to switch to another, so there continued to be pleasant days of variety, instruction and hardening up for bigger things to come. There was always so much to tell Eleanor in the evenings. The years began to slip away. I hadn't felt so fit since I was 20.

I like to remember the large fencing projects at the far end of the ranch or work on the telephone line. We would take the truck and a couple of saddle horses if there was river work. Into the truck would go the tools, posts, wire and grub-box. Joe didn't believe in dull meals like tins of beans and Spam with bread. The box always held a surprise.

By the time we were hungry enough to eat a steer raw, Joe would get a good fire roaring, cook up a wonderful meal in a sheltered spot and we would have a royal picnic—tired, ravenously hungry and full of fresh air. These meals, eaten Indian fashion squatting or lying before the fire on a pair of chaps, the fall air crisp and clear, twisting smokes while we had those extra cups of coffee, were the highlights of the life on the Deer Creek. And Joe usually had some good stories to tell of the early days.

At the end of three months we drove to Medicine Hat for Eleanor's physical check-up. Everything was fine. Tip was pleased to see us looking so well. I also paid off the note at the garage for the motor. But we were glad to get back to the ranch.

When the first winter blizzards hit the country we climbed into our saddles with a vengeance. Crowding on extra sweaters, buckskins, coats, wearing chaps and "neck rags", I began to feel that here, at last, was action. After an early breakfast the three of us would be off, fording the icy river, rounding up little bunches of cattle together into a big drag and driving them miles into the teeth of the blizzard to winter grass. Joe taught me that you cannot get the feel of the weather by scraping the frost off the window and looking out at the bleak landscape or by reading the thermometer. If you hustled outside, properly dressed, and got right to work the cold was always much easier to bear than it seemed at first sight and shudder. When you were riding in open country, slowly stiffening up under the cutting wind and believed you couldn't go much farther, you had to hang on just a little longer to reach a coulee or river bank out of the wind. Often when you leapt to the ground from your horse the first impact was painful, for you couldn't feel your feet at all and imagined you were standing on stumps.

I found out how tough those range Herefords could be, what great little rustlers the weaned calves are. After the main bunch had been moved we went looking for stragglers. At one place we found a dozen big steers stranded on an island. They had forded the river to the island but the thin shore ice stopped them from returning. Having eaten all the grass and palatable bushes in sight to keep alive, they were now huddled together in a miserable phalanx, humping their backs against the cold. We couldn't budge them until our horses had crossed and recrossed to mark a trail and break the ice. We had to do some riding and crowding to get them going, swinging lariats against reluctant hides.

It wasn't an easy winter for greenhorns but the tough spots were never so bad as we feared. We were a jolly crew, taking delight in wholesome fun. Joe was considerate and kind to Eleanor, more like a big brother than the boss. To Dane he was "Unca Joe". After lunch and a hard morning ride he would proceed to the living room for half an hour on the couch, waking up right on time. Then he would walk into the kitchen, look at Eleanor sheepishly and mutter apologetically: "Well, I had to rest my horse."

We had wonderful evenings in the living room with radio and books and good talk. We were more contented than we had ever been in our years of marriage. Joe let us send to Calgary for our trunks and cases of wedding presents that had been stored there since the Swift Current days. He trucked them 40 miles to the ranch from the railroad and let us store them in an empty house. For the first time we had everything together.

When the Christmas holidays began Joe's wife Muriel and their three children arrived at the ranch. Dane was overjoyed at the games with his new playmates. Muriel and Eleanor together cooked up all sorts of surprises. The Gilchrists treated us as though we were their closest relatives. Muriel brought up the question of the baby's arrival in March and decided that a good three weeks in advance Eleanor should move to town with her, where trains and buses were handy for the dash to Medicine Hat. She insisted on having Dane too, saying she was lonely during the day with her three away at school. Dane and Muriel were firm friends from the start. He called her nothing but "Gilchwist".

Eleanor and I began to talk about the future. We wondered how long we could remain with these fine, understanding people without imposing upon them. Another child might make a big difference and it didn't seem fair to Eleanor or Joe. We felt it was time to get in touch with a Veterans' Land Act office and in January I wrote to Lethbridge. We reasoned that they could not very well advise us to return East or that we were unlikely to qualify since we were working for Joe and he was satisfied. We had to start some time.

The reply came that a field man would call the next time he was in the district. By the end of January I had sent them my discharge from the Air Force and my War Service Gratuity statement. We were very busy at the time hauling feed to the cattle and two extra men were in the bunkhouse with spare teams in the barn. We didn't have time to think about it, worry and plan. On February 14, 1947, we received an important communication. The regulations required the veteran desiring to be qualified to appear with his wife before the Regional Advisory Committee. Our appointment was fixed for February 25 at 2:45 P.M. in Lethbridge. This was our big chance, if we were ever going to make the jump to a place of our own. With the way the weather was shaping up and the baby due in a few weeks it was running things pretty fine. I showed the letter to Joe and he suggested I combine the trip with Eleanor's move to town. In spite of the heavy work we continued studying Professor Ewen's textbook on animal husbandry and in the evenings we had long talks with Joe in our attempt to prepare ourselves for any questions that might be asked to test our knowledge. We had to submit the names of three reputable stockmen who could vouch for our experience and ability and had picked as our victims

Harry Hargrave, Joe Gilchrist and Eugene Burton of the V-T Ranch, known locally as the Will Rogers of Medicine Hat.

We had the car started early on the 25th to warm it up and managed to get to Milk River. We left Dane with Muriel and proceeded to Lethbridge. We were quite jittery about the test before us and poor Eleanor was terribly self-conscious of her appearance. I hoped with a fervour akin to prayer that we wouldn't let any of our friends down. If we couldn't impress these people it would be so hard to turn back, defeated. When we arrived at the office Eleanor puffed upstairs and I found her a seat on the bench where other applicants were waiting. I gave our name at the counter and glanced through the glass partition into the board room where the Government chairman was flanked by a prominent farmer and a rancher. At the other end of the long table a young couple were sitting on the edge of their chairs, the man twisting his cap nervously. I would rather have been waiting at a dentist's office for a long and difficult extraction. Would we be able to convince them?

Like all ordeals most of it was mental. The Committee were very kind and considerate. We stumbled over the questions about previous experience by remembering that Eleanor as a young girl had spent summers on a farm in England and I had done about the same in Ontario. As we talked about our present work I quoted Harry, Joe and Professor Ewen. When they went into my service in the R.C.M.P. I had an inspiration. For a time while I was stationed at Manyberries the Provincial Government had appointed me deputy stock inspector so that I could clear shipments of cattle out of the district.

I vividly remember my first inspection.

When I was transferred to Manyberries, I came under the avuncular interest of the late, great Leo Hester who was born at Zephyr, Texas, in 1884. Coming to Canada in 1903 he began punching cattle when he was 19. He joined the Alberta Provincial Police in 1923 and was absorbed into the R.C.M.P. in 1932.

It was a sad day for Manyberries and the ranching fraternity when I took over the detachment and Leo was moved to Lethbridge. He didn't have much time to train a newly appointed novice stock inspector, so designated by an unwitting government. However, he did try to ingrain in me his particular brand of warmth and kindness and cowboy savvy.

"Don't worry," Leo had said. "If you play the game, these folks, good or bad, will help you survive. You know you can't read a brand and they know it. When you get to the corral, climb the rails, push your stetson back on your head and shout to the boss to run 'em by. Get the count right, the brand on the forms, collect the money. Nothing to it. You'll get by."

The dust had barely settled on the trail to Lethbridge when my first challenge came up. An important rancher named Murray, running the Top Hat brand, drove up in a large car. He was shipping 750 head of yearlings from a distant siding to Saskatchewan. I grabbed the brand book, tried to remember what Leo had told me, sneaked another look at the form and followed Murray across the prairie.

The siding was busy with cowboys riding herd and cattle milling, the train waiting patiently. All eyes were on the green-horn. I climbed the rails, doing it just like Leo had suggested, but when I shouted "Run 'em by!" the cowboys stopped and stared. Murray held up his hand, shrugged, jumped into the corral and stood as pivot so the steers raced past me one at a time. I had a good tally, carefully marked the brand on the certificate, remembered to check for horns and worked out the total. Murray wrote out a cheque and handed it over.

"Powerful good brand reading," he said dead pan. "The Top Hat brand happens to be on the other side of the critters."

Obviously if the government had appointed me a stock inspector I must know something about cattle. I forgot to tell the Committee I had been there only a few months. They were very pleasant and nice. At the end of the interview we shook hands all around and we were told that the committee would write to us when they reached their decision.

Leaving Eleanor with Muriel and Dane at Milk River I returned to the ranch. We continued hauling feed, opening frozen water holes and fighting the cold. Joe took over as cook.

Then a curious thing happened. I must be careful setting it down because even for us, looking back, it is hard to believe. Fortunately I have the letters before me now.

Remember that when we first arrived at Harry's station I had taken a trip into the Porcupine Hills with Harry and Professor Ewen. The latter had been very much taken with a ranch we found at the end of a long day of enquiry and inspection. Now a letter arrived from Professor Ewen, dated February 27, two days after our ordeal before the Committee, stating that with the acquisition of a house and daughter he was afraid he could not go through with a deal for the ranch we had seen. He thought the size would be right for us; the price was good and he sent me the post office address of the owner. Was this fate again, pointing the way? Joe thought we couldn't afford to miss any opportunity. I lost no time in getting off a letter to that address. Then I received a communication from the Veterans' Land Act dated March 1. The committee agreed it would be to our advantage to gain further actual experience by working on a ranch. It would be in order for us to work for Mr. J. D. Gilchrist for this season. Although the letter didn't turn us down it seemed to rule out the possibility of closing a fast deal. I continued working harder than ever on the ranch, feeling very fit and confident that everything would work out for the best. If I had time to think at all, my concern was only for Eleanor. She had put up with so much to keep me happy that I could not fail her now, whatever the future had in store.

Muriel telephoned that Eleanor had left for Medicine Hat and everything was fine. Eleanor was shy about using the telephone and we agreed not to try getting in touch or writing until it was over. The days at the ranch merged into a blur of heavy slogging with frozen stacks and intense cold so that after the evening meals in the warmth of the kitchen I had to fight an inclination to drop asleep at the table.

In the next mail that came through was a letter from the Porcupine Hills dated March 7. The owner of the ranch which Professor Ewen had recommended had decided to sell in the spring. He was getting on in years, had spent 40 of them on his ranch, and I guessed the long hard winter had helped to convince him it was time to get out. He was asking ten dollars an acre and was running 225 head of cattle through the winter. The ranch consisted of 1,440 acres of deeded land, 160 acres of lease, with a permit to graze cattle on the forest reserve in summer. The school was two miles away.

I wanted to write or telephone Eleanor about it but remembering our agreement, decided it would not be fair to raise her hopes. After all, the Government had not qualified us and I was sure if we burst in on them so soon after the interview with a big deal pending they would get very sticky. Then I began to jot down figures on the back of an envelope. Assuming we could get the Government to approve the deal, what would their backing amount to? Their pamphlets stated they would pay up to $6,000 for a place if we put up ten per cent. We had 20 years to pay back the balance at a nominal rate of interest. That meant I would have to give them $600 first to get the $6,000. I put the car down at $800; we could cash in two insurance policies for $1,400; the trailer might sell for $1,000. And when I left the Air Force we had bought industrial stock now worth $1,400. That gave us $4,600. If the Government came in with $6,000 perhaps I could close the deal for $14,000. The difference between what I needed and what I might get was $4,000.

I didn't bother Joe about the details, merely showing him the letter from the owner and telling him I could get within $4,000 of buying it. He figured I should look at it anyway and told me not to worry about borrowing money to get started if it was a good place. He said that when he and his brothers started out they had borrowed a large sum on their name alone which had taken them years to pay off. I realized that even if we could swing it we would find ourselves with a ranch and no stock, but I hoped to be able to keep some of the owner's cattle on shares or make some kind of deal with a cattle buyer. I was ready for one more gamble. I remembered Eugene Burton saying to me in Medicine Hat: "If you find a good ranch and need help I'll throw in with you." Well, I had to drive to the Hat when the weather changed to get Eleanor. Perhaps Joe would let us run up and look at the place. It wouldn't cost us anything to ask.

As I came in with a sleigh at noon on March 20 one of the new men came out to tell me there had been a telephone call from Medicine Hat. Eleanor was fine and our family had increased. It was another boy—eight and a half pounds! Joe said he was our hot-cake baby. Howard Leslie, a neighbour, said: "That guy Campbell sure is getting set up for ranching. When he gets a place he's going to have lots of help." Eleanor wrote a letter five hours after the baby was born saying how thrilled she was, that he would be a fine rancher because he had such enormous hands. She had decided to call him Timothy Gray, she said, and he hadn't shown any objections. I began to write notes to everyone I could think of, in a few adding that we were going to look at a ranch.

Gradually the weather warmed up, but for quite a while the roads were too bad to attempt getting as far as Medicine Hat. Besides, Joe needed me. Finally, when the baby was three weeks old Joe thought I could get away that week-end and on the return I could drive around by Lethbridge. If things were breaking right he advised me to take Eleanor up to look at the ranch in the Porcupine Hills. Saturday morning we had to de-horn calves. As soon as the last one went through the chute Joe turned to me. "What are you hanging around here for? I thought you wanted to get away and see the new cowboy!"

I sprinted for the car without waiting to change clothes, reaching the house where Eleanor was staying two hours and 45 minutes after clearing the first gate at the ranch. I had so much to tell my wonderful wife. It was spring, and we were going places. If we got the breaks.

Chapter Six

IT WAS comforting to learn that Eleanor had been staying with Augie and Ethel Sauer. The day Eleanor entered hospital she had gone for a walk and dropped in to see Ethel. They had sat in the kitchen sipping tea and watching the alarm clock until it was time for Eleanor to go to hospital. Ethel had insisted then that she come to their home until I could fetch her.

Augie had arrived from Denmark as a boy to seek his fortune in the new world. He had done well as a cattle buyer and owner of ranches. He was a colourful character, a square shooter well liked by all stockmen in the south country. When I was in Manyberries as a young policeman trying to figure out what the job of stock inspector meant, Augie had dropped in to the detachment to have some carloads of cattle inspected. In the hungry thirties cattle on the hoof fetched only a few cents a pound. After buying a couple of carloads at the going rate, Augie then offered the rancher and his wife double the price for any steer or cow they could run through the living room! They managed to get one or two over the obstacle course. Everyone had a lot of fun and after that I am sure many more ranchers decided to sell their stock to Augie. He was friendly and considerate and I was always glad to see him in my district.

When we arrived in Medicine Hat from the East in the fall, I had spotted Augie driving down the main street and had followed him home. As Eleanor's mother was Danish, I wanted her to meet the big fellow. We had spent half an hour with them on that occasion.

And now here they were, the best of friends. Eleanor looked lovely that day. We stood at the door and gazed at each other with eyes full of pride and joy, Ethel beaming in the background and Augie booming: "Well, what are you doing out there? Don't you want to see your son?" He propelled us through the house to the bedroom where Timmy was asleep.

They left us alone for a big hug and Eleanor whispered: "My, but Ethel is a sweet person. They couldn't have been nicer to us and I have never been in a happier home. You would think the baby was theirs, the way they show it off to all the visitors. Oh, darling, is this world of ours full of wonderful people and how does it happen to be so perfect? Could we ask Augie to be godfather for Timmy? It's the only way we can thank them." I was pleased she had thought of that, told her this was the West and the people had always been that way.

We took pictures of the two families and then I told them about developments, being careful not to draw too glowing a picture of the ranch as I remembered it. Augie's opinion was definite. "You kids go to Lethbridge and talk to the officials. If you think it's what you want don't let anyone stand in your way. Then go up and see the old fellow at the ranch. Don't let them scare you or think you can't pay for it. Buy it if you can and worry about it after." If Augie had told me I could walk on the ceiling that day I would have tried it.

After getting away early Monday morning I found the chairman of the Committee who had interviewed us two months before. This time we had more bounce. I explained that we had intended remaining with Mr. Gilchrist at least until the fall but the arrival of Timmy rather complicated the arrangements. Then I told him about the ranch we wanted to inspect and how we had come across the lead. He said we had better tell our story to the Director, Mr. Miller, and get his opinion. We were shown into a private office. Mr. Miller appeared, all beams and smiles. Fortunately he had been to the ranch in question and knew the owner. He said it was a fine place. He checked our file again, said my name was familiar and wondered if we had not met when I was in the R.C.M.P. It would have been comforting to establish a friendly tie with the past but we could not connect any previous relationship. Mr. Miller said it had been worrying him since our case had come before his office and some time he would get to the bottom of it. I fervently hoped that if there was something in my past it would not be bad. We didn't bring up the problem of financing the deal. Mr. Miller told us to go ahead and look at the ranch, then come back and see him. He didn't say yes and he didn't say no. So far we were holding our own.

We headed west towards the Rockies, but I couldn't have found the place unaided if we had been on a treasure hunt and my life depended upon it—which it did. At the post office we were told to cross the tracks and take the road north into the hills. The ranch was quite close, within 12 miles of the village the letter had said. The lady in the post office had mentioned Squaw Butte, and away in the distance we could see a height of land which might be the landmark. I watched the engine temperature climb as the car struggled up the hills and over the little bridges. Finally the road ended at a gate through which a track led into a hay meadow.

I opened the gate and followed the trail. The ranch looked larger than we had imagined. We were in a big green bowl with alpine slopes of clean, park-like grass on three sides topped with evergreens. There was Squaw Butte, sure enough, towering over us dead ahead with all the land sloping south from the rugged little peak. We spotted the house, a friendly, tidy building, freshly painted the colour of ripe corn trimmed with maroon and protected by a belt of trees. Off to one side was a new cabin. We noticed a large stock dam, a trim arrangement of corrals, barns and sheds. It looked awfully large and expensive, spread out there in a picture setting overlooking the valley behind us where strip farms reached to the Rockies about 40 miles away. It was April 15, a heavenly day. Higher up, patches of snow showed, clinging to the base of the trees and filling the coulees.

Eleanor held Timmy up, saying: "Look, darling. Daddy may get us a home after all." I didn't have to ask Eleanor how she liked the layout for her eyes were fairly shining.

But we were a frightened pair of youngsters. We knew without proceeding farther that this would exceed our wildest dreams for a place of our own. And having travelled so far, putting up with so much, the thought of losing it would be a major set-back. We debated whether to go ahead. It really looked like too big a proposition for our limited resources and all the backing we could get. We both felt we could look for the rest of our days and not find a setting that held so much appeal. Any other place would be an anti-climax. We should never be able to

The ranch: "the house, a friendly, tidy building... protected by a belt of trees."

forget the perfection here before our eyes. I remembered the figures on the back of the envelope in my pocket. If we could sell this and if we could get so much for that. There were too many ifs! Turning to Eleanor I said: "Let's get out of here before we break our hearts."

As I turned around Eleanor stopped me: "No. Wait a minute. Remember what Augie said to us yesterday." We sat there in a panic of indecision until the owner came out of the house and waved us on. I put the car into gear and drove ahead.

While Eleanor went into the house with Timmy I travelled up the valley with the owner to feed some cows. It was just starting to green up; the earth was stirring sluggishly from its long sleep. Mr. Rhodes pointed to hay fields that were sod-bound and required working. The place had advantages of scenery, good grass and a temperate climate. The altitude couldn't be definitely established but we accepted it as around 3,800 feet. It was swept by the warm chinook wind, which bared the western slopes and high ridges for winter range. This was important. The disadvantages were lack of roads and schools. It struck me that the district abounded in small, family-size units where good homes

were established. There were no large spreads of the kind that
made fortunes overnight, yet the people had not been forced on
relief in the hungry thirties.

When we began to discuss business I didn't dare look at
Eleanor. We both felt we were there under false pretences. Mr.
Rhodes told us that another party had sent word they were
coming up to buy it but my letter had caused him to wait until
he saw us. We made a lot of the fact that he came from
Yorkshire, some 15 miles from Eleanor's home. He told us he
would sell for $14,000 and agreed to go along with our deal
through the V.L.A. if we could give him a definite decision
soon. We got along fine that first interview and before leaving
went over quickly some of the equipment now on the place,
the things we would need for a start. Remembering the
briefing Augie had given us I asked him to throw in a team
and a set of harness. He hesitated but finally agreed. I
promised we would let him know as quickly as possible after
our interview with the V.L.A.

As it was too late to make Lethbridge we stayed that night in
Macleod. Tuesday morning we were right on the button when
the staff arrived. This time all the doors opened to Mr. Miller's
office. By the way he looked at me I knew he had dredged up
something from the days gone by. Thank heaven, there was a
twinkle in his eye. He turned to Eleanor. "Mrs. Campbell, this
may come as a surprise to you. I have been digging through my
scrapbooks at home. Here are some Calgary newspapers with
pictures of your husband which may interest you. Let's see, it
was in 1935 when Constable Campbell, your husband there,
and three other Mounties shot it out with three bandits up in
the mountains near Banff. Two of the policemen were killed as
well as the three bandits. Now what you don't know, Mr.
Campbell, is that the car the bandits held up in trying to get
through the mountains to the coast, just before the shooting
started, contained my brother-in-law and his wife, whom you
do know."

From now on we had a friend in court. Mr. Miller could not
do any more for us than for any other applicant but at least we
could tell him everything. And we did. It appeared that we
could split the ranch up, the V.L.A. buying and holding in our
name half the ranch, or part of it up to the value of $6,000. We
could make our own arrangements to buy the remainder for
$8,000. It would all be our own when we had completed the

payments to the government and ten years had elapsed. The clause withholding full title for ten years was apparently to stop a veteran from speculating on a quick sale.

We ran into more luck on this occasion. I told Mr. Miller that we would never be satisfied with any other ranch or type of country except the place we had found and that I was sure we could work out the details from our end. He advised us to get back up there as soon as possible and to have Mr. Rhodes sign an Offer to Sell listing the land and buildings. If the Offer was made for 90 days he would have it appraised and decided upon within that time. Then I brought up the question of our being qualified. By a splendid coincidence the head man for Alberta, Mr. Allam, was then in the building. He agreed with the general idea of the deal. We stopped worrying about being qualified and, indeed, were only reminded of it when we received a certificate dated May 3.

As we drove back to the Deer Creek we speculated upon our chances of having the other knots untied as easily as this. We had to get Rhodes to sign the Offer to Sell but felt we should not mail it to him. While he was considering it someone else might appear with a better one. The trailer must be sold right away. We told Joe all about it and I got in touch with an agency in Lethbridge to sell the trailer. We soon got back in the groove working for Joe. He took a great interest in Timmy, insisted on getting breakfast for the crew several mornings a week and found time to help Eleanor with the dishes. We were now busy with irrigation. Harold was working at it from dawn until dark, and the days I helped him decided me that irrigation was fine anywhere but on our place.

I let one Sunday go by, then asked if I might take the trailer to Lethbridge. Joe didn't mind. I hoped to make a fast run, then continue on to see Mr. Rhodes and get him to sign the Offer. The day was very poor for such an ambitious trip, a steady downpour of rain and mud holes in the road. The old nemesis of flat tires dogged me this wet Sunday, so I didn't make it to see Rhodes.

When I explained to Joe my bad luck in not getting Rhodes to sign the form he advised me to keep after it. So I took a chance and mailed it, trying to forget the details hanging over us, the figures and the sharp pencil work Eleanor and I had gone over time and again. Revising and hoping, one minute burning with conviction that everything would work out, the next minute in the depths of misery over the gap of at least $4,000 that made it seem hopeless, we waited fearfully for Rhodes' reply.

The calves were arriving, and with irrigation in full swing we tried to submerge our doubts in hard work and give Joe better value for our presence. The next week-end Muriel and the children came out to the ranch, so we had no time for conferences or plans. The mail arrived on Saturday. A thick letter was addressed to Eleanor and myself. As she was busy in the kitchen I sneaked over to the bunkhouse to read it after the noon meal.

I had to go over that letter three times before it would sink in. And then I couldn't believe it. A cheque had fallen out of the envelope, but when I retrieved it with shaking hands my eyes couldn't make out the figures. I wiped the moisture away, fumbled for a cigarette, got hold of myself and read the letter for the fourth time. I must be dreaming. If this was true, could I make Eleanor believe it? The writers said they had followed our journeyings with great interest and congratulated us both on the arrival of Timmy. They thought the work we were doing and the sacrifice we were making were worthwhile and the news that we had found a ranch had made them wish to speculate on our venture. It was heartening to think that a young couple today would cut the strings of modern living in the city to go back to the fundamentals that had built up this young country. They had come to the conclusion, although we had not asked for help, that it would be fun if they could come in on the adventure. Would we tolerate silent partners if the Government had no objections? They enclosed a cheque for $5,000, but if this was not quite enough we were to write and say so. The letter pointed out that if we had decided to start out in business, running a bowling alley or a string of tourist cabins, they would not have been interested in the least. But the thing we were striving for seemed to them to be as good for Canada as developing a new oil field. They would be much happier to have this money at work helping our plans than in a bank to be invested in something they would never hear about.

Nothing like this had ever happened to me before. How could one say thank-you for a letter like that? Eleanor would find it impossible to believe if I told her verbally. This girl from England, who had left security and social position to keep a restless husband happy in search of an indefinable longing for a way of life, after all the wandering and uncertainty, the work and struggle, would she see this as the turning point? I walked slowly over to the house. I couldn't take Eleanor away for a talk. It would have been fun to interrupt the house full of guests and share this letter with Joe and Muriel. But somehow the letter seemed sacred, its message for us alone. Eleanor had to go through the experience of reading it alone first. I tried to calm myself, slipped the letter to her and whispered that she must go off by herself to read it. I am afraid it alarmed her, for it might just as well have been bad news and I gave her no hint of the contents. But I am sure she shared it with Timmy when she was feeding him. The rest of the day he was perfectly contented and good as if all the tension in his Mummy had given way to calm and peace.

These good people insist on being anonymous. They consider their help only a small part of the story. And they repeatedly assure us they have been more than repaid in the letters that flow continually from us. But they have been firm on one point, that we should write down the tale of our adventure to encourage others. And because they have saved all our letters I am able to quote part of Eleanor's reply after receiving this thrilling information that removed so much of the risk to our plans. As you read her conservative lines please bear in mind that she had been overwhelmed time and again by the kind words and actions of the Burkes, Whytes, Volways, Hargraves, Gilchrists, Sauers and a legion of Good Samaritans.

Eleanor wrote: "I know I can't put on paper all that I feel and would like to say. In all the rush of this week-end with never a chance to discuss things with Gray, he and I have shared, undeclared, the purest happiness and peace knowing that these dreams and plans of ours are coming true, with nothing to stop us now, only made possible by your wonderful offer. Why you should want to do this for us I will never understand. With you two for partners we shall have all the greater incentive to make a success of the venture. I know I feel I could lick the world now! . . ."

It was time we stopped running around in circles. If we were ever going to make the jump, this was the moment. We were not the same pair who had arrived at Harry Hargrave's the previous September. We laughed at the memory of our predicament when the motor packed up and we thought about working on the station. Joe had shown and taught and shaped us to appreciate the real values of life on a ranch, the balance between the financial and spiritual dividends. Everyone with whom we had come in contact had added something of value to our new character. If we worked hard and continued to learn we might be as happy and contented as Joe, not striving for supremacy over the next man, neither jealous of a neighbour nor dissatisfied with our lot. We could be so wrapped up in our own little world of creation that we would actually be at peace with the rest. These thoughts made us very humble.

We wanted to go on but hated to leave the Deer Creek. We discussed the possibility, in making the deal for the ranch, of asking the owner to remain there during the summer while we stayed on with Joe until after haying. We put it up to him.

"It will take you all summer to get the feel of the place before winter closes in," he said. "I could use you here but you'd better get settled as soon as you can."

We had to make one more trip into the hills. If we could persuade the owner to let us move in and begin working the place while the V.L.A. wheels started grinding, we could pick up all our cases, trunks, boxes and bags and move for the last time.

Chapter Seven

THIS SUDDEN change of fortune bewildered us. All the details, the difficulties, the juggling around with figures trying to make the impossible happen disappeared into thin air. From the mere fact of our now having money or convertible assets to make the purchase possible we assumed that everything would soon be settled. Looking back, this sounds like utter folly but we had never been so certain as now that the scheme must fall into a pattern of our choosing. It had to go our way. We began jumping ahead of ourselves in our plans.

Not until we were speeding along the highway the following Sunday towards our ranch did we realize Mr. Rhodes had not returned the Offer to Sell which had been mailed to him. We were pulled back into the same old rut, however, when we had two more flat tires. A Sunday driver took me to Macleod to have them patched and a taxi returned me to Eleanor and the stranded car. Early in the afternoon we turned off the highway for the climb to Squaw Butte.

As we imagined, or as Joe had warned, several parties had been after the ranch since our first visit. As the roads improved we could expect more visitors to build up the opposition unless we acted quickly. Mr. Rhodes told us one of the parties had offered more money! Hoping it was an offer of part cash with time for payment of the balance, we said that we were ready now for a straight cash deal. We added that the Director of the

V.L.A., whom Mr. Rhodes knew, would be coming up soon to complete the business as we had agreed. We acted as though it was taken for granted our offer stood and for the moment we did not mention the Offer to Sell.

We spent the night in our home-to-be. Eleanor and I slept little, whispering to each other the things we wanted to see and ask about, the strategy and line of talk we should adopt in getting the paper signed. We kept running to the window to look at the view, in moonlight so bright we could see the Rockies. Then we would do a ghostly jig, throwing our arms wide and trying to shriek at each other in an excited whisper: "Just think! It's almost ours."

Next morning when we asked Mr. Rhodes to drive around with us he suggested we view the summer range and the farm land. The summer field looked immense.

"Does all this belong to the ranch?" I asked.

"Oh yes. There is just as much again over the hill," he said. We had not grasped the acreage involved and were quite awed to think of all the land we might own one day. To Eleanor it all seemed more lovely on this second trip, perhaps because she had not dared to let herself go the first time she viewed it. Now that the place was within reach she began to take it all in. She had a good look at the house as well and decided it had possibilities.

The visit had gone very well, but before we left it was necessary to find out exactly where we stood. Should we be business-like and precise, asking for a straight answer, or would this afford them a moment for pause and doubt? Or should we try a little gentle psychology? The Rhodes were an elderly couple. Several people had warned us that they had been on the point of selling two or three times previously and had backed down at the last minute. Obviously they were attached to this place and would be reluctant to leave the home to which they had devoted the best years of their lives. Perhaps the other prospective purchasers had been too anxious about how soon they could move in and take complete possession. If the owners could be made to feel they were wanted and welcome around the place for an indefinite time they might not panic at the thought of finally having to leave their ranch for good. If this reasoning was correct they might not back out of the deal once again. It looked to me as if this was the best method of approach. We had returned to the house and were seated in the kitchen.

"Mr. Rhodes," I said, "we will never find another ranch as nice as this. We can appreciate how you picked the site, homesteaded, added and improved upon it so that it will always be known as the Rhodes' place. Eleanor and I can understand how you and Mrs. Rhodes must feel at having to part with it. You know how we have worked to find a place like this. We would like to buy it and carry on the work as you had planned. If you would like us to be the new owners Eleanor and I would be grateful if you could both stay on, at least until the hay is up, to advise us and show us how you operated. We would not like you to feel you had to move away and lose contact. You will want to spend your winters in comfort and security without the work and responsibility, but you will always be free to return and visit when you wish. If you would like to sell under those conditions we will move up here in a week or so with our things and live with you. It will take the V.L.A. a little time to complete the deal. In the meantime we can be working the place together. When the place changes hands it would be a great help to us if you remain here so we can have the benefit of your advice. How does that plan strike you?"

"That's the way I want to sell," he said. "We don't want to begin thinking of a place to live right away. After 40 years in one spot it's hard to move in a hurry at our age. If you would like me to stay I will be glad to see you settled in and help in the running of the place."

"Well, that's fine," I said. "Until the deal goes through we will be helping you. In the meantime you've got yourself a man and you don't have to pay wages. We will share the food costs. Mr. Miller, Director of the V.L.A. in Lethbridge, will have the ranch appraised in a month or two and then they will buy it for us. He asked me to have you sign the Offer to Sell form which will start the ball rolling."

The form was filled in, signed and witnessed. I told Mr. Rhodes that through the V.L.A. he would be paid in full for the ranch. That would leave us with the place but without any stock. We talked about keeping some of his cattle on shares but he was not too keen. He did say, however, that he would sell us some cows with calves, 30 or 40 head, and he would give us four years to make three annual payments. It looked to us as though we had everything covered.

Driving to Lethbridge with the precious paper Eleanor and I tried to recall the things we had seen, the surprises in buildings, the fine cattle, the lovely scenery that unfolded from any angle, the dream-like quality of our amazing luck. Then we took hold of ourselves. We were committing the rest of our youthful years to hard work, no luxuries, precious little furniture. Our own interests would have to be subordinated to paying off every cent. Yet we were going into it with joyful hearts. Joe had taught us what was ahead, working from dawn to well after dark—no 40-hour week, no holidays—seven days a week. If we weren't dragged down the first few years by crop failures, drought or falling prices we knew we could weather the storm. There would be no time out for illnesses—we couldn't afford to be sick. The Government was giving us 20 years to pay back their loan and we hoped to have the silent partners repaid in three to five years. But when it was all cleared, look at what we should have! A fine little family ranch, real stability for our children, a business in which they would grow and develop, all cleared for them if they should decide to carry on. And best of all, a place for us to retire with the help of the boys. Oh yes, even then we had decided this was where we wanted to spend the rest of our days. We should then have a little cottage where in the declining years we would have the comfort and luxuries we were prepared to do without now.

Back in Lethbridge we waved the paper before Mr. Miller. He congratulated us and said it was indeed a fine spread. I warned him about Rhodes backing out of deals in the past and said we were moving in within a week, if we could, to work with him. Because of the bad roads during the winter the office was behind with the appraising and it would normally take five or six weeks before they could get around to our choice. Mr. Miller was prepared in view of this to try to come up himself within two weeks.

Eleanor dragged me straight to a store to buy garden seeds, saying: "Mr. Rhodes had the garden all ploughed and ready. I can hardly wait to get my hands into that lovely black loam."

We were treading on air. "How about it, El?" I said. "Are you ready to move for the last time? Would you like to change places with anyone in the world at the moment?"

"I really can't believe it, but I hope to come down to earth in time to get the packing done."

Somehow she managed it, and if Joe ever reads this I trust he will realize with what sadness our joy was tinged at leaving the Deer Creek and the fine people there. Muriel and the children were coming out next week-end and we tried to get a truck to help us move the following Tuesday or Wednesday. However, the storekeeper in Milk River who was arranging for this transport telephoned Saturday afternoon with the information that all trucks were busy during the week and he had managed to get one to take us Sunday!

We had a real send-off. A three-ton truck was piled high with our cases and trunks. Joe gave us a sack full of seed potatoes for our garden and as we all gathered before the house to move off, called out: "Just look at them! They drove in here with a few suitcases last fall and now they're pulling out with half the ranch."

Eleanor couldn't let it go with a handshake. She turned to the wonderful "Gilchwist" and said: "Muriel, do you mind if I kiss Joe good-bye?" And to Joe: "Is there any rule against kissing your cook?" We were all feeling sad. If we hadn't turned to go at that moment tears would have been in evidence. This was the first time we did not enjoy moving on.

The first week we were busy getting settled, storing our things on the verandah and in two small bedrooms in the main house, helping with the chores and gardening. On Wednesday Mr. Rhodes went to town to see his lawyer. On his return he told us about meeting a rancher who had just heard he was selling. When the fellow realized we were here waiting for the deal to be completed he told Rhodes he was coming up to offer us cash to change our minds. Mr. Rhodes then told us that six other parties were after the ranch, including some from the States. The weather turned wet, the roads became impassable and we spent too much time sitting around wondering if the appraiser would get out.

On the following Sunday I helped two neighbours brand their calves. The next afternoon I started riding for the mountains with the spring cattle drive. We stopped the night at another ranch, started at daylight with the neighbour's bunch added to ours and picked up a third neighbour with his cattle on the way. It took all day to trail them about 25 miles into the mountain forest reserve. We spent the night in a cabin with the Stock Association rider, talking of horses and cow men, sleeping in saddle blankets on the floor. It was a trip to remember always and afforded escape from the tension of awaiting developments.

We rode straight home the third day and to my dismay I learned the appraiser had been out. It was unfortunate that I had not been present to answer his questions and he did not seek the answers from Eleanor. She was worried, and more than that, apprehensive. Mr. Miller, to whom we had told so much, did not make the trip and it was obvious the new man did not have all the details. He told Rhodes this was the largest deal the Government had handled so far in the district. To complicate matters, a quarter-section of land adjoining had been sold for $18.50 an acre. Our ten dollars an acre deal was pending, but what if there should be a loophole somewhere?

I questioned Eleanor further. She said the man had been here most of Tuesday and as he was leaving she ran out to ask him what she should tell me. He said some papers would be mailed for me to sign. I was very tired from the long ride, confused with the various accounts of the visit from the appraiser. It didn't sound right. Could there be further obstacles to jeopardize our slim chance for success? I did not believe so, but Eleanor felt our plans were approaching a crisis.

The first thing that resulted from the inspection was a letter asking for more details on my financial standing and working plans. Curiously enough at the same time Rhodes told me he could not sell us any cattle on time as he would have no guarantee of payments. The coincidence was significant but we were not disturbed. Once the deal was through I was positive that Augie Sauer or some Medicine Hat rancher like Eugene Burton would offer just as good a proposition. I sent an account of our financial standing to the V.L.A., mentioning the silent partners, telling them everything we had explained to Mr. Miller. I sold the car quickly for $900 and purchased a second-hand army jeep. The agency got rid of the trailer for $1,200. We sent off letters about cashing our insurance policies. We sold all the personal effects we could market in a hurry, including a new suit of mine and Eleanor's electrical appliances. I hated to part with a fine leather suitcase that had travelled with me since September of 1939.

The appraiser had obviously found a lot of loose ends. We had believed his job was concerned only with the state of the ranch and its earning capacity. Why should the V.L.A. be writing at this stage for more details? We had told them everything, they had allowed us to move up here and nothing had changed our standing since then. Well, we had sold the car and trailer; everything we owned was here. But time was running out on the Offer to Sell. Mr. Miller had certainly been wise in advising us to make it for 90 days. They would have to use dynamite to get rid of us, we were so well dug in. But the delay was giving the owner understandable concern. After we had moved to the little cabin other buyers began to appear openly and sessions went on in the main house. We began to look like squatters and cold fear began to displace our high hopes. We now had just enough money to buy the ranch and if any other conditions were imposed we should be at a loss to meet them. We began to suspect everyone. Mr. Rhodes tried to call off the deal and offered to pay us for our time working as ranch hands. He was very positive that we could make no deal for cattle with him or anyone else except on a cash basis.

It was almost the end of June when the roof fell in. A letter from the V.L.A. stated that after reviewing our case the Board could not proceed further unless we could stock the ranch with 40 head of cows and their calves owned by ourselves. They had to be convinced we had a reasonable chance for a financial return the first year. We stopped fencing, farming and gardening long enough to realize we were in a spot such as we had never before experienced. I felt a very real persecution complex for the first time and said to Eleanor: "You know we're licked. Let's retire in dignity while there's still a chance to get out of this mess without hurting anyone else."

"What kind of people do they think we are?" she said. "No one is going to push us around now. You'd better start for town and keep going until you come back with an answer. I'll hold the fort here. If both of us leave now our stuff could be put off the place, but I think we have some kind of common-law rights as long as we hang on. Besides I've put the garden in."

Next day I left for town and I wasn't coming back without an answer. That's what the girl said. My girl.

Chapter Eight

WE FELT the world had turned against us, not the world of our friends but a world of officialdom and strangers. It was a funny sort of persecution complex. There wasn't anything definite you could put your finger on, but a number of little incidents, piled on top of a good imagination, began to add up. Strangers in a new country, we were being called with a weak hand. We were so close to getting the ranch and winning our objective that this new condition of buying a bunch of cows and calves first seemed an obstacle of major proportions. Once the ranch was in our hands I could go anywhere and buy cattle or take them on shares. It was an easy sort of deal to swing. But to make the purchase of the ranch conditional on my having cattle first, before I had the ranch to bargain with, knowing the exact state of our finances, was to my mind at the moment tantamount to telling us we could go no further. The cards were definitely stacked against us. If I had been in a reasonable frame of mind and had driven to Lethbridge first we might have threshed it out. Understandably or not I was very sure someone in the Government was waiting to pounce upon me and talk me out of it.

I don't believe Eleanor fully understood the seriousness of our financial position. When she told me to drive away and come back with an answer that would satisfy the authorities, she had probably been made overconfident by our amazing luck in the past and felt I could pull off another miracle. I had been caught up in her mood and felt I would return with the solution. But driving along the highway, not thinking very clearly, the old doubts and fears took hold. In the back of my mind was the certainty that once the ranch was ours we could work out any kind of deal. As the matter stood we were on the brink of disaster.

I turned into Pincher Creek. Was there any use in going to the Canadian Legion and talking to fellow veterans? I didn't know any of them well and besides they had their own troubles. The lawyers in town were working for Rhodes. I did not know any business men and there were no ranchers around to whom I could turn for ideas. With a chip on my shoulder from nervous apprehension and no clear plan to argue from I went into the bank and asked to see the manager.

"It's like this," I said. "We are on a good little ranch and the V.L.A. approves, but they won't complete the deal unless I own 40 cows and calves. I have enough money to buy my share of the ranch but nothing for livestock."

The manager shook his head sadly. "You veterans read these pamphlets overseas and look at the nice pictures and imagine how wonderful it is going to be when you get home. But it isn't like that at all."

"Is there any way I can buy some cattle?"

"Yes," he said. "The best proposition for you is a farm improvement loan. You pay ten per cent down on the cattle, the Government guarantees the rest and you pay off the loan in a certain amount of time at a reasonable rate of interest."

They had me there too. I would have to borrow more money but had never in my life been in so deep as I was at the moment. The V.L.A. would probably take another look at the picture and turn thumbs down. The bank manager had correctly pointed out there was no guarantee that cattle would not go down in price. Everyone was sure there would be a post-war recession and no one was expecting it more than the rancher. To base the purchase of this ranch and its survival on the buying of 40 head of stock, with prices expected to go down, and tie it up with anything as strict as a bank loan was simply courting disaster. I didn't want any of it. So I left.

It took me a few years to learn that the bank manager was himself a veteran of World War One, that he was a hell of a good guy and that it was time somebody pulled me up short with a few home truths. I didn't enjoy it at the time but I have realized these facts since. Everyone else had been patting us on the back, increasing our daring and elan. This man made me realize that the ranch with its potential earning value was sitting on one side of the scales and borrowed capital on the other, nearly in balance. One bad decision or a freak change in our fortune would upset it. I recalled Professor Ewen's last letter in which he warned me that we had to buy a ranch now. We could not afford to wait for the prices to go down. And he had it figured that there were three years of steady prices ahead in which to reduce our capitalization. Against this I remembered the words of Gene Burton: "Don't let the banks get into you, fella. Lots of us old-timers spent our best years working our heads off for the bank." And there was Eleanor holding the fort with the simple faith that I would wheel up to the door, jump out waving my arms and call: "Everything is fixed, Buckwheat! We are saved again!"

Walking down the street of this prosperous little town I wondered where to turn. For the first time I was alone and frightened, a complete stranger. The nearest friends who knew what we had been through were almost 200 miles away. As I crossed the street a big smile lightened the face of a passing priest and a strong hand grasped mine. What on earth was I doing here and why did I look so worried? He was a husky Irishman who as a student had played such good baseball in the States that a semi-pro team had tried to sign him up. But he had become a missionary priest and taken a vow of poverty. We had been good friends when I was in the R.C.M.P. and he was working in the relief-stricken coal-mining areas of the south. Although I was a Scottish Presbyterian we had shared an interest in sports, books and common experiences in our work. He had seen me off to war and we had exchanged a few letters. But that was years ago.

I told him the story briefly. Now *he* looked worried. We climbed into his car and drove away from the town to park and talk it over. He said if he had some time to work on it he might rally some help. I told him we couldn't borrow money as we were already involved too deeply. He reminded me of his vow of poverty, but said he owned this car and offered to sell it so I could put up a payment on cattle. His attitude gave me courage. I told him we might lick it some other way and we parted with his promise to come up and help with the haying. I think that I revealed some of my persecution ideas or the suspicion of a double-cross into his mind, for he reacted as a good fighting Irishman would. When I left him I was ready for another round and just waiting for the bell.

Driving back to Cowley I decided to telephone Eleanor. But what could I tell her? We couldn't waste time, every day was valuable, and here I was cruising around. I had settled nothing. If a solution could be found I would have to drive to Medicine Hat to find it. I thought of Augie and his voice booming: "You kids buy it if you can and worry about it after." I thought of Tip and his infectious enthusiasm. They would be the boys to see.

At the telephone office in Cowley I put through a call to Augie's house. Ethel answered, said Augie would be in that evening. This was Saturday. I told her I was leaving Cowley right away and would drive straight there. She said Augie would be waiting for me. Now I had something to tell Eleanor. I put through a call to the ranch for my wife. The operator turned to me and said: "I have spoken to the ranch but Mrs. Campbell isn't there any more."

I blew up at that piece of information. "Sure she's there," I said. "She was there when I left this morning and is expecting me to call." The operator rang again, told the party at the other end to have Mrs. Campbell come to the telephone right away, or else! It was good to hear her voice. I tried to sound cheerful. Was she all right? Fine. I was just leaving for Medicine Hat. I had something cooking. Augie was waiting to see me. I would return as soon as I possibly could. Eleanor was equally cheerful. She would hang on, and here's to success. We couldn't say any more.

I burned up the road to the Hat, giving the old army jeep everything it had and arrived about 11. Augie was waiting and we talked until about three in the morning. Augie got mad.

"What's the matter with that bunch in Lethbridge? Why can't they let you buy the place and leave you alone to run it your own way? We'll get the cattle for you, don't worry about that."

I tried to explain about the series of incidents that made us think we were being squeezed out of the deal and although we couldn't pin down any evidence of connivance between all the parties concerned, unless I could come up with something solid for the V.L.A. Board, with no loopholes, they might withdraw once and for all. Augie was distinctly embarrassed.

"Right at the moment I can't help the way I would like to," he said. "All my money is tied up until next winter in cattle."

"Believe me, Augie, the last thing I wanted from you is financial help. I drove down here because there isn't a friend in that country I could talk to, and you know the angles. Maybe you could come up with an idea I haven't figured."

I had not eaten since breakfast and Augie cooked up a meal. "Let's go to bed," he said finally. "Maybe we can sleep on it and come up with a plan in the morning." It was very late and I had a splitting headache, but in that friendly home I slept like a baby.

I was awakened by the aroma of bacon and eggs and good coffee. Ethel was cheery and full of fun, and we had a pleasant breakfast. She would not let us talk business or worry until the meal was finished. As Augie and I twisted smokes in the living room I knew by his silence that he was worried. I began to feel badly about coming down to bother him like this with our troubles. Finally he looked up.

"What do you figure we should do first, Gray?"

"I don't know, Augie, but I remember Tip Volway told us when we had our ranch one of the big fellows in the short country would give us a start with cattle. I don't want to do it this way but if I could show on paper that I had these cattle, and no strings attached, I think we could force the thing through. It won't be long until the time limit is up on the Offer to Sell."

"Let's talk to Tip," he said. "Phone his house and ask him to meet us down town."

I called the Volway house, told Tip I had a knife in my back and someone was getting ready to twist it, that Augie and I had been trying to get it out and we would like to see him if he could get down town. He said he would drive right to his store and we could talk in the office.

We started to toss it around once more. It seemed like an improper subject on this peaceful Sunday morning. I was sick and tired of the whole thing, but they were a couple of great guys who had gambled with life and won. They were getting their teeth into it. When I mentioned one of the big ranchers trusting us with the cattle Tip thought it was a good idea.

"To hell with it," said Augie. "We can do it right now without leaving the office. I haven't got much loose money, but say we each put up $500 and telephone a few other guys for the same amount. How about that, Tip?"

"Sure," said Tip, "we can get it covered in half an hour." And he grabbed the telephone.

"Wait a minute, fellows," I said. "Eleanor and I would rather give up the ranch than borrow money from you boys. I didn't drive down here for that. Joe Gilchrist and others told me about starting up like this and getting a bank behind them on their name alone. This country is healthier than it was in those days and there wouldn't be as much risk for a bank. I bet a good manager who is interested could help me convince the V.L.A. and put the thing across. And I'm willing to bet with his prestige and the right amount of bluff we won't have to sign papers or borrow until we have the ranch in our hands. Eleanor and I don't care how hard we have to work as long as we can leave the ranch cleared of debt for our boys. The whole problem is to find someone like that with enough nerve to help me cut the red tape."

Tip jumped to his feet. "I've got it!" he said. "You know Hutch, Augie. He was a bank manager here for some time. Right now he's in Lethbridge waiting for a new branch to open. He always wanted to be a rancher and he knows the business. Besides, he'll probably have more authority to take chances looking for new business."

Tip chuckled as he picked up the telephone. "This is the kind of thing he likes and if he can't work it out nobody can." He put through the call. "Hutch? This is Tip. What are you doing, sitting around in the hotel? Look, I've got a friend here in the office. You don't know him but he's got a problem. Sure, I'm sending along a new customer for the bank. Can you see him today? Okay. Listen to his story and give the boy a break. If you want any backing I'll sign any notes you agree on."

Augie grabbed the telephone. "This is Augie Sauer speaking. I want to sign the notes too."

When Tip had hung up we parted at the front of the store. I raced around the block, found I needed gasoline and pulled into a service station. While I was checking the tires a car stopped at the corner. Tip's head appeared through the window opening and he beckoned me over.

"Did you have something to eat, boy? I forgot to ask. Do you need any cash?" I told him I had enough but he shoved his hand in his pocket and thrust ten dollars into my hand. "Take this anyway. You may need it. You can send it back any time. And don't forget, Hutch is a right guy. Tell him everything. He's going to be interested. Don't forget to give our love to Eleanor and don't quit now." That was the last time I saw Tip. We wrote him a few letters and returned the money.

It must have been about 3:30 Sunday afternoon when I arrived in Lethbridge and went to Hutch's room. I was feeling very dull, the sort of tiredness that was more mental than physical and prevented me from summoning any enthusiasm. Yet there was no restraint or tension between us. Hutch poured me a drink. It was the one thing I needed. He poured me another and got me talking. I had made up my mind to answer routine questions, leave out the details and refrain from any attempt to build up the adventure and romance that Eleanor and I had enjoyed until now. But Hutch was more than a bank manager. He was the kind of man that helped make the West, one of the old school though young in years. Before I knew it I had told him where I had been in the R.C.M.P., the years during the war, all about Eleanor, the first job, the drive, Harry Hargrave, Joe Gilchrist and all the rest. I answered so many questions my head was spinning, but we had a lot of laughs. If anyone was going to pull me out of this slump Hutch was the man to do it.

"Well, what do you think?" I said finally. "Should we put our tails between our legs and crawl back where we came from—or should we stick?"

"Meet me in the morning around 9:30," he said. "We're still building the new bank and I'll be down there getting in the road. The two of us will call on the V.L.A."

In the morning I was slightly hung-over and nervous as we climbed the stairs. Mr. Miller was in his office and I introduced Hutch. The bank manager waved his hand and said we were all fixed up to buy the cattle in a way that would be acceptable to the Government. Mr. Miller was relieved and asked for it in writing. Hutch wrote out a statement to that effect. Mr. Miller said he would send it all in to Edmonton and would try to rush things through. When he received clearance he would telephone me to meet him in Pincher Creek.

Back in the new building, amid ladders, workmen and blue-prints, I asked Hutch if he wanted me to sign anything. He suggested we wait until we found out what was going to happen. We shook hands on that and I left for the jeep. I started the engine, then shut it off. Had we covered every-thing? All the Government had was Hutch's statement. What if they decided to write again asking precisely where the cattle were and for a new report on our finances? This would consume more time but we couldn't put the boots to the Government to hurry them up, and if the Offer to Sell expired, and there were only a few weeks left, nothing could save us. Tip had said: "Don't quit now."

If there was going to be any more fighting I should look up an Irishman. And I knew one in town, the fighting kind, Arthur Beaumont, K.C. He had been a police magistrate and before the war we used to meet frequently for dinner and bridge. In addition to his hilarious accounts of his exploits during World War One and his early years in Canada afterwards, I remembered his great willingness to drop everything and throw himself into a fight for poor, unfortunate, helpless little people. Perhaps he would like to hear our story!

"Bejasus!" he said when I told it to him. "We've got to move quickly. Why didn't you look me up before this started? I want to meet this bank manager and we're going to see Miller. Then you are going to take me up to the ranch." He cancelled his appointments and I raced down the street after him. "I'm going to do all the talking," he said. "I'm Southern Commander of the Canadian Legion. During the war I helped the Government draw up some of these regulations and I'm going to threaten the whole weight of the Legion behind me if there's any funny business."

He talked to Hutch privately, and told me afterwards he knew enough about banking laws to feel Hutch was sticking his neck out. Hutch said he realized this but hadn't the heart to turn me away. Beaumont told him he was my lawyer now and promised to dig up a better plan for both of us. Hutch remembered Tip's and Augie's promises to back any notes but the lawyer wanted a firmer business and legal foundation.

He stormed into the V.L.A. shouting, "Where's the bloody S.S.B.?" (After World War One the V.L.A. was known as the Soldiers' Settlement Board.) I cannot remember what he said except that he was going out to the ranch and that he and the Canadian Legion were very much interested in the case. On the way to the jeep I spotted Harold Haugen on the street. He explained that he had left the Deer Creek and was looking around. I asked him if he would like to visit us for a while and agreed to meet him when I returned with Beaumont.

The indignant Irishman had jumped in with both feet without knowing a fraction of the details. I had talked and explained so much to Augie and Tip and Hutch the previous day that I was trying for short-cuts in my narrative. Beaumont became more puzzled as we progressed because I was talking in chunks, with no sequence, and not helping him much. He was perplexed over the reason for the drive to Medicine Hat, why the cattle deal with Rhodes should fall through, when I remembered to tell him about the silent partners. During the last five miles of the drive he suddenly said: "For the first time I'm beginning to see daylight. I'm getting the picture now. But why go to Medicine Hat and other people after starting up with the silent partners? Keep all your eggs in one basket, boy. Don't try to complicate things."

Arriving at the ranch he met Eleanor at the cabin, said that he was spending the night, the camp cot would be perfect, he loved strong tea any time, and his idea of luxury was to sit by the oven door "measling his shins and sipping tay." He had Eleanor laughing so that she forgot to ask how things were going. Before settling down, however, he said to me: "Take me over to the main house to meet the owner. I'll do the talking and don't interrupt me. I'm going to tell them things that will surprise you." He certainly did. Apparently he was our lawyer and had a large trust account of mine. Everything was going through as originally agreed upon, including the purchase of 30 cows with calves to be picked from the herd now on the place and they were to be paid for in three annual instalments, without interest charges, commencing one year from the sale of the ranch. When Rhodes protested that he had no guarantee and once my brand was on the animals he had no come-back, Beaumont said he would produce a guarantee from the bank to pay each instalment on time whether or not I had the money and that this guarantee would satisfy his lawyers. He added that we had the money to pay for them but everyone was going to stick to the original agreement, verbal or written, all the way down the line.

He returned to the cabin rubbing his hands and proceeded to entertain us hilariously during the evening, drinking strong tea and "measling his shins". Eleanor saw to that. The next day he attended to details we never realized existed, beat up our flagging hopes with Celtic zeal and worked so many miracles we dubbed him the Wizard of Oz. When he left he took with him all our headaches.

On the drive back to Lethbridge he said: "Boy, you found a gold mine." I told him about Harold coming up to visit, and said we had so many commitments now we had better take out some insurance against our lack of experience by trying to hire Harold for a year anyway. He thought it was a good idea. Because I couldn't pay wages I asked him if he would draw up a contract later, when all the trouble was over, offering Harold a percentage of the net income.

The Wizard then told me he would be in Calgary by the end of the week and would check the titles of the land. He told us to go ahead and work the ranch as though it was ours.

We did just that. Harold returned with me. It was July and we were late getting started with the haying. We seemed to be working day and night. We had to borrow a team of horses here, hay forks there, and all the neighbours began to rally around. Rhodes would not let us use any equipment until the purchase of the ranch was completed. It gave us a fine chance to discover how good the neighbours really were. And it was fun.

The only cloud appeared in a letter from the V.L.A. with a legal form to be signed by ourselves and the silent partners. It was an undertaking that we were not to pay them in money or kind until we had discharged our debt to the Government. Beaumont said it was a "low blow" but we had no choice except to bother those good people, and I mailed it to them with an apologetic letter. They returned it with the cheery notation that we could get the Government out of the way first and let them be real partners!

At the end of July 1947, Rhodes returned from town. He came over to the cabin in the evening to tell me he had signed all the papers. Everything had been completed, but his lawyer wanted to see me. He did not know what it was for, but it was important that I do so. We were very busy, so I drove to town early, hoping to return for the best part of the day, and was waiting for the lawyer when he arrived at the office. He was very apologetic, said all the documents were drawn up and that he wanted to see the deal go through quickly. But three more conditions had been imposed. I had to sign an additional legal paper, agreeing to the conditions set forth before the papers could be sent to my lawyers. Those were the instructions from his client. The conditions were as follows: 1. Cash for the cattle (There's that knife again!). 2. Possession of the house until November 15. 3. The right to keep all their possessions on the place until April 1948, and full use of the cabin.

The lawyer asked me to sign. I shook my head. He wanted to know what I intended to do. I said I would telephone my lawyer and let him know.

When I explained the new conditions to the anxious Irishman I had to hold the receiver a foot away from my ear. He shouted that I was not to sign anything or mention the matter to anyone but to tell the lawyer he would be along the next day. He asked me to meet the bus.

I went back and put in a pretty good day at the ranch. But Eleanor was worried. I told her the Wizard was coming out and he was planning to remain a couple of days. Our cabin had one bedroom, a kitchen and a small pantry. Eleanor, Dane, Timmy and I slept in the bedroom, and Harold in the kitchen on my Air Force camp cot. Harold offered to sleep on the mattress placed on the floor so Beaumont could have the cot.

After the Wizard dismounted from the bus he called on the lawyer and asked him to come along. We drove to the ranch. Beaumont was magnificent. He talked to everyone like a Dutch uncle with a brogue. When he had finished, all were eager to return to the original conditions. He gained possession of the papers and I drove him to Lethbridge Sunday evening to spend the night at his home.

Monday morning early we called on Mr. Miller. Beaumont gave him an account of the latest tactics and threatened to sue for everything. He said we simply had to get the final okay from Edmonton before something else turned up. Beaumont wasn't fooling when he threatened to sue, but he didn't want any time to slip by for the effects of his warning to wear off. Mr. Miller admitted he had been worried the last few weeks by the delay in Edmonton. He didn't know as we were talking that things were happening at that very moment.

The clerk who checked the mail came rushing into his office and put down the last piece of red tape—final authority for Miller to close the deal! There it was on his desk and he beamed at us in triumph. It could not have been more timely. Heaving a sigh of relief Beaumont asked: "Can you finish this today?"

Miller said he would telephone Rhodes' lawyers and have all the principals meet in Pincher Creek that afternoon. He asked me to give him time to clear his desk and I walked out with Beaumont. As he turned to go to Court he wagged a finger at me: "Don't sign any papers but the ones Mr. Miller hands you." I grinned back at the genial Irishman and promised.

Then I walked around the streets in a daze. The business had been so long drawn out, and yet it had ended so suddenly. I don't know just where I went but I remember fighting down an urge to stop citizens on the street to tell them the news. Finding myself down at the railway station I sent off a vague telegram to Eleanor, not realizing that she could not begin to guess the drama was approaching the closing scene. "Bringing home the bacon. Love", I wrote. The date was July 28, 1947.

Then I drove to Pincher Creek as Miller was following in his own car. When he arrived we assembled in the lawyer's office. I had a mad impulse to ask them to hold everything until I fetched Eleanor from the ranch so that she could witness the last chapter in the struggle. We finished signing all the papers at seven o'clock that evening.

It was too bad I couldn't borrow an airplane to shoot up to the ranch. I pushed the jeep hard, expecting to find Eleanor tip-toe with excitement. Her calmness infuriated me. Wasn't this a wonderful climax? Wasn't what wonderful? I found that my telegram had left her completely in a fog about developments. She thought I had bought a couple of weaner pigs! Bringing home the bacon, to be sure. What a gal!

Several years later, I asked a V.L.A. official about our case.

"Maybe you don't know how lucky you were," he replied. "We still figure you should never have been passed and I can tell you now it was touch-and-go for a long time. The only thing that got you in was the fact the records showed you had been a stock inspector in the Mounted Police!"

Chapter Nine

HAROLD DECIDED to remain with us on a yearly contract and we were soon immersed in long days of heavy work, trying to catch up on lost time. So many fine days and precious hours had been spent running around the country pulling irons out of the fire we had to let everything else wait for the urgency of saving our hay. We had a team and rack, two hay forks, a mower and rake. Because we could not afford any breakdowns caused by my inexperience, Harold ran the mower. We worked around the clock, from five in the morning until ten at night. It was a real struggle to get out of boots and blue jeans in the evening before falling asleep. In spite of hot weather, nose flies bothering the team and bull-dog flies attacking man and beast, we kept at it. We forked the hay on the rack, built large loads, hauled to the stack yards and forked the hay off. We built the stacks as high as we could pitch hay. But the method was too old-fashioned and slow. It looked as though we would be working at it until the first snow storm. In the past, Mr. Rhodes had put up hay in this fashion but he had used several teams and many men. More progressive outfits had long since been using stackers and sweeps run by horses or tractors. Harold explained the various methods and advised getting a stacker. Mr. Beaumont had made sure we would have a few hundred dollars in the bank for emergencies, so Eleanor and I debated if a stacker could be so classified.

One evening I drove to a neighbour's place to buy Eleanor a present to celebrate the completion of the deal. I returned with six ducks which we launched with appropriate ceremony in the large stock dam in front of the house. I also brought news of an auction sale south of Pincher Creek. A farmer was selling out. Sometimes at these sales a man can pick up a piece of machinery very cheaply if he keeps his head, and this one advertised two home-made sets of stackers and sweeps for horses.

During July, between crises, we had attended a local sale just over the hill about two miles from our place and had wonderful luck. We had purchased a young saddle horse for $20, a bench and some pails for $1.50 and a fair kitchen stove. This was our first experience of a farm auction sale and we were elated with the results. We found out later that the Bougerolle brothers, our neighbours to the west, had wanted the saddle horse and had, in fact, started to bid. But when they noticed me bidding they had stopped. They had heard we were running into tough luck and figured we needed the horse. Heady with the success of buying a horse so cheaply and badly needing a stove, I started to bid on the one in the cabin. A man north of us also started to bid lively. We were the only two interested. When he saw it was the new people who wanted that stove he walked out the door and left me to bid alone. We got it for $8.50.

Remembering how well that first auction had turned out for us we decided to try for a stacker to speed up the haying. Harold and I arrived early for the sale and spent an hour looking at all the machinery on display. The stackers were made of logs and heavy bridge timbers; it looked as though moving one would be a big engineering job. We debated the feasibility of taking it apart, moving the sections and rebuilding at home. But the more we sized up the contraption the less we liked the idea. As the sale progressed from household effects to animals and tool and harness, winding up with the big machinery, I asked other men for their views on the possibility of moving one of the heavy stackers. One chap told me he had a "slide overshot" horse stacker and sweep, factory built, at his farm much closer to our home which he would sell for $100. He had just bought a tractor outfit. He would also lend us a strong trailer our jeep could handle for hauling the outfit home. I spoke to Harold, and as he thought it well worth looking at we arranged to stop in after the sale. We spent the rest of the day there watching other men buy at reasonable prices tools and machinery we could well have used but felt we could do without for the time being. If we were going to lose no time improving the hay land, however, we would need a plough, so I told Harold to bid if he thought there was a bargain. At the end of the sale he slipped in a quick bid for an old sulky plough with good shares. Such ploughs were so out of date in this rich and modern district we got it for $2.50. It was the kind used by the early homesteaders to break the land. Flushed with success we bid again on a binder, in good working order with new canvasses and rollers. It was knocked down to us for $9.50. When someone told us a new canvas cost eight dollars we felt even better.

On the way home we looked at the factory-built stacker and sweep, decided to buy and arranged to pick them up next day. Now we really began to make time with the haying. Harold ran the horse sweep while I raised the sweep load on the stacker with the jeep. Then I built the stack while he was out getting the next load. We put up our first big high stack in five hours. Using the old method we had discarded, handling the hay twice as much and damaging the leaves, it would have taken us three days or better to put the same amount of hay in a number of smaller stacks. It was hot and heavy work for the stacker, but it was child's play when compared with the old time-consuming system. We began to catch up and think of other things besides hay. I recalled the words of an old-timer who had cautioned: "City folks holler for a 40-hour week and I figger a man in the country is entitled to a day off. Don't you folks get in the habit of working Sundays. It's all right for an emergency but I did it for years and I know it's a bad habit to break." We decided to try taking a day off.

The valley between the Porcupine Hills and the Livingstone Range of the Rockies is called the North Fork. That is the North Fork of the Old Man River whose headwaters come rushing out of the mountains through the breath-taking gap about 30 miles from the ranch. If you climb the hill to the west you can follow the whole lovely valley for miles north and south with the naked eye. Directly across, so massive and close you feel like reaching out to touch it, is the Livingstone Range. A great many of the early settlers who came out from England chose this valley and from a scenic point of view I think it was a fair exchange. Some had money, built fine homes and imported good horses and stock. Others started by homesteading. But all were sportsmen and in those free and easy days they played a lot of polo. They also built a tiny log church, known as the Livingstone Church, part of the Foothills Mission. This church was about 14 miles from us and during the summer, weather permitting, a service was held the first Sunday in the month. Mrs. Mowat, the wife of George Mowat, our closest neighbour on the north, who had left a desk in London about 45 years ago and settled in the North Fork, telephoned Eleanor to ask if we would care to attend the service in August. We thought it would be a nice thing to do in the calm and peace that had descended upon us after all our adventures.

When this Sunday came it was a lovely day, cool, sunny and clear as though the air had been washed by some gigantic air-conditioning unit. All scrubbed and shining and in our best clothes, we drove over Cabin Hill to Mowat's in the open jeep carefully, lest we get dusty. Then we transferred to their car for the drive to church. Here we were, going to church with our neighbours in our own community. We were going to meet many of the old-timers and their descendants. It gave us a warm feeling, a fresh reminder that we actually belonged after so much wandering.

Mr. Mowat described the early settlers, the young Englishmen who came out for adventure bringing polo with them. His own brother had followed him out to become the Anglican vicar in the Foothills Mission. As this was to be a special service we were to meet a larger number than would normally attend. Some of the young people were to be confirmed. The Bishop of Calgary was expected. We found the little church standing all by itself in the middle of a field, with hitching posts and stables adjoining. People were arriving in cars and trucks, in wagons and by saddle horse, dressed in their Sunday best. Mrs. Mowat took Eleanor around to introduce her to the ladies while George had me meet some of the men. There was "Posthole" Smith. The nickname had been picked up in the early days and Posthole was proud of it. It had to appear that way in the social column of the Pincher Creek *Echo* or people wouldn't know which Smith was meant. His brother was known as "Dropper" Smith. There was Harry Gunn who came out in 1890. He had been one of the stars on the famous Cowley polo team which had travelled to Winnipeg and down through the western states. The team had distinguished themselves by winning an international match at Seattle and probably caused many people to wonder where the devil Cowley was located.

We leaned over the hitching post while George reminisced about the early days in his English accent. "We had a lot of fun then," he said. "It was quite a community of old countrymen. Some of them had fine houses where they gave very correct and magnificent parties. Everyone was invited whether you were struggling on a quarter-section of land or managing a big place. It was a joke to see the well-dressed men from the Saturday ball at work the following week. In those days we had two outfits— greasy old cowboy clothes and our white ties and tails. This little church was always well attended on Sunday. Everyone would ride or travel by buckboard to the service very sedately. But as soon as church was over they would gallop and whoop their way in a mad race to the river bottom where they played polo the rest of the day.

"I will never forget one lady just out from England to visit the Kemmis or Sandeman ranch—you know, the Sandeman wine people. She was alone in the house when she answered a knock at the back door. It rather horrified her to see a run-down Englishman with a good accent peddling meat. His hands and arms and shirt front were all bloody. He had just killed a beef, and as he couldn't keep it all on his bachelor establishment he was riding around to the neighbours to sell the surplus. The lady thought this man had quite come down in the world. When they took her to church on Sunday and then to the polo in the afternoon, she admired the very handsome person in immaculate white riding breeches and polished boots, well mounted, who was captain of the winning team. But when she was taken up to be introduced she was horrified to learn he was 'the butcher' who had called a few days previously. It was a good joke for quite a while."

I kept thinking of the old days as George had described them when we entered the church. It was a typical rural service such as one could expect in a church used once a month during the summer. Someone was hammering up a curtain and the Ladies' Aid were putting last-minute touches to the flowers while the bishop hovered discreetly in the doorway. But it was a lovely service. For us it was Thanksgiving. As I looked around at these pleasant faces I couldn't help thinking that although the old days of polo and fancy parties were over, the same kind of people were here, living the life that had been created by hope and fortitude so many years ago.

After the service the whole congregation was invited to a buffet supper on the lawn of the Lynch-Staunton ranch where all sorts of nice people came up to say hello and welcome us. As we drove back with the Mowats the worry of the preceding months began to fade as though it had been a bad dream. Our plans, formed in another kind of life, were actually taking shape. We were finding security. Peace was in the valley, contentment in the hills. Here was a new life to be developed; the main risk was over. We only had to prove ourselves with these new friends. Eleanor and I held hands. We didn't have to talk. Timmy was asleep in his basket and Dane was barely hanging on to consciousness. It was ten o'clock when we got home. The ranch looked different. It had taken on new stature. We had arrived in our spiritual home.

A letter from the Provincial Government sent me off to town. They had approved a brand for us. In years to come, after it had been established and handed down to our sons, the brand would be as well known as our own name. I had the blacksmith make us the branding irons—the Seven, the C and the Bar. As I threw them in the jeep for the trip back I felt they would complete the cycle. We had the ranch, and when we put our brand on the cattle it would really interpret for us the true meaning of the mysterious mass of legal documents and deeds I had signed.

The Rhodes were still in the main house, so I went over to fix a day for the branding. We decided to stage it on Sunday. We would need a crew of five or six, and Eleanor had to plan on two meals, served in relays in the cabin. Needing a good roper we decided to ask Fred Hewitt, an old-time cowboy who had worked on the big Walronde outfit and had travelled in the Welsh Brothers rodeo down East one or two seasons before settling down on his own place. I drove over to ask Fred, whose ranch was just beyond Mowat's. Then I got word to Jim Carney, at whose place we had bought the ducks. Mr. Rhodes said he would get hold of a few others.

In addition to the roper there must be a man to tend the branding fire and hand the irons through the corrals to the man branding. A couple of husky lads are required to wrestle the calves, one with a leg lock on the head, the other stretched out behind the calf to secure the hind legs. You need a good man to mark the ear and castrate, and one to check the horns, dehorning with knife and caustic or dehorning paste. I had to purchase a vaccine gun with spare needles and a fresh supply of vaccine for blackleg and malignant edema. Each calf had to be vaccinated at the same time as it was branded. Normally these operations would be completed much earlier in the calf's life, often in two stages, before the end of June. But here it was August, in fly time and hot. The calves were just that much larger and stronger and we figured the "rasslers" would have to spell each other off.

We had everything assembled before Saturday but Eleanor's job really started then. She had to plan large meals, make a number of pies, have everything ready by Saturday night. We insisted she had to attend the branding and take pictures, so she decided on baking a huge ham the day before.

It was almost time for evening chores on Saturday. I had just checked the supply of wood for the branding fire, assembled shovel and crow-bar for the pit, collected branding irons and lariats, looked over the roping corral and the chute when I noticed trouble by the blacksmith shop. The pigs were out! We had recently purchased two little weaners and had fenced them in by the pig house until they became accustomed to their new home.

I ran towards them, calling to Eleanor for help. We had to keep them together and try to drive or entice them back into their quarters. Eleanor came running. We knocked down the little fence, got them corralled without stirring them up, and together nailed everything back into place. I walked back with Eleanor to the cabin for the milk pails while she explained that her preparations were completed. Poor Eleanor! . . . The sight that greeted her at the cabin was heart-breaking. Her lovely ham that had been left cooling on the table had been dragged outside by the dog and partly eaten. Fortunately for the culprit we couldn't lay our hands on him at that moment. Eleanor lamented tearfully that now she wouldn't be able to watch the branding but would have to spend the day standing over the stove. And we should have to serve stringy pieces of beef instead of tender slices of ham.

We awoke to a lovely calm day, were out at five to do up the chores in mounting excitement. Mr. Rhodes and I were to remain at the corrals. Harold was to take a couple of riders to round up the herd in the summer range, and while his helpers held the cattle in a bunch Harold was to cut out the cows with calves he selected for our basic herd. Then he had to drive them through the gate into the horse pasture which leads down to the corrals. They hoped to get going early, before the heat of the day and the flies should stir up the critters and make them balky. As Harold started up the horse pasture he met Jim Carney riding down and together they disappeared from sight.

Down to the corrals I hauled a pail of hot water smelling strongly of disinfectant, the vaccine, syringe and needles—all the paraphernalia we would need. Fred arrived and we squatted on our heels before the fire pit talking cow and hay crop. Henry Neufeld walked over from his ranch on the east boundary. I wanted to start the fire and begin heating the irons but Fred said: "Plenty of time. The irons will get hot enough between the time the herd is corralled and we get the cows cut back." So we twisted smokes and waited. I wanted to be everywhere at once— out riding with Harold and at the same time checking things at the corral. But we just waited.

About nine o'clock we could see cattle and horsemen milling around at the top of the horse pasture. I wanted to get busy right away. But Fred just said: "Plenty of time yet. They're going to be quite a while getting the right calves with the cows they want." Indeed, it was quite a job and I didn't realize until a year later how difficult it is to ensure you have them properly paired.

By 11 they were starting down the pasture and we disappeared out of sight, leaving the main gate wide open. The cows were suspicious and did not cooperate in taking their calves away from their playground. Once inside the main gate they had to be moved into the smaller roping corral, and then the cows cut back. Here the matrons pressed up against the little corral, bawling at their calves and the little ones answering so continuously it was difficult to hear or understand what anyone was saying.

As soon as the irons were almost red hot, the syringe tested and filled with vaccine, the boys checked each other for jobs and positions. Then the boss nodded and said: "Let's go."

Fred rode into the corral, shaking out his loop, and hind-footed a calf. As the little animal ran out full length on the rope, bucking and plunging, it was dragged over to the side where the irons were waiting. The wrestlers sometimes used an extra rope to secure the head, and by pulling tail and foot ropes on opposite sides they upset the calf. Then they would dive for head and hind legs, stretching it on the correct side. If a head rope wasn't used it took a good man to grab the calf by flank and neck, lift the animal and slam it to the ground. Quickly Harold approached with the first iron and after brushing the hide clean of dirt pressed on the Seven. Back to the fire to exchange his Seven for the C and on it would go, the C for the Bar—and he was through. At the same time Jim had his knife and disinfectant

Branding: Eleanor at left in white cap, Gray with branding irons, Claude Hammond holding calf. (PHOTO BY GORDON CRICHTON)

at work if the calf was a bull, turning it into a steer. Another man was at the head, cutting the horn button and rubbing in caustic, while yet another was shooting into the neck or shoulder five c.c.'s of vaccine. As each man finished his job he stood clear to replenish his supply of vaccine, check tools, clean knife or coil a spare rope out of the way. A tally man marked up the score, divided into steers and heifers. When all the jobs had been checked the wrestlers jumped clear and the roper went after another calf.

As the hot day wore on we changed jobs around and it turned into a sporting event with the interest mainly on the roping. We tried roping on foot, and after dabbing the loop correctly took a couple of quick turns on the snubbing post in the centre. Men were leaping and racing out of the way as the calf usually raced around the corral, winding up on the snubbing post before it could be stopped. Another rope on head and one forefoot, so the animal would not choke, stretched to one side of the corral, made it easier to handle the larger, more energetic calves. It was easy to get tripped or knocked about. Rope burns and bruises from the hind foot of a protesting calf made their appearance on legs, arms, shoulders, even necks.

It was a tired, hot and dusty crew that finished the last calf. We walked up to the cabin for our dinner, some of us limping from bruises. In the shade of the cabin there was beer in a wash tub full of cold water from the well. It tasted like champagne. We ate heartily in spite of the heat. The job was half finished. The cows had to be run through the chute and branded in a primitive type of squeeze. At last it was completed, and Fred Hewitt put the final word to an active, exciting and satisfying day.

"Well, Gray, now you're in the cattle business." I looked at his new car and his well-dressed wife and children, thought of his comfortable little home over the hills as he added: "Everything I got out of this world was provided by those Herefords. Just hang on to the old cow's tail, boy, and she'll pull you out of your troubles."

These were our first cattle, as nice a little bunch of cows as any man would want to start with. When everyone had left, Eleanor and I strolled down to the corrals in the cool of the evening and looked at each animal before turning it into the bull pasture to be kept separate from the Rhodes' herd. We took a long look at the brand, 7C—, on the right hip. Not one calf looked ill or as though it had suffered more than momentary anguish. Eleanor had taken some snapshots and wondered if the brand would show up. There were 30 cows with their calves at $125 each pair. And we had bought one of the bulls for $200. That made it $3,950 worth of stock in the corral. A year from now we would have to make the first of three annual payments for them. Would the price of beef go down suddenly and sharply, forcing us to sell the whole herd? If it held steady and if we could pick up more cattle either on shares or by running them at so much a head per month, we might scrape through, selling the calves out of the cows and holding the 30 head of matrons in our herd. It was going to take us a long time to build up. I'll bet some of the neighbours must have wondered this day if we were going to make it with only 30 cows for a start. I could see now what the V.L.A. Board meant when they insisted on our having a herd first.

Eleanor must have sensed my thoughts. We turned the thirsty animals out to water and grass, then walked up the valley until we were standing on a knoll looking down at the buildings, corrals and strip farms in the distance. "I hope our branding parties will be bigger and better in future, old thing," I said, "and that you'll be out there with us all day taking part in the fun."

"Remember what Fred told you," she replied. "You're in the cattle business now. All we have to do is hang on to their tails and they will pull us through."

I wondered. Would Fred start out like this today?

Chapter Ten

THIS IS great country for winter wheat. With a reasonable winter, wheat seeded in the fall gets a better start than spring wheat and the farmers are able to harvest it ahead of the early frosts. By this time everyone with winter wheat was busy cutting his crops. We remembered Jim Carney who had lent us a team of horses and a set of harness for our haying and also helped us brand. Harold and I decided to keep on the right side of the ledger and when we heard Jim was about to stook his grain we went over there for two days. I had never done this sort of work before and was dismayed to see the long rows of bundles lying on the strips. We worked without forks, which means more bending, and Harold set a terrific pace which almost played out the rest of us. We finished the stooking in two days but it nearly wrecked me. The Carneys were very grateful. It was the largest crop they had cut in years.

We had just settled down at home again when Angus Maufort, our neighbour to the south, paid us a call. George Mowat was behind with his haying. His best hay had been lying in cocks on the home place. Angus explained that George had suffered a bad accident some years before that had slowed him down and he wondered if the three of us could go over there and give George a day. We left next morning with a team and wagon and three strong backs to put up most of the field. We forked the hay into wagons by hand but George and his hired man operated a stacker to take off the loads. After sizing us up on this job Angus wondered if we could help him for two days to get his clover bundles stacked. He offered to pay us going wages. We couldn't continue working for good will, so I made a counter proposition. Angus kept pigs and I wondered if he would trade us a finished pig for our work. He thought that was a fine arrangement and for our part we needed meat for the winter. A pig would help. So we moved down there with team and wagon. Harold did the stacking, being an artist at building bundle stacks, while Angus and I spent two days hauling loads of bundles to him. I began learning how to pitch bundles. The lessons were credited towards the precious pig.

Rhodes finally left the main house and when we returned from working out I thought all we had to do was move our things over. But Eleanor took us on an inspection tour and laid down the law. Left for us was an old bed, some shelves in the pantry and the linoleum on the kitchen floor—we had bought that. Eleanor began pulling paper off the walls, showing us layer after layer of old wallpaper underneath. She took us to the bedrooms and made us look at greasy finger marks on woodwork and walls. She made us inspect the floors, she pulled up the linoleum, and when she finished talking we realized we would be lucky to get in there before the end of September.

While we spent a few days fixing fences Eleanor dusted and swept the house. Then with a knife she scraped the woodwork. When she had removed the old dirt she put on rubber gloves and with plenty of lye in the water scrubbed the floors. Then she painted walls and ceilings and woodwork after papering some of the rooms with a strong building paper that would take a cheap casein paint. Her first complete success was with the little boys' room which she transformed into a bright, cheery place. After scrubbing, painting and waxing the floor she closed up the room before tackling the next job.

It was no place for a man, so we cleared out. Eleanor suggested that if we were out of the way and she didn't have to plan meals for us she would make better time. As Carneys were about to start threshing we joined their outfit for three days. They paid eight dollars a day for a team and wagon, six dollars for a man. I let Harold take the team as I didn't know how a threshing crew worked. If you have a team and wagon you throw on your load with the help of the field pitcher, rest while you drive in to the machine, then pitch off the load. Then you rest while the team takes you out to the field where the field pitcher helps you load again. I was the field pitcher. There wasn't any rest for me. In fact, I could hardly keep up with the six teams that kept coming at me with horrible regularity. Thank heaven it lasted only three days.

We slept at home, stumbling around in the dark to do our own chores, downing a hasty breakfast and rushing by jeep to get on the crew by daylight. As the outfit travels from one farm to the next the wives go along to help the next neighbour with the meals, and the women vie with one another to provide the best grub. The tables literally groan with the food and I have never eaten better than on a threshing crew. At night we would return home, utterly fagged out, to find that our milk cows had strayed and in spite of complaining muscles we had to search for them in the dark.

After finishing the three days in that outfit I would have been content to rest on my laurels. But when we returned home with our team and wagon Eleanor announced there were two calls for us. Angus wanted to know if Harold could take his place on the Dumont crew and Gus Dingreville wanted to know if we could come down there. Working for Angus would help to buy that pig. If Harold joined his crew I would have to show up at Dingreville's. Harold left at noon with team and wagon next day to put in ten days. I spent another day hauling and splitting firewood for Eleanor, then went off for a week of threshing. Harold slept with the crew this time but I had to hop nimbly back and forth by jeep to keep up with the chores at home. This time, though, I played it smart. I grabbed a wagon. They could catch some other dude for field pitcher. We needed the money. And as in all hard jobs I found the body quickly toughened up to it so that each day I had more bounce. But, thank goodness, the work came to an end. Being with the Dingreville crew was fun but our own place needed attention.

Back home we got out the bargain binder. In the spring we had hurriedly seeded a field of 30 acres to oats. Being without a seeder we had followed the old biblical custom of seeding by hand. Now the oats were maturing rapidly. When Harold first inspected the field he wondered just how it had been seeded, the pattern was so peculiar. Now we had to test the binder. While Harold checked and assembled the parts I went over the machine with an oil can as I had watched it done at Carney's. When all was ready we intended to pull it with the jeep and try it around the edge of the field. With Harold on the seat working the levers I drove around in low tractor gear. It worked beautifully until at the first corner the platform bit into the earth, breaking two slats. Slowly we returned to the blacksmith shop. Eleanor noticed our return but was so afraid things were not going well she didn't let on she saw us. Quickly we replaced the slats, raised the hitch and were off again. Now Eleanor appeared from hiding to wave, so we stopped to insist that she come out with us and see it working. She protested that there was bread rising on the stove but we were firm about it, so carrying Timmy she got into the jeep with me. Dane jumped on the back and we climbed the hill to the oat field again. We must have looked a queer crew—Timmy gurgling happily on Eleanor's knee, the rest of us shouting and pointing as Harold put the machine in gear, manipulating the levers furiously. Everyone was excited and happy that it should work. We cut all around the edge of the field for feed. The trial decided Harold that the oats would not be ready for another week. But the machine worked; it hardly missed tying a bundle. Harold had to make only minor adjustments. Indeed, it was a very good buy.

Before we could cut our oats, however, an early mid-September storm hit the country, knocking the grain flat with heavy, wet snow. We were building a new fence around the house at the time and thought of our cattle still on the summer grass. As we had fenced our haystacks up north it was clearly time to move them to winter grass. Mr. Rhodes had taken his saddle horse away and we had only tried the young, $20 horse once, so Harold and I set out on foot. We found most of the cattle bunched together out of the wind on a steep side-hill where we could work them along a fence line to a gate in a corner. Some had broken through the fence already but most of them were standing dejectedly in a sullen group. We slithered and crawled our way up the slope, Harold cutting off at an angle to move the few head already through the fence along with the main bunch. Just as he disappeared over the top I flushed a little black bear cub just ahead of me, higher up among some rocks. He scampered like mad over the top in line with Harold and I wondered how the two of them would react at the meeting. As the little ball of fur disappeared I thought it was going to run between Harold's legs. Harold told me later the bear must have thought he was surrounded as he tried to go several ways at once!

We moved the cattle without trouble and returned to the house. That was a mistake. Eleanor decided she could put us to work. She had one room left—the kitchen. We stripped all the paper off the walls, pulled thousands of tacks, swept the walls and ceiling of an accumulation of dead flies and dust and rolled up the linoleum for scrubbing. Eleanor figured that after applying hot water, soap and elbow grease to the floor and walls and re-laying the linoleum over the entire floor we could move in. Papering the walls and ceiling could be postponed until winter when we could help more easily. At any rate we should enter a clean house—she was sure of that. After some sandwiches and tea Harold went out to try the new horse while Eleanor and I finished the kitchen. Another day of scrubbing and it would be over. Then we could really unpack—for the first and last time, we hoped. It had been a tough month for Eleanor, working hard and fitting in with our comings and goings, but she was delighted with the results!

We moved at the end of September, on Eleanor's birthday. Her comment was: "What better birthday present could I have?" After being in that tiny cabin so long, four of us in the bedroom, Harold in the kitchen, with very little privacy and no elbow room, we could now spread ourselves through six rooms. We didn't have furniture but we had the rooms and enough beds to go around. There was a kitchen table and five plain chairs. My old saddle box and camp cot now served for extra seats. Once in a while we would look in the mail-order catalogues at the sumptuous beds with spring mattresses, the chesterfields and easy chairs and think that some day, if we held on to the cow's tail long enough, we could certainly improve our living conditions.

In the meantime wasn't it enough to think we had the ranch and 30 cows with calves? Of course, they weren't paid for, but we were on the way. We were still strong and healthy. The things we could see and touch were in our name, and the work we had done threshing, the heavy, muscle-screaming work, was going to help feed us through the winter. Moreover, Harold and I had $96 coming to us. If there was a pinch later one of us could always go out and work. We had an enormous potato crop and a fine garden. We were making our own butter and had our own hens producing eggs. No, we wouldn't be hungry.

When the snow disappeared we were blessed with lovely Indian summer. The hills donned their red and yellow and brown garments. The wood smoke from our fires hung lazily in the air.

Eleanor with a puppy. (PHOTO BY CATHARINE WHYTE)

We dug up garden produce, storing it in bins down in the cellar. Indian summer is almost as thrilling a time to be alive as it is in the spring when everything is greening up.

When Eleanor was alone one day an Indian arrived, the first to visit. She wondered how to handle him as she watched him tie his horse to the hitching post. It was Jim Crowflag, a minor chief of the Piegans. The timber limits of their reserve bordered our north fence. Jim was quite tall, old-fashioned and courtly in manner, with long braided hair tied with coloured ribbon hanging in two plaits, one over each shoulder. He spoke good English and was very fond of children. Eleanor asked him to stay for a meal and he spent the time questioning her about England and the life there. They got along fine. So did Jim and Dane, who was wide-eyed and slightly awed at the majestic sight of this native aristocrat. Eleanor told us later it was sweet to watch the two of them conversing, Jim so gentle with the little boy. I remember meeting the old Indian in town a year later and his first question was: "How is Dane?" At the end of the meal Eleanor took our cigarette machine, rolled Jim a smoke and presented it to him. It was just the right gesture.

Our relations with the Indians were always happy. Occasionally on a fine Sunday Jim and Bob Crow Eagle would drop by on horseback, stop for tea and a smoke, play with the children on their horses and ride away. Experience with the Plains Indians seems to bear out the saying that their religion consists of horses, dogs and children.

A younger Indian also arrived once when Eleanor was alone the first fall but did not have such a prepossessing manner. When he asked for some shells for his gun she gave him what few we had. In telling us about it later Eleanor feared our ridicule but I believed that only time would tell. He did come back a week later but stopped only long enough to give her a roast of venison. The Indians never broke faith with us.

When our oats were ready for cutting they were so flat the binder was useless without attachments. Gus Dingreville thought of us and offered his set of pick-ups as well as a quiet team to go with our old veterans as we needed four horses on the binder. Angus sent over his set of pick-ups also. With this added equipment Harold started cutting the oats. It was fun working at home, stooking oats of our own for a change. When they had cured sufficiently we had to haul and stack them. While the oats were in the stook we had feed racks to make and the corrals to fix for weaning.

At this time we fell into a couple of nice little deals. Gus had told me one day: "You should have another milk cow for your kids." We were milking Shorty, one of the beef-type cows bought from Rhodes. I told Gus we had to wait until we could afford it. "No matter the money now," he replied. "I let you have an old Jersey. We got too many cows. You try her out a couple of months and maybe you pay me next year. It no matter." I rode down to look at the animal. She was quite old, due to calf the next March but still in a fair amount of milk. Gus said he would sell her for $75 with all the time to pay I wanted. So I wrote him a demand note and chased the cow home. About the same time the chap who had sold out his small farm that summer called and wanted to know if I would pasture the saddle mare and colt he had left. Since we needed a horse I couldn't charge him pasture. He then offered to let us have another colt out of the mare for her keep. So now we had two horses to ride.

Fred Hewitt had always been good to us, helping with our first branding and some friendly advice. After the branding I told him to be sure and call us if he needed help some day and sure enough he got in touch when it was time to stack his green feed. I rode over on the young horse and joined Fred with three other neighbours. We were working in some well-wooded valleys. I was helping Fred with the stacking when one of the men on a wagon called out: "Hey, boys! There are some deer in the next pasture." Those hill-billies seem to work in the fields with a hunting knife in their belts and a gun handy. The work became a bit disorganized. Someone shoved a gun into my hands and pushed me off with a man I had just met. He was an old hand at deer hunting and we snaked to the top of a small hill on our bellies with our caps turned backwards. I thought he was crazy, for I had watched the deer high-tail it into the woods at right angles to our course. But he whispered: "They'll swing back around. Get ready for one quick shot when we top this ridge. They won't wait." Sure enough there they were, and we brought a young buck back with us.

It was very dark and snowing heavily when I started for home. I couldn't see the trail through the woods but left it to the horse as we climbed around the edge of Squaw Butte. Into the woods we went and out on the other side to start the descent for home. I had a haunch of venison in a sack over the saddle horn, feeling mighty good from the activity and good fellowship of the day. Through the soft snow haze I could see the cheery warm lantern light slanting on the fresh snow away down below and I could imagine the warm kitchen with the smell of fresh bread and supper on the stove. The horse perked up when he came to our fence and whinnied softly. Eleanor and the boys would be waiting with a big welcome, and I had a surprise for them. I thought it must have been like this in the old days. It was one of the delicious little moments that seem to crop up without warning to convince one that, taking the bad with the good and averaging it all out, it was indeed a very rewarding life.

Harold and I stacked our green feed. We talked a bit about our operations to date. I was sending Hutch, the bank manager in Lethbridge, regular letters and perhaps a too-glowing report about our adventures. Now I felt like writing him about trying for a deal on more cattle. We estimated the amount of feed we had stacked and were then putting up. We figured we could handle a couple of carloads of cattle. I wanted to write Augie but sounded Hutch out first so that I could give Augie an alternative. If the bank agreed I could get Augie to buy me some and sign a note at the bank, or if Augie felt like it I could winter some of his. Hutch wrote back with the okay to sound him out. I wrote to Augie in Medicine Hat. He telephoned me from Claresholm, asking if I could get over there next day.

Harold and I rode to Cowley. It was cold and blustery. Then Harold turned around and fogged it for home with the horses. I took a bus to Claresholm, had a meal and spent the evening in the hotel with Augie talking cattle. He asked about our grass, the feed we had put up, what we were running in the way of stock and how we were standing financially. I explained what I had to pay the V.L.A. next year and how much I had to pay off on the cattle we had bought from Rhodes. Augie wanted to know what I was paying Harold. When I told him Harold was working on a contract Augie felt we needed a lot more cattle to make it worthwhile for the boy. But he didn't say what he had in mind that night.

The next day he took me to my first cattle auction. It was quite an education. Individual ranchers were selling more cattle in one lot than we had on the whole ranch and buyers were snapping them up without batting an eye. Augie wasn't interested most of the day, but he slipped in a fast bid and caught a couple of carloads of choice heifers. That evening he remarked casually: "If I was sure they were bred I would let you have them, but they had better go on cover crop."

Then he told me he would send us some big steers, a couple of carloads, early in December. In the meantime, if I could get a truck to meet me at Granum, he would send me back with a load of calves. I tried to find out what the arrangement would be but Augie was vague. He said when he found the steers he would ship them, then write us about a deal. He figured we could make money on steers but until he had bought them he didn't know how the deal would go. I told him that Hutch agreed I could buy anything that seemed reasonable and I was sure I could give him a cheque for the calves. "We'll talk about it in the morning," said Augie. "Just get on the telephone for the truck and tell him to meet us at Granum tomorrow about nine o'clock."

We met the truck and travelled in convoy to a farm. Augie had moved a bunch of cows and calves up from the short-grass country around Manyberries and we chased 15 head of blocky little calves up the chute into the truck. Augie was chuckling as he waved me to the truck and told us to get going. "Don't you want a cheque now?" I asked.

"Pay me when you turn them over," he shouted. "I stole them anyway."

"But how much are they, Augie?"

"Forty dollars each," he replied.

It wasn't so bad buying Dingreville's old Jersey cow for $75. I could make that much threshing. But here I was riding with $600 worth of little dogies. What if some of them should get pneumonia and die? Were we jumping into deals too quickly? All of them on the cuff too. I always had these worries when I went to town. Back on the ranch we never seemed to have time to worry. We were busy all the time, we were happy and the ranch always gave us faith. It wouldn't let us down.

This was Friday. With considerable snow on the highway I didn't think the truck could take the calves right home. At Cowley I telephoned Harold to ride with our horses to Dingreville's. I was sure of getting that far with the truck and we could unload them there and trail them the three miles home.

It was about seven when I reached the Dingreville place. We dumped the calves off into a snowbank. They had just been taken off the cows and we wondered how they would behave. But after some preliminary skirmishing with the horses we got them strung out. We made the last mile home in bright moonlight.

On Saturday we had our first good look at them. They were a fine lot. We put them through the chute and snipped the ends of their tails for identification. Then we rounded up the rest of the herd and drove them into the corral, cut back the cows and had all the calves locked up for weaning. Most ranchers wean in the late fall, the latter part of November or early December. This gives the cow a better chance to come through the winter stronger, and have a larger calf in the spring, and the rancher generally feeds the weaners well during the winter to keep them growing. Now it was almost the last week in November.

Sunday morning the weather seemed settled. We decided we could take a chance on branding the new arrivals and at the same time vaccinate all the calves for hemorrhagic septicemia to prevent the danger of pneumonia or diphtheria. Although we had worked around the district by now so that we knew most of the neighbours we had not paired off with any of them to exchange work regularly. We could do with help this day but we rather hesitated to ask anyone. Everyone had been terribly kind in lending us equipment and giving us advice but we felt that in some measure we had paid them all back. Harold had picked up with Marcel Dingreville, the son of Gus, and we thought he could ask Marcel to give us a hand that afternoon. Eleanor volunteered as well. By taking more time to do the job and using several lariats we thought we could get through the work. Branding the new calves would take time but when that was finished it wouldn't take long to run them all through the chute for the vaccinating. It was the same old thrill all over again but this time it was more fun because of the surprises. We had reckoned without the neighbours. Before we could take all the stuff down to the corral and get the fire going they started to arrive. When we spotted the first sleigh coming up the valley Eleanor began stoking up the fire and mixing a batch of hot biscuits. They crowded into the kitchen and when we pointed to our few inadequate chairs, the boxes and camp cot, they all laughed at our embarrassment. Single riders appeared and Eleanor began to panic at the thought of our six cups and insufficient cutlery. The cowboys in their high-heeled boots just squatted on their heels, flicking cigarette ashes into the cuffs of their jeans. The second sleigh load brought the Mowat family, four of them, and as they shook off their wraps they announced cheerfully that they had spotted four more riders coming up the valley! Everyone had another good laugh at our predicament. They seemed to crowd the kitchen so that Eleanor couldn't get organized and you simply could not move around to pass the tea and biscuits. Six families were represented, and three nationalities. I couldn't tell you how many were present but children were swarming everywhere and the only way we might have counted them was through the cattle chutes.

It must have been our house-warming and we didn't know it, or just a great big Porcupine Hill-billie gesture, entirely spontaneous, to let us know we were accepted. No one party seemed to know the other was coming. Finally Bill Lagarde rode up on his famous horse Pancake with a saddlebag full of elk steaks as a present. He had just returned from his annual hunting trip in the mountains. It made a lump in our throats to sense their friendship and kindliness. All the men came out to the corrals for the sport of pitching their skill against the lively calves. We vaccinated 45 of them. They represented a potential of $5,000 in stock. Of course, here on the ranch I didn't doubt for a second our faith in the future or recall my town worry about buying Augie's calves for $600 on time. We then branded the 15 in about an hour. Marcel tried to throw one calf alone. It was so heavy he went down with it and they wrestled on the ground. Panting, he turned to me.

"Say, fellow, how much did you say these dogies are going to cost you?"

Bill Lagarde. (Photo by Lloyd Knight)

"Forty dollars apiece," I replied.

"You didn't buy them—you stole them."

We adjourned to the house for more food, scalding tea and good talk. It was a wonderful day to be alive and ranching in the Porcupine Hills.

The first week of weaning is tricky. Day and night you have the cows around bawling continually for their calves and the hungry little ones bawling back. The noise can be heard from the house at all hours. All the gates to the corrals have to be left open or the cows will walk through the fences anyway, and you just have to sit it out patiently until they get used to the idea and move off to graze. When they start drifting off you think it will be quiet in a few hours, but the old cows suddenly remember their calves and come trotting back to take up the chorus again. This reminds the others, so that the noise picks up, dies down, and repeats in waves. That is why you always hope for good weather during weaning. The cows won't eat and drink properly and if a blizzard comes up suddenly it certainly pulls them down.

Fortunately, our corrals held for our first weaning. One must also be careful in handling the calves. The new ones had been brought a good many miles in a cold, draughty truck and the vaccine we gave them takes a few weeks to have any effect. Harold practically wrapped them in cotton wool. Alone, I would have shovelled the feed to them and the odd one might have had trouble handling the roughage. But Harold stayed out there from early morning until late at night giving them a little feed at a time to clean up. One calf which developed a cold was put in a barn out of the wind, in a special, straw-filled pen we made. It kept its appetite, had warm water and ten c.c.'s of vaccine. We saved it.

Angus rode up one day just at the end of November to have his hair cut. There was a dance at the school that night to raise money for the children's Christmas party. The school was a little over two miles from the house. We had talked previously about going but we had no place to leave the children and disliked the idea of taking them along. Apparently it was the custom, in a country where baby-sitters are as rare as ulcers, to take the whole family to the dances. We were lukewarm about dancing, feeling that we had enjoyed our fling before starting a family and that it would be better not to begin again now. We intended to send our money with Harold and wondered if our absence might give an impression of stand-offishness in the district. After talking to Angus we decided we must go.

Eleanor baked a cake, we all had hot baths and got the big sleigh with the old team up to the house. The sleigh had a large platform without sides. We hoisted Timmy's pram aboard and also a large packing-case for all to sit on. We wrapped everyone up in blankets. The sleigh whooshed softly through the snow in bright moonlight. It looked like fairyland with the evergreens standing out sharply on the hilltops and the team trotting friskily, throwing a spray of snow over us. They were snorty and eager. As we neared the school we could hear the bells of other sleighs approaching from the west and south and our interest heightened as we tried to guess who it might be. Harold tied up the team while we lifted the pram to the ground and took a peek at Timmy. He was sound asleep. So we wheeled him over by a window and left him outside in the moonlight.

The school was crowded with friends from near and far. The orchestra consisted of a father and son. The boy, about 14, played the accordion while the father beat what looked like an Indian war drum and wore bells on his feet to add a tinkly touch. Everyone was dressed and scrubbed and shining. Children were racing around the schoolroom madly in and out of the dancers. The music wasn't suited for modern dancing but it was an inspiration for the Spanish waltz, heel and toe polka, schottische and the square dances. Eleanor had not been in town for more than two months and I was so accustomed to seeing her in blue jeans I marvelled at how lovely she looked in a proper dress. In fact, she was the belle of the ball. I couldn't do the local dances but I asked Bob and Eb Burles if they would whirl her around and they taught her the whole series from square dances to polkas. Dane and I sat on a bench admiring our "bootiful mummy". Everyone asked where Timmy was, and soon there was a procession of neighbours going outside to have a look at him asleep in the moonlight. With his pink cheeks he looked like an angel, and judging by the remarks that were passed to us from people who had gone out to visit him the wee scamp must have been holding court.

As Dane got over his shyness he joined the other children in their excited games, and they simply played until they dropped in their tracks. Then they were wrapped up in overcoats and tucked away on a school desk or bench. The ladies provided sandwiches, cake and coffee for which the men paid 50¢. The children who remained awake filled their tummies with cake and milk. It was a grand party for the whole family. There was no need of stimulants for jaded spirits. There was a refreshing absence of formality and an abundance of good manners. Eleanor had been feeling low all week with a touch of 'flu and was just on the mend. The party seemed to do us all more good than a week-end in town.

On the way home we were singing like a bunch of school kids and the horses were fighting for their bits to get home as quickly as possible. I remembered my own youth with one or two sleigh rides laid on in the city, just for the children, with a chaperone or two, and most of the ride along the city streets. How artificial it seemed now! Our boys could have this kind of a party any time they wanted. And we could always make it a family affair. I thought of these highlights and also the children's bath by the hot kitchen stove, the smell of fresh bread baking in the oven, the games they played outside on the fringe of the grown-up jobs, the pets they had, the machinery to play on, the buildings to climb and hide in. Dane and Timmy could always have this to look back upon. And as long as we were capable they would always have this to return to, some anchor in a changing world.

And soon it would be Christmas.

Chapter Eleven

EARLY IN December we began thinking of Christmas. Eleanor made cakes, puddings and mince meat. We had a turkey fattening. Eleanor wanted desperately for our first Christmas to be perfect, an occasion we could always look back upon. And she was determined to establish the right touch which could develop into a custom for the family. To humour her, and because it was right, we made a ceremony of everything. We did not have to buy a tree, we had them right on the place. And Eleanor didn't want us as an afterthought to turn around and cut down any tree. The whole family must turn out to pick the right one and we must make an occasion of it.

That meant the team and large sleigh. She bundled the children up and we all started out with axe and saw. We drove up into the hills and along through the woods. On the west slopes the wind had bent the trees and we had to look farther afield for the right kind. With cries of "Timber!" and youthful play the unanimous choice was cut down. We also gathered green boughs to decorate the house and returned in triumph for a tea party. We set the tree up in our empty living room. Although the children did not realize it the tree was pathetically bare. Eleanor could find only one strand of tinsel but she rolled up bits of coloured paper into balls and also hung up some of Timmy's toys and rattles. Dane also stuck branches in the snow outside, tying fat and peanuts on the tiny limbs to make

Christmas trees for the birds. The boys were well satisfied, which was the main thing.

A few days later Augie Sauer telephoned from Medicine Hat. He had been working for three weeks trying to pick up some cattle for us and would be shipping in a few days. He wanted to know if our trails were good enough from the railway shipping point. We assured him they were and that we would be ready for the drive.

Eleanor and the boys had not been to town for three months, so I ran them in with the jeep. They had a lovely time in Pincher Creek looking at the toys and decorations in the stores. Dane was thrilled with an electric train. Opening our mail during lunch we found a letter from the silent partners. They warned us they had shipped two parcels which we were to open before Christmas as the packages inside were labelled with instructions. We hurried through our shopping and dashed to Cowley, worried about getting the parcels from the railway station. It was five P.M. and the station usually closed at 4:30. As luck would have it a freight train was in and the station office open. I staggered to the jeep with two enormous boxes which we had difficulty squeezing into the vehicle. We tried a shortcut, hoping to get home more quickly, and high-centred the jeep on a hard-packed snow drift, which lost us about 45 minutes.

Home at last Harold announced that Augie had telephoned again to warn us he had shipped two carloads of steers which would reach Cowley next morning. It was too much excitement. Eleanor kept me up late that evening opening the boxes and sorting out parcels. The ones for Christmas had to be hidden, the rest opened now as the letter directed. Eleanor became a little girl again when she found all the proper things for decorating a tree, especially since she had that very day looked so longingly at the decorations on sale in town. There was enough to transform the whole house. In addition to large parcels for the tree there were many intriguing small things wrapped up for little boys' stockings. Other items included maple syrup, candied peel, nuts and fruit, such extravagant things which we had not even thought about for this Christmas. For Eleanor, striving for perfection, the picture was now complete. And she was deeply touched by the care and thought that had been put into the parcels. We went to bed in a very excited frame of mind. And tomorrow there would be more adventure. Augie's cattle were arriving.

The whole outfit was up before five o'clock. Harold caught the saddle horse while I milked, fed chickens and turkeys, watered the calves and turned them out to their pasture for the day. We telephoned Dingreville to see if Marcel could ride with Harold. After breakfast Harold took off about 6:30. I loaded the jeep with oat bundles and arrived in Cowley about 7:30. When I checked with the station the agent advised me the cattle would arrive on the way freight about two o'clock that afternoon. It was a difficult job hanging around, just waiting.

I called Eleanor and found she was having a wonderful time. Dane was helping her strip the tree and they were decorating it all over again. She told me that Dane thought the little glass balls were too precious to handle and was just skipping around the tree directing her where to hang them. I warned that the cattle would be late and I would telephone again after they left to give her time to organize a hot meal which I would pick up for the riders.

At last the train arrived and as the first carload moved down the chutes I noticed Harold for the first time get really excited. There were 41 steers: 24 two-year-olds and 17 yearlings. We didn't know yet whether they were to be boarders at so much a head per month or if it was a share-profit deal. That they were coming on the ranch and would boost the total stock to 117 head was the important thing. The ranch was beginning to look like a business. These steers could add to our income, improve our chances of keeping the cow herd intact next year. We might be able to meet our debts from Augie's cattle and the calves. No wonder Harold was excited.

After unloading we fed them the oat bundles and let the critters rest in the yards for a couple of hours. They had spent a long time in the stock cars and were "gaunted up". We talked about heavy gains in weight when we could roll the feed into them.

Harold and Marcel started them on the drive around five o'clock. They were going to take it easy as the steers would likely try to graze on the way and would stop to water at the river. I drove home and picked up a box of hot food that Eleanor had prepared. The cattle had moved well at the beginning and when I found them had covered some five miles. The boys, who were cold and hungry, welcomed their meal and a smoke in the jeep. The toughest part of the trip proved to be the last few miles because some of the animals wanted to bed down. But they arrived about midnight at the ranch where I had another meal ready for the lads.

We branded them next day and after turning them out with the calves in the smaller pasture for a spell we soon settled them down on the winter grass with the main herd. We had taken a firm step forward. It was with great satisfaction that I could write to Hutch and Arthur "the Wizard" Beaumont telling them of these developments, for back in July they had only taken my word that we would find this sort of break. I also wrote to Augie reporting their safe arrival, enclosing a demand note for $600 on the calves he had given us.

Christmas was upon us before we knew it. We had been making trips to town by saddle horse, returning with parcels and mail stuffed in sacks hanging from the saddle. The mail seemed to have more value, somehow, coming 12 miles from the post office by saddle horse. Everyone remembered us. There were letters and parcels from England, California, Ottawa, Australia, Kenya—and from all our friends in the West. "What lucky little boys!" said Eleanor, as she tucked parcels into hiding places. "You would think their parents were wealthy. Do you think it will spoil them? We must ration them out and make them last until the New Year or their birthdays. If there are duplicate toys it would be fun to take some around to the neighbours."

I can remember a later Christmas when the cattle broke into a haystack on Christmas Eve, holding up festivities until noon next day, but this first one was indeed perfect.

We had the boys bathed and in bed early but their excitement was boundless. They had to hang their stockings and set out a lunch of peanut-butter sandwiches and a glass of milk for Santa. We promised that their hero, Bill Lagarde, would be up in the morning to help them open parcels if they settled down quickly to sleep. Edgar Burke had sent us a bottle of sherry, so we sat quietly drinking a toast and listening to carols on the radio until Dane and Timmy had surrendered to the arms of Morpheus. As Harold had gone out to a party we were alone in setting the stage.

Eleanor sneaked into their bedroom and came out with the stockings which we filled with the tiny parcels, sorted in two piles. We blew up balloons and hung them, with extra decorations which Eleanor had been saving, around the bedroom so there would be surprises to greet them as soon as they awoke. From all the secret hiding places we brought forth the many

interesting parcels and placed them under the tree. It was
midnight before we got to bed. And as we fell asleep we
murmured to each other how precious was the scene in the
nursery, so gaily festooned, the boys asleep in their innocence
with the fat red stockings tied to their beds.

We were awake first, listening for them to stir. Then we heard
them talking. It was still dark and they had not noticed
anything. We could hardly bear the strain. It seemed like half
an hour before Dane made the first discovery. "Timmy,
Timmy!" he shrieked. "Look!" Then an excited squeal.
"Mummy! Daddy! Santa's been here!" We rushed in to watch
Dane open his stocking and to help Timmy with his. It was fun
for us as well because we didn't know what was in the stockings.
Eleanor had breakfast ready in no time. Dane took note of the
fact Santa had finished the lunch they had left. The boys
seemed to think that was all there was to Christmas and were
quite content until Dane chanced to go into the living room,
and came running to tell us that: "Santa's been in the living
room too!"

It was only right they should open a few parcels but we kept
the main ones until Bill arrived. When Dane, after watching the
electric train in the store and talking of nothing else since, found
he had a real wind-up train and tracks, you can imagine what he
thought of Santa Claus. Bill took him outside where they found
the sleigh tracks Saint Nick had left in the snow.

Eleanor and I had discussed the modern thinking that tended
to shield a child from the fantasy of believing in Santa but now
we weren't sure. If there wasn't a Santa Claus somewhere, then
there must be a fairy godmother. Didn't we feel it ourselves? As
long as we didn't lie to the boys or impose on them our own
conception we were quite convinced it was normal at their age to
create an image out of their own lively imagination.

On a later Christmas the boys received a toboggan and spent
part of the day sliding. After they had been tucked into bed
Christmas night and all was peaceful, Bill, Eleanor and I sat
around reviewing the day and drinking hot rum punch. About
ten o'clock Bill thought he had better get home. We all went to
the door and gazed upon a night of pure magic. Fresh white
snow reflecting a full moon from a sky that was almost blue,
without a trace of wind, sparked us to mild lunacy. It was so
bright out you could read a newspaper. The Rockies in the
distance were etched in bold relief.

"Bill," Eleanor said, "you can't go home now. We must try out the toboggan." And the first thing I knew we were climbing the hill to the rocks behind the house. Of course they put me in front and we raced down the hill at terrific speed, right to the fence of the horse pasture. I had snow down my neck, in my mouth and ears and up my sleeves to the elbow. They thought it was funny, so we had to roll around and wrestle until they were equally submerged. Then we had distance and speed competitions, singly and in pairs, and every other type of childish fun we could think up. When the toboggan hit a bump all the occupants would go flying and sliding on their own.

We waved Bill down the road about 1:30 in the morning, soaking wet and helpless with laughter. He whooped it up so that he must have startled half the coyotes in our part of the hills.

Christmas in the Porcupines was not a one-day affair. We had to travel by sleigh to Dingreville's for an enormous dinner and games with half a dozen families present. We repeated the performance at Bougerolles. The hospitality amazed us. It was indeed a fine community. Christmas to us seemed to have lost the commercialized and formal modernization that editorial writers decry so often.

The Mowats had wanted us for Christmas Day but understood our fierce determination to spend it on the ranch. Mrs. Mowat thought Eleanor would be lonesome so far from home. The following week, however, we went directly over the hills by sleigh and team, Harold riding the saddle horse so he could nip back and do chores. We enjoyed a splendid dinner, then played cards and had some good talk before bed. Next morning Mrs. Mowat thoughtfully gave Eleanor a treat which she had not enjoyed in years—breakfast in bed. We returned home that afternoon very much refreshed.

It is easy to slip into a nostalgic mood over the old days and use it as an excuse to cover up lack of progress. I don't want to give the impression that we preferred it that way or that living in the country as we did has any special merits or appeal as a "way of life". It may be entertaining to read our account of the happy landing at Squaw Butte but it is well to remember that the ranch was evaluated by very capable men. And we tried to farm it and rotate our pastures on the latest principles.

But had we walked into a set-up with the latest machinery, been able to live in a modern home with all the furniture we required, the latest gadgets and services, I don't believe we would have had half the fun out of the venture.

From Eleanor's point of view, the home, she used to admire the inside of modern country dwellings and wonder if we would ever aspire to all the labour-saving devices and comfort that is possible. We started with a pump in the garden, hauling pails of water to the house. We filled tubs for washing, had to stand pails in the kitchen overnight to prevent them from freezing in winter. The coal dust from the stove settling on the water made it decidedly unpleasant. Whenever any visitor talked about what we were missing we could not imagine lights, running water, inside bathroom and everything laid on. After a few years Eleanor felt she could be content with just a small pump in the pantry. She had a gasoline-engine washing machine as had nearly all our neighbours. The fact that I put the pump in and piped the water from the well satisfied us both. It wasn't a running water system but it was a big achievement in our eyes, and for the rest we would rather make our improvements in the machinery and stock line that would pay us dividends.

A large modern home on a ranch doesn't add one cent to the earning capacity of the place. In fact, it may handicap the re-sale value. Joe Gilchrist used to say time and again: "When you look at a ranch for sale don't spend your time on the house, seeing how comfortable you can be. Look at the business side—the grass, soil, shelter for the cattle and the carrying capacity. If that is good you can work it to provide the home later. Some of the best ranches may have only a shack on them." I thought about it one evening when I turned on the radio for the news and caught another blast of propaganda on the air. This time it was a large plumbing firm in the big city advertising a choice of bathroom fixtures in a wide range of colours. I pictured our House of Parliament at the back, built by a specialist of the Chick Sale school. Edgar Burke had described it as the only privy in the world with a million-dollar view. Of course we were horribly out of date, but did it shorten our expectancy of life or cause us any real discomfort?

I remember bath night, as it was then.... It takes a bit of planning around here. But sometimes one just gets in the mood for a bath. The winter has been kind for a spell and I have just finished the evening chores, toning up my muscles by cutting into a stack of feed for the calves. All the critters are doing well and I'm feeling fit and at peace with myself. Catching a glimpse

The ranch house, with the pump on the well, and the privy with the "million dollar view" behind the woodshed. (PHOTO BY LLOYD KNIGHT)

of lamplight from the house as I walk up from the corrals and sensing the good meal waiting in the cheerful kitchen heighten my sense of general well-being.

Balancing pails of milk and chop for the pigs, I reach the back shed intact. Soon I can relax. The cheerful hum of the cream separator announces my return. The boys rush out with a welcome and Eleanor appears with a dish for milk.

"How about a bath tonight, Mummy?"

"A splendid idea. But keep your overshoes on. We'll need more wood, coal and water."

I kick the snow and shovel around the drift for the wood pile and cut up some kindling. In the shed at the back I fill a bucket with stove coal and a grease pail with lumps to keep the fires in at night. Do I turn a tap for water? I do not. A pump perhaps? There is one at the well but the darn thing freezes up, the casing cracks and it always needs priming. So in hill-billy fashion I lower a bucket down the well tied to an old lariat, filling cream cans, canning pots and pails. After hauling water, wood and coal, I locate the tub in the dark shed and everything is lined up for the ritual.

In the Porcupine Hills we are really up to date. We have a bath tub—not the round wash tub that was our initiation and despair, the kind that slopped water over the edges whenever we tried a new position, the cramped, frustrating little tub that caused you to wash in sections and continually try to invent new procedures and positions so that you didn't have one part of your body in hot water while the rest chilled in the icy air. No, we have a full-length bath tub. Almost full length, that is, four feet long and 13 inches deep. It cost us about five dollars plus freight. It was such a change after the wash tub we were convinced it was just as good as anything in the city. We hardly noticed it was galvanized iron instead of white porcelain enamel. When we spotted it in the catalogue it was immediately ordered for Christmas and the family took on a new standing in the community.

You know what a country telephone line is like, the party line that irresistibly draws one during a winter lull to listen in to an exchange of news and views. Sometimes when the rings aren't clear several receivers are lifted from hooks just to make sure for what party the call is intended. The station agent started us on the road to fame by calling up to announce the arrival of our bath tub. I can imagine and, mind you, I am only imagining, that someone's wife put down the receiver that day, turned to her husband reproachfully and said: "Those new people have ordered a bath tub. They must have put in running water." And quite likely the husband replied: "Sure, they always had it—running through the roof! Ha! Ha!" However, word got around that we had acquired a bath tub, and when we started home with it on the sleigh we met Angus by his gate eyeing us curiously.

"What on earth have you got there?"

"A genuine bath tub, Angus, and it cost only a few dollars more than a wash tub. I guess this is the first time they've been advertised since the war."

"Keep on going, friend. Don't let my wife see it or she'll want one." So I went giddy-yap up the trail.

But the station agent was soon handling a procession of similar articles. (Note to mail-order houses: All you have to do is spot one such item in each district. As long as the wives hear about it—and they will—you have got yourself some business.) We had to chuckle when we noticed them at our station waiting to be picked up.

Mind you, not all these tubs came into the district as a blessing to clear the way for progress. George Mowat, having to follow suit grudgingly, laid the blame squarely on the first customer.

"See here, old chap," he said, "I've been 40 years and better in these hills and no big troubles—just dry years, poor calf crops and weak markets—until you came along. We always managed to make a living and we could wash out of a bucket, the horse trough, an old gas drum or the creek. Now we have to get a proper tub. Do you know how much water that takes? Dammit man, you are plumb ruining our way of life."

Later on some of them were put to better use. I noticed one outside a house in the spring, full of rain water caught from the roof. And on very hot summer days ours made an excellent bathing pool for the boys to play in out on the lawn. And it did take too much water for every bath!

For bath night we clear a space in front of the large kitchen stove. A blanket is spread on the floor, the tub is brought in to warm up, a large bath towel is hung by the stove and steaming pots of water are kept waiting their cue. Soap, brush and face cloth are set out on the blanket and all doors leading into the kitchen are closed against draughts. The tub is filled and the last act before the ritual of ablution is to open the oven door. A blast of hot air pours over the scene of operations. The stage is set.

How good it is to soak the frame after a day of riding and forking hay! The combination of soapy water, steam and hot air from the oven makes one realize the endless preparations are well spent. Could spirit and body be more in harmony if one had all the benefits of the city cousin? Or would one have to exchange his daily round of fresh air and exercise for a desk job to achieve them?

I thought of the children having their nightly baths on the kitchen table, an assembly-line procedure when they play and clown for us and we notice the development of their sturdy little bodies. I thought of the articles on water conservation, the cities that suffer a shortage of our most precious and fast-dwindling commodity. Our bath water isn't chucked out the door when we are finished. More often it is saved for washing floors and other purposes. When you watch the seasons come and go and work the land you become conscious of water tables and their importance.

We realized how old-fashioned we were one time when we went to the city and took a hotel room. We thought it would be fun to introduce the boys to a proper bath. But when we started running the water at full throttle through the taps Timmy was terrified at the noise and wouldn't go near the monster.

So I said to Eleanor: "There's nothing like a bath on the ranch. Could you imagine everything up to date with lights and running water?"

"I could," she replied, "but it wouldn't suit the character of the house. We would have to add a room or take valuable space we're using now. I could actually be satisfied with a pump in the pantry until we're old. After all, to modernize completely you would have to consider how many cows in the herd would be working full time just to keep it going."

"Never figured it that way. Trouble is we read too much and that radio keeps butting into our affairs. But I know what we can do to improve things and make the work easier for you. We can compromise like the politicians. I'll buy a new lariat for the old bucket at the well."

That was when she fired a pillow at my head.

Chapter Twelve

DURING JANUARY we received a letter from Augie Sauer giving the weights, prices and shipping charges of the big steers. He suggested we keep track of the feed we used and feed them oats as well as hay to ready them for an early market at the beginning of summer, even if we had to buy the oats. After all these charges were deducted we were to split the profit 50-50. Nothing could have given us a better start for the New Year than this news. Without putting up any cash or speculating dangerously we stood to make half the profit on two carloads of cattle. If the price dropped we would only be out our work and the cash value of the feed—most of it the hay we worked so hard to put up the previous summer. With the normal gains in weight, 200 to 250 pounds an animal, the price would have to drop very far indeed before Augie would lose his investment. The news gave us a tremendous lift. Just think if the price should go up! We fell to work with a will.

Some of our best hay was stacked on top of a hill with no way of getting it out except by a steep climb and descent. Normally we could wait and feed cattle up there. But we were concentrating on the steers. We had them cut out separately in the horse pasture, with their own salt and water, and Harold made them long feed troughs where they ate their daily ration of oats. We bought more grain at the elevator in town, hauling it out by sleigh. And with the steady old team we had inherited with the place we began to make a trail through the deep snow to the good stacks of hay. The steers were getting feed from stacks closer to the corrals but we intended to feed them everything we had and this meant moving down the hill-top stacks. Obviously the team could not take the slope straight up and down, so whenever we could spare the time we made practice runs, angling up to our objective, packing the trail well and judging from the sidling as well as the tipping tendency of the sleigh what amount of hay we could reasonably put on for each trip. When Harold decided the trail was right we tried our first load, using chains wrapped around the sleigh runners as brakes. Dane came along to help. During the descent, while Harold did the driving, we hung over the top side as you would sailing a dinghy in a stiff breeze, Dane putting all of his 35 pounds into the effort. We roped on the loads and it took ten trips to bring down one stack. Curiously enough we did not upset on the steepest part of the descent. But we did tip just about every trip, on the level when the runners on one side hit a hard drift.

Winter is the best time to break horses. We had started with the old team, Prince and Brownie, that Mr. Rhodes threw in with the deal. And when we had finally bought the place we purchased three other workhorses at $50 apiece. They were "rough broke", which meant that in addition to having been halter broken they had had the harness on. They might have had more than that but it was safer to assume the minimum. In winter one can harness a green team to a sleigh and start driving them with the least amount of noise and annoyance to the horses. The pull isn't too hard and then they can gradually be worked with loads so that they become reasonably safe for normal farm work. And they should be well broken in by the time they are hooked up to a mower.

Harold felt we should start breaking a second team so that as soon as the frost was out of the ground they would be ready for the sulky plough in breaking the sod-bound hay land. The plough would require four horses and they had to be hardened up for it.

Brownie and Prince, the old team, had been together so long you could not leave one in the barn and take out the other without having trouble. You also had to turn them out to pasture together and most of the time they walked along in the same position they were driven, Brownie on the left. Prince had an aggressive way about him and he was always mean to every other horse on the ranch except his mate Brownie.

We gave the green horses their first lesson in the corral, tying them up outside, which was safer, before putting on and taking off harness. The next lesson was driving. We planned to make it easier by harnessing one green horse with a veteran. We had just returned with the sleigh from hauling feed and as Harold turned it ready for the next trip he thought we might try out one of the new mares, called Babe, with Prince. We harnessed Babe in the corral again, then hooked her up with Prince. Brownie was very indignant. Then Harold drove his mixed team around the corral, turning and backing, starting and stopping until he was satisfied. He called me to open the gate and gently we hooked them up to the sleigh. Prince was strong enough to hold Babe from running away but we didn't want to spook the green horse by carelessness or break any of our old harness.

Now if we had tried to tie Brownie up in the barn there might have been trouble. I figured the best thing to do would be to tie him in the hay yard where he could watch Prince practising with Babe. The green horse was nervous and trembling but I threw open the gate from the horse pasture and Harold started them off quietly. I slipped on to the sleigh as it passed and we were delighted to notice that Babe was keen, a good worker, and that she settled down quickly. We were in sight of Brownie all the time, but as Harold let them out and headed up the valley we could hear Brownie nickering and then whinnying violently. As I turned to watch him he was pulling at his halter rope, head and ears well up, trying to stand on tip-toe to keep Prince in sight. Harold decided not to give Babe too much the first day and we soon returned, well satisfied.

While doing evening chores we wondered about Babe. Since we wanted to keep her working we decided to let her out with the team. As soon as she stepped out of the barn Brownie took after her. It was unusual to see him turn mean—Prince, yes, but not Brownie. This time he was the aggressor and he chased poor Babe up and down, biting her neck. Prince joined in the attack. Babe lost her head and ran into a fence. She went down and Prince stood right over her. While Harold and I watched, hoping they would get over it and settle down without injury, Babe got to her feet, slipped clear and headed for the other side of the pasture with the team in hot pursuit. Coming to the fence she cleared it with a nice jump and kept on running in blind panic.

With looks of smug satisfaction the old team turned their backs on her and walked sedately over to queue up for the evening meal. Later when we returned the mare to work we had to keep her with the steers. I had observed jealousy in people when a stranger comes between friends but had never seen an instance like this in the horse world.

During a spell of good weather Mrs. Mowat telephoned Eleanor about the quilting bee. It was well on in the winter and Eleanor had not been out much since Christmas. In town she used to do anything to get out of a hen party. But now she really did want to see a few women and moreover she wanted to learn how to quilt. So when she asked us if she could ride over safely we assured her there would be nothing to it.

We were so pleased she could get away to this party we had the mare saddled up and tied to the hitching post at the house by dinner time. I offered to do the dishes, so Eleanor set off right after the meal on the trusty old mare. We watched her climb our big hill and disappear. When she returned about four o'clock we all greeted her, eager for details of the nice time she had enjoyed.

"Home never looked so good," she said. "I managed to ride about half a mile, but when the trail got so steep the mare was gasping for breath I got off to walk and I never did get on again. We ran into such deep snow I had to pick the way for her. We made Cabin Hill at last and half way down I was up to my waist in snow and the mare was up to her shoulders. It got worse and worse. We plunged and heaved until the poor old girl became exhausted and refused to go any farther. By this time we had both had enough and decided to go home. But our troubles weren't over yet. I couldn't find a gate to get us out of the field and on to the road allowance. In the end I had to tread down the wire at the weakest part of the fence and persuade the mare to high step over it."

Eleanor went to bed before eight that evening and next day she ached all over. We felt rather guilty about letting her start out alone on such a trip without checking the trail first. It was just an incident in our first winter and almost as stupid as the time Harold took Eleanor to town in the jeep. I was baby sitting, and when Eleanor telephoned from Maufort's that she would be along soon I let Dane, four years old, go outside to meet Mummy. I thought he would wait by the gate nearest home but he kept on walking and was at our lowest gate, a mile from the house, when a blizzard and drifting snow came upon him with startling suddenness. He was just about buried by the time the jeep passed him and he would not have been noticed at all if it hadn't been for the dog who ran out in front of the jeep. We were lucky that time for it might have taken days to find him, the snow was drifting so badly. Dane was sufficiently impressed by his experience and our warnings to be most cautious after that.

In February it took two weeks of work, including Sundays, to move all our hay in close to the buildings. Having listened to tales of disaster in the past we thought it wise to prepare for the worst. We expected some bad blizzards before spring and believed that we might be caught unprepared with inaccessible stacks of hay beyond our reach and weakening cattle around the buildings. So in addition to the ones on the hilltop we moved stacks from a mile north and a mile south of the house through steep coulees that would most certainly fill with drifting snow. By February 17 it was a mighty nice feeling to see all the feed in place for any emergency and everything squared away for the next storm. We estimated there was enough hay to last another 35 days at our present rate of feeding.

We couldn't keep our thoughts away from spring. In addition to the daily round we spent many hours sawing wood by hand, hauling logs from old cabins we had pulled down and filling the woodshed so that we should have a back-log when spring work started. Eleanor spent two enjoyable evenings culling the seed catalogues and making out the order for her garden. She was anxious to try growing tomatoes, celery, green peppers and eggplant. For the flower garden she ordered Iceland poppies. By March 11 she had a feeling that spring was only a few days away. In the light of our experience after that, which saw us battle through unusually long and severe winters, it is easy to laugh at our mistakes. But they were not stupid mistakes, just over-anxious and eager ones. Could you guess how she predicted that spring was close? The weekly washing usually took three or four days to dry. Out on the line it would promptly freeze and it was a matter of thawing out the frozen garments little by little until they were dry enough to iron. When for the first time she had a washing that she managed to dry and iron on the same day Eleanor decided it was time to start planting the seeds indoors. Harold caught the bug as well and started checking over the sulky plough. In the fall, pulling it with the jeep in the garden, we had hit a rock and Harold was worried that we had bent the frog and beam. We got the forge going in the blacksmith shop and after much heating and hammering got it fairly straight. To make certain, however, Harold took it down to Bill's place where they worked on it again.

Toward the end of March we began looking for signs of green grass. Everything seemed to be working to plan. The cows were heavy in calf and the steers looked fine. We began to pray for good calving weather to avoid losses. Cows are deceiving. They look fat, but when they have dropped their calves you notice with alarm that they are emaciated, thin and bony. I had just read an observation of this common mistake and looked at them again and again for signs of weakness. Some days when they walked by to water with the icicles jingling on their hides we were thankful that the loyal Harold was with us. Calving was going to be a tricky business.

Just when we were feeling calm and confident on this point a fog rolled up the valley to swallow the outline of hills, fences and buildings. The temperature dropped sharply and a nasty southeast wind whipped up, bringing a blizzard. We glanced anew at the stocks of feed and studied the calendar to estimate the days of winter left. We remembered the tales of old-timers recounting disasters in the past and began to wonder if we were going to pull the animals through.

Early in April, with Eleanor's seeds sprouting in the house, the neighbours began telephoning to ask if we had any feed left and if the calves had started to arrive. We had been cutting down on the daily ration of hay and moving the cattle out to find grass to supplement the difference. We realized it was a poor year for early calves when we heard that one neighbour had lost ten, another four and several one or two each.

It was dark when I started evening chores on April 9. Harold had gone riding to look over the herd and returned about nine o'clock carrying our first calf! He had packed it more than a mile, up a steep hill and down the other side, sliding and falling, with the mother in hot and worried pursuit. What a thrill it was to see the little bundle of life bedded down on some clean straw, dry and warm! We made an elaborate tally sheet beside the calendar in the kitchen and proudly marked up the first calf. You work hard all year for this one crop and after eleven months of planning and slogging away for the one objective, calves, you feel that you have a right to expect some help from the weather. Every time a calf is lost or a cow fails to produce you sadly write off a year of work and struggle for one of your units. For the cow is the basic unit on a ranch, and when you haven't got too many of them the loss of one calf seems immense.

It was natural, the first year, to fuss over the herd and try to do too much. Had we, with more experience, left the old range cows alone to find their own hide-outs and shelter spots and not tried to improve on nature, we might have had more success. Since those days we have known cows to drop their calves in 40° below, during a blizzard, and somehow manage to dry and warm their offspring and save them. Only hard, realistic experience will bring a man to the point when he knows just when to interfere for the good of both cow and calf and when to leave them alone.

Next day four calves were born in quick succession. I found the second one lying in a pool of water between two trees. With the sack I always carried on the saddle I dried it off and after packing it a while threw it over the neck of the horse and rode for home. The cow followed for a way, but when the calf and I both got on the horse she must have lost the scent and returned to the trees.

The horse was very patient with that calf over his withers, kicking at him. Sliding and slithering in snow and mud we made our way down the slope. From the hen house Eleanor and Dane saw us coming and there was great excitement at the sight of the second calf. Eleanor opened the gate, we put the little animal in the dry shed we had prepared and I started off to look for the mother. But she had disappeared.

I continued riding until I found four cows together, one of which looked like the mother. But after chasing her to the corrals and bringing out the calf, she turned up her nose. I began to panic that I never would find the mother. I tried three others without success. I felt that I had stirred the cow up so that she would never claim her calf and the little one would die. Just as I was getting desperate, on the last try of the day, the cow I had chosen pricked up her ears and hurried toward the calf. He gave a little bleat and there was no doubt this time the way she licked his face and remained contentedly beside him. As I came in for the noon meal at three o'clock that afternoon I began to wonder for the first time if we were interfering too much with nature.

The cows who were showing signs of calving in the next few hours we moved into the horse pasture for the night where we could check them first thing in the morning. Although there wasn't any natural shelter, they could use the sides of the sheds to break the wind if a storm came up, and we could move them into the corral, a place we later realized as the worst possible spot for a good range cow. In the morning it was cloudy and threatening snow. One of our cows in the horse pasture had dropped her calf and it was lying in a wet spot, dead. I began to accuse myself, for the cow might well have chosen a better place out in the hills among the trees. Breakfast was a gloomy affair that day.

But just after breakfast when I was looking the matrons over again and turning them out to graze another cow began to have a calf. I shouted for Eleanor, ran to the barn for a lariat. I was convinced the beast was having trouble, and we fussed around the milling herd trying to keep her back while I was wondering how we could get her shut up or at least rope her and snub her up somewhere. Our fussing got all the animals stirred up. I wondered why in blazes the cow in question would not lie down. Then, right before our eyes, we saw the miracle of birth and forgot the poor little dead calf in trying to help the latest arrival. We dried it off with a sack and moved it to a dry bed, the mother coming along quietly.

The first calf, born April 9, was getting thinner each day and weaker on its legs. It could barely keep up with the mother. Eleanor and I got them into a small shed and closed the door. We put a loop on a hind leg of the cow and stretched it so she could not kick. We managed to get a large halter on her head and snubbed that up. Then I tried milking her—and she became wilder. One of the teats would not work until I had pulled off the scab. When we had the milk flowing Eleanor brought the calf up and we got him started on his breakfast. It was a relief to see the little fellow tie into a meal, switching his tail with delight, to see the thin little sides swell out and the cow quiet down. It was another victory, but with a heavy heart I went out to skin the dead calf. Determined not to call it a total loss Eleanor intended to tan the hide with a recipe of her own, half Indian and half *Winnipeg Free Press*. She had the weirdest collection of chemicals and nostrums which, combined with much elbow grease, she hoped would turn the trick.

The weather was decidedly unfair for our first calving, but had it been too easy we might have become careless in the following years. The unusual conditions probably afforded us a concentration of experience we might not have acquired otherwise in such a short time. It kept us thinking of other calves being born out in the hills and the need for constant supervision and fast action. Never since have we hoped so hard for a break in the weather. We were told that at this time the previous year the grass was green, that with the proper conditions it could green up in a few days.

We tried to hang on, save ourselves from losses and keep the cattle from slipping back. Augie's steers simply had to keep their weight, but for an early turn off to market we had to have green grass now. The most despairing sight was to stand helplessly by and watch the cattle constantly on the move, marching back and forth, up and down the hills, past the house several times a day, searching for another blade of green grass. They would get a small taste of it, eagerly search for more, and then go on the march in single file again, milling around to tear up any tiny shoots that were discovered. Their system seemed to demand grass. They had no taste for hay now. It was grass they wanted— green grass. And the weather was standing still. It wasn't winter and it wasn't spring. If it would only do something. . . .

Suddenly the weather changed, but not the way we wanted. One of those storms that all ranchers fear, an April blizzard, descended upon us. The cows that have calved are weakened, they are losing their winter coats and the rest are trying to make milk. Then you face a blizzard that with a diabolical twist of fate discourages all your good efforts and intentions. It was our worst storm of the winter and the snow piled right up to our windows. No forecast came of its clearing. It was like kicking a man after knocking him down. The only bright spot for us was that no more calves were expected for a week or more and that those we had were flourishing.

However, we learned that we couldn't let a little thing like our first winter get us down. In the long wait through the deadly hours of twilight before spring the months of blizzards and cold behind us had faded into insignificance.

Chapter Thirteen

OVERNIGHT, IT seemed, spring started busting out all over. With the most startling, dramatic suddenness the warm chinook wind came pouring over the mountains from the south-west, licking up the snow with a greedy tongue. The world of white disappeared. The warm wind unlocked the earth from its long sleep; we could feel it stir and come alive sluggishly. Heat waves shimmered, and higher up brought the melted snow from the steep coulees in clear, merry little streams that joined together in a mad, headlong dash for the valley below. Our dams filled right up, the first time the large one in front of the house had held so much water, and the overflow rushed wildly through the lower pastures.

The rapid thaw created havoc for some good people farther down. Claude Hammond had a shed and some buildings washed away but managed to move his garage to higher ground when it threatened to go down Tennessee Creek. Our ducks, who had been so bored all winter, lost no time getting into the large dam and amused us with their antics. They refused to come in at night and all hands were employed keeping an eye on them to find out where they were laying.

Eleanor began a collection of turkey and duck eggs to set under broody hens. She kept them warm in boxes under the kitchen stove, turning them every evening. And she was "proper mad" that our hens would not turn broody and nest on the eggs.

When Gus Dingreville had brought up his income tax forms for me to type he had presented us with a couple of broody hens they could spare, but after the trip over our rough road one of them had been shaken out of her broodiness. Eleanor could have used six more.

The space behind the kitchen stove and under the oven became an important scene of operations on the ranch. At various times it sheltered new-born calves, who were chilled through and had to be fed a raw egg and stimulant through a frosty night under its benevolent warmth. It harboured the weak peepings of baby chicks and ducklings just breaking out of their shells, boxes of little puppies and kittens. It was a corner that attracted the boys like a magnet. They would lie on their stomachs for long spells, gazing with wonder at the new world of hope and struggle.

The house was deserted during the day. Eleanor could only retreat to the kitchen for the meals. She built a coldframe outside our bedroom window to which the garden plants she had started in the house during March could be transferred. Harold and I donated a whole day to Eleanor, raking the lawns and yard by the house, removing the ash pile, the tin cans and the accumulated debris. We hauled fresh earth to bank around the woodshed and the garage and flat rocks for paths while Eleanor tore up the hop vines in front of the house. In their place she planted her Iceland poppies, sweet peas and lilac bushes. And all the time we worked for her we were restless to hook up horses to the plough and begin breaking land.

As soon as we could break away from Eleanor's type of spring fever, on the excuse that we had to plough up her garden first, Harold and I got busy with the sulky. We oiled and greased it, rigged the hitches and tightened bolts. Then with a brick and coal oil we scrubbed rust off the share until it was smooth and shiny. A clean share is easier for the horses; it doesn't pick up dirt and it turns the sod over clean. Harold was still worried that it might not plough straight, in which case we would have to take it to a blacksmith in town.

At last we were ready, and he decided to try it with Prince and Brownie alone on a small piece of land in front of the house. When the team was hitched up Dane and I raced ahead to fetch Eleanor from her garden. Harold turned on to his line and settled himself in the seat, called to the team and threw the levers so that the share dropped into the soil, cutting its way to proper depth like a warm knife in butter. Eleanor and I danced with joy while Dane dashed along in the furrow behind, very much excited. Tippy the collie raced around almost under the horses' feet as they pulled evenly, heads down, breaking the first furrow. We were all pleasantly intoxicated by the feeling of spring. We knew that no one else in the district would consider working on the land so early in the season, but we had a large job ahead, breaking some 25 acres of old hay land in a rich bottom. If we were going to take off a crop of oats by fall we had to start now. The others had tractors and large modern machinery and they only had to work summer fallow. We had land to break.

When Harold made the turn and started back towards us he was wearing a big grin. The museum piece that had cost us $2.50 worked perfectly. It was a fine feeling to be starting spring work on our own land. He then ploughed around the trees by the house and turned up the patch for Eleanor's garden while I took the young team, hitched them to the stone boat and began cleaning out corrals and feed racks. Right after the noon meal we intended moving down to the big field to start ploughing with the four horses. The 25-acre field was half a mile long and we expected it to take about three weeks to plough and disc. With interruptions from the weather and other sources we could not say just when it would be seeded, but as long as the horses could stand up to the work we hoped to spell each other off at the job.

When the weather clouded up at noon we turned to the radio for a forecast. Rain or hail or snow could be expected! See what I mean? We had to forget ploughing and move our last remaining stack of hay into the horse and cow barns to keep it from spoiling, as the top had been taken off. In the middle of the afternoon George Mowat arrived, riding over Cabin Hill with his son and daughter. Mrs. Mowat had to remain at home to run the brooder stove for 150 day-old baby chicks. We discussed our plans for the year. George told us of the close calls some neighbours had experienced, getting down to their last fork-full of hay before the weather moderated.

Next morning a thin blanket of white lay on the ground. But it was warm and we spent the morning in the blacksmith shop, sorting trays of bolts, checking the post drill and wrenches for any emergency break-down. After the noon meal we hitched Prince and Brownie to the sulky. Harold started down the road while I followed with the green team. It is quite a trick to hitch

Layout of the ranch: the oat field on the left of the stock dam; the little round corral was used for weaning calves. (PHOTO BY LLOYD KNIGHT)

four horses abreast to pull the plough. Watching Harold I wondered if I would ever get on to the complicated system and if the time would ever come when I could do all the jobs myself. There seemed no end to the business of learning and the multitude of trades to master. It made me think of the costly mistakes I should most certainly have made without Harold's help during the first year and reminded me that his presence was the best insurance we could buy.

The question came up of how to place the two teams to the best advantage, as Babe or Gertie, the green horses, might cause the old team to wander from their straight line and make a crooked furrow. Unless the start was right, with a half mile to go, the ploughing could end up in a horrible mess. And how long should one work the horses for the first week until they had hardened up? I had not thought of that.

I expected Harold to make a round, down and back, and then check his horses. But he started easily as if he had all the time in the world. Half way down the field he stopped to look at his furrow, check the horses for harness and hitches, before proceeding to the bottom. After making the turn he stopped again and sat down to roll a smoke. He didn't seem to be in a hurry at all. On his return he seemed pleased with the team. He gave them a ten-minute rest. They had done a mile, but the two furrows made such an insignificant mark in the field that I began to revise my estimate of the time the job would take and wonder if we could really get it seeded for this year.

"Were they hard to handle, Harold?"

"Babe tried to wander, but she'll get over it. And that Gertie isn't pulling her weight. I might have to change her around with Brownie."

"It seemed to take so long. Do you think we can finish the job in time?"

"Sure, if we keep at it. I'll have to poke along like this for about a week until they get hardened to it. We'll have to keep graining them and we might be able to borrow another four horses, but we wouldn't have enough grain for them all. No, I think we can tough it out with these horses unless one of them gets sick. I'll keep on until dark and give them lots of rest."

"Okay, fella. I'll go riding and check on the calves and I'll be out later with some sandwiches and coffee."

This business of calving was a much safer proposition now. They all had an even chance. One only had to ride around, and if a cow looked suspicious it was smart to pass just close enough to look at her bag for signs or check a new calf to see it had sucked. If these signs were normal you could tally another. The exception was the odd heifer having trouble with her first calf.

I saddled the young horse and started out. The older calves were in a group, lying on the warm ground in a perfect pastoral setting or racing in circles kicking, bucking and bunting at imaginary butterflies. The cows with older calves join up together on the range. Coyotes were always lurking on the fringe of a herd, though I knew of no authenticated cases where they killed a newborn calf. Certainly they clean up the calving grounds and will feed on a dead calf, and I knew one case where they worried a heifer who was down having trouble with her first calf and another where they ate a still-born calf right near the mother, who was helpless. Some cowmen call the coyote a nuisance and a danger. Others like them around to keep nature in balance and clean up carcasses.

If you want to see range cows on the fight at this stage, just take a dog out amongst them or walk alone on foot. The cows, as

I say, join up with their calves, but they also have to spend many hours out grazing to keep up the flow of milk. Obviously the calves are safer in a bunch and the cows cannot all leave together. So they arrange matters just like any well-organized society. They leave a couple of baby sitters. Joe had told us about this but we thought he was pulling our legs. When the opportunity arrived to observe this in our own herd I spent many hours trying to figure it out. Each day a different pair of cows was with the calves. Did they run a duty roster? How did they know which cows were on duty for a particular day? Had they some means of communication? I never could find out. However, it is done. They manage to change the jobs regularly and each day I would find a different pair of mothers lying in the midst of the calves, chewing their cuds, while most often there wasn't another cow in sight. Most would be grazing, some would be away over at the water, others would be taking salt. What discipline made the calves remain behind with the baby sitters? Why didn't one lonely calf walk away looking for its mother?

And don't think for a minute that you can get away with anything. The old girls know and trust the rider who appears daily amongst them. But try to dismount anywhere near and they will be on their feet. Approach one of the calves and the peaceful scene changes abruptly. I have tried it alone and also with the collie dog. The moment the old cows on guard smell trouble they let out a bawl. The calves get to their feet and group around the baby sitters. Over the hill the rest of the mothers appear like magic, on the run, and with short little soft moos they call their own calves, pair off and disappear out of sight. If you follow one the cow will put her head down and paw the ground. That should be warning enough. The wild ones aren't even scared of a horse. City folks generally show more respect for a bull out on pasture but he is a sissy compared to a good matron with her calf.

With or without calves the range cattle usually keep together. A cow or young heifer will only go off by herself to drop a calf. This day I noticed one alone and tried to ride by at an angle without showing too much curiosity. Out of the corner of my eye I could see a calf had been sucking. I expected to see that or the cow "making bag". Now I wanted a look at the calf. As I rode up into the trees the old girl was watching me unobtrusively. She was a cunning one. I hid in the evergreens, changed position before peeking out at her and noticed her start around the side of the hill on a trail. She was either going to check on her calf or lead me away from it. I moved along the hilltop to keep her in sight and was perched on a rim-rock when she spotted me. I backed the horse up. When we looked again she was nowhere in sight. We moved along the edge but there was no trace of her, and as she had been quite a bit below us on open ground it seemed as though she had just vanished in a few seconds. I stayed on top but moved back to a point where I could see the place we had picked her up. It was uncanny, the way she had given us the slip. As we turned I did a double-take as we nearly bumped into her, standing by a tree right on top beside us. She must have moved quickly to get there, and after staring at us defiantly she pretended to be interested only in grazing. I tried to move her or get her excited but she would not let on. She had us buffaloed, and she knew it.

When I finally found the calf, about 50 yards away and well hidden, I decided to show the cow who was boss by moving them into the bull pasture for observation. It was a big heifer calf and lay doggo as a baby elk, which has this same instinct to lie rigid when danger is about.

I lifted it to its feet and it showed plenty of life. The trouble was to steer it. Of course I should have left it alone but I started it down the hill. It kept veering back to its bed and the old cow began to act belligerent. After chasing each other on and off the hill several times I finally worked them to the flat west of the house where Eleanor saw the struggle and came out to help. The cow saw her, charged full speed, with head down. My good wife looked like the bear cub that tried to run in several directions. There wasn't a tree or fence to climb and I had to put the horse into high gear to get between the cow and Eleanor. The horse just managed to turn the old girl and I had to escort my wife back to the house, both of us scared, while cow and calf trotted back to the trees. It had been my fault entirely. But we were learning.

We didn't lose any more of our own calves, though probably it wasn't my fault we saved them. But we had one more loss. Angus had come up with another deal for us. He wanted Harold to give him a hand for a couple of weeks digging a well to get water on his summer grass. He offered us a shorthorn heifer, which we could use for a milk cow, and her calf. In this case we collected the wages long before doing the job and moved them up home. As the calf had been born recently we started right in to break the heifer for milking. We tried to play the game of "range dominoes", as Mr. Bennett had described it in his book, by matching up the shorthorn calf with the range cow whose calf had died. But the cow would not have anything to do with the stranger although we spent many hours tying up the cow, keeping her alone in the barn with the calf, roping a hind leg and dragging up the calf to start the meal. Sometimes the game works and they settle down together so you can turn them out on the range to their mutual advantage. But this girl was stubborn and continued to fight. The calf was willing but only made headway so long as we were there to supervise and hold them together. Perhaps there was too much supervision. We tried every trick in the book, including the old dodge of dressing the new calf in the hide of the one that had died, hoping the mother would accept it on scent. But it didn't work. The calf had been kicked so much it gave up trying altogether. We had to switch it to a "pail bunter", raising it on skim milk.

One day the bull came along and opened the barn door. The calf bolted, found his real mother and filled his little tummy to bursting with rich milk. It was a terribly bloated sick little animal that night and Harold worked late trying to save it. When we went to bed that night he thought it had a chance, but it was dead in the morning. So Eleanor had two little hides to tan.

All this time the grass was greening up at a terrific pace, the buds were coming out in the trees, and among the cattle you could hear the tearing sound as they ripped up the tender shoots. The grain farmers lamented the late season but everyone conceded it was a perfect year for grass and hay crops. Harold kept on with the ploughing, up and down, rest ten minutes, up and down again. On the half-mile strip the belt of rich black loam gradually widened. He did not want me to spoil his nice straight furrows, so I was allowed to make only one round at a time. I kept working at the cattle and repairing fences where the big drifts had knocked them down.

An old cow showed up with bag trouble—too much milk for her small calf—and had to be milked once a day. She was big and tough and it required time and patience to get her snubbed up. One day the rope loosened. She didn't so much strike me as lift me bodily in the air with a hind leg and when I stopped falling I landed on a very hard rock. That put me on light duties and I took the opportunity of travelling to Lethbridge with some neighbours. It was fun to see the Wizard and Hutch again. The former told me the V.L.A. were very much pleased with our progress. I walked into the Government offices without a care in the world. This time there wasn't anyone ready to shoot us down in flames. Mr. Miller had the same old smile and twinkly eyes. He wouldn't let me go as we talked and talked about the highlights of the winter. He was impressed by the number of cattle we were running but we didn't try to figure anything out. Both of us knew we had a heavy load of debts but it was impossible to estimate our probable income. There were too many factors involved for the sharpest of pencils.

Early in May Eleanor came running out in the rain to tell us some thrilling news she had picked up on the radio. The Minister of Agriculture, according to a news broadcast, had opened negotiations for the export of beef cattle to the United States. It sounded like just the break we needed. How good it would be for us we could only guess. At the best it could bring our prices up to parity with the American market. The least we could expect was for our prices to hold firm.

It was just a year since we had first laid eyes on the ranch and a fine Saturday afternoon reminded me of the fact. I asked Eleanor to come for a walk, ostensibly to look for more calves. We strolled up the valley reminiscing.

"Do you remember when we first drove up here and thought it was too big a place for our resources?"

"Yes, and you tried to turn around and drive away, you coward."

"And you, my precious fool, repeated Augie's words about buying it anyway and worrying about it after. He didn't know we had no right trying in the first place."

This was light-hearted banter, but it was spring. We had never felt so sure of ourselves, so healthy, tanned and hard. We were both working harder than we had ever worked in our lives but we had never been happier. Edgar Burke had written to remind us of the struggle ahead and had added that we would always be looking for the day when we had it cleared and could turn around to buy ourselves furniture, a car, clothing or do anything we wanted with money. But he warned that we,would look back on these years, when we were struggling for our ideal, as the best. He ended by hoping we would stop once in a while to realize we were having the best fun right now.

Turning back toward the house, walking arm in arm and marvelling at the beauty of the place and the wonder, which will remain always, of the peace it brought us, we stopped on a rise above the house. The picture spread before us was framed by green hills angling from east and west. The dam, smooth as glass, reflected green slopes and blue sky. Below the dam the freshly ploughed field took on a new aspect. Eleanor swears the soil had a purple tinge to it. It looked so clean and neat. On the slope above it the willow and Saskatoon bushes reminded us of heather and the flat field on top had young brome grass growing thickly. On the other slope across the valley from the ploughed land we swept our eyes over the horse pasture and fixed on a pair of black and white statues. They hardly moved, and we knew that Prince and Brownie were trying to get in the act by completing as pretty a picture as anyone could wish. In the middle distance to the south the strip farms were changing colours as the machines varied the pattern and in the far distance the foothills rolled up to the turrets of the Rockies. Very clearly we could make out the Gap leading to Waterton Lakes National Park and at the end of the mountain chain, way down in Montana, Big Chief stood proudly by himself, looking like a bluff and hearty friend.

Eleanor broke the silence. "Oh, but I wish I could paint and had the time to drop everything and just stay here for a couple of hours to capture all that colour and beauty."

But our life seemed to swing sharply from the sublime to the ridiculous. Eleanor and I had a yen to try some fruit trees. Shortly after our lovely walk with its touching moments I used the plan as an excuse to satisfy a hidden frustration. I was going to plough land on my own. I was going to show Eleanor what a man she had married and prepare new ground for the fruit trees. We had an old walking plough that would need only Prince and Brownie. Harold was away for the day, so without telling anyone I hitched up the team and hauled the plough into the garden. After making one horrible pass at it, when the plough insisted on twisting and turning, popping out of the ground and digging in too deeply, I called for my good wife and asked her to handle the lines. She tried to drive the team while I wrestled with that infernal implement. I couldn't get the hang of the thing and as my temper mounted it became obvious the blame should be put on Eleanor for faulty driving. Any husband knows the trick. It is one of the cardinal rules in marriage for supporting the male ego.

The more we tried the more I criticized and the wilder the plough snaked around, in and out. I threw off my shirt to fight it, and Eleanor left in disgust to continue putting in potatoes. I tied the lines together, put them over my head and really settled down to fight. I was plain mad by this time and the steady old team settled down to following the best furrow. At the end of each row I collapsed on the grass, fighting for breath. It was like wrestling some 200-pound giant. But I stayed with it until the strip was black and had to do the chores very late in the dark. Eleanor and I weren't speaking so light-heartedly that evening; in fact we hardly said a word, and next day I was stiff and sore. Imagine anyone in his right mind wanting to be a farmer!

Harold had been in town trying to get the jeep fixed, and when I showed him the plough next morning he said it didn't have a breaker bottom and could not turn the sod over properly. He ran over the ground with the sulky repairing my mistakes.

I had figured the only way to learn was by starting with the walking plough to get all the angles, then riding the sulky on a post-graduate course. Each year I did some work with the walking plough and finally caught on to it, but the initiation could have been a lot easier had I known about some minor adjustments. Bill came up once and caught me practising, dropped a bar about four holes and after that the share didn't dig in too deeply. From then on it was easy to control. But from that time, whenever I began to act big and talk like a successful rancher, Eleanor interrupted with: "Don't forget your experience with the walking plough." Perhaps that is why most ranchers seldom lose their modesty and humble bearing. The business is full of walking ploughs.

We had the land ready for seeding by the first week in June but heavy rains delayed the final job. When Harold finished ploughing I did the discing in a couple of days with the same horses, and then he dragged the field with large planks. Rain continued to plague us until the middle of June but we were fortunate in not being so dependent upon the weather as grain farmers. We wanted this field for feed, and green feed would suit our purpose as well as threshed grain.

We had come full cycle on the ranch. From now on everything we did had a precedent. The jobs were looking familiar and our big interest was in improving the procedures and mastering the trades.

Chapter Fourteen

ELEANOR'S POULTRY business started to pick up. In the garden beside the house she had a regular nursery with special little houses for the baby fowl and this gave us all a chance to study their living and eating habits. There were 24 chicks, ten ducklings and nine turkey poults. Of all these the ducklings proved the most interesting and amusing. Ungainly as they are on land at first, they are forever chasing butterflies and insects through the grass. We raised them all in the garden, fearing that down by the barn they might be wiped out by coyotes and chicken hawks.

In those days we had quite a few peculiar ideas about animals. For instance, we believed that ducklings should not be allowed near water in the early stages of their growth. Where we picked that one up I cannot say, but the family was horrified when I scooped up a few of the little ones and dumped them into the rain barrel for an experiment. Even though they swam around happily Eleanor was not entirely convinced, conceding them only a pan of water to play in. However, as in most cases, the animals themselves soon taught us the truth. After many weeks of care with the first hatch we stood speechless when a mother duck took her day-old brood waddling in a solemn, ludicrous procession towards the dam where they entered the water and proceeded to cruise in line astern. Another queer idea was laughed into oblivion.

Eleanor clipping the wings of the turkeys so they could not fly away. (PHOTO BY LLOYD KNIGHT)

When an early hatch began to arrive Eleanor brought them up to the kitchen, to the great delight of Tim and Dane. One particular egg seemed to be a dud, but when I suggested throwing it out Eleanor was indignant. It fascinated her and she kept close watch. When more than a reasonable time had gone by she gently made a tiny crack in the shell. There was a slight struggle inside, so she peeled off a piece. More struggle, and more help from the budding scientist supported by an interested audience of little boys. And weren't they proud when the little spark of life teetered uncertainly on the palm of her hand and they all rushed out to show me the triumph! Eleanor named it "Little Albert", kept it warm in the house and fed it pablum for a few days. She took a lot of teasing for wasting her time. "He will never make much of a duck, I know," she said. "He's much smaller than the rest to start with and he doesn't grow so quickly, but he is well worth his feed in entertainment. Take a few minutes to watch his antics. He's just like a Walt Disney character."

During the early part of the summer that was his role exactly—falling into buckets and holes, tripping over a blade of grass, trailing behind the flock, always getting lost but always trying valiantly to keep up with the rest, stumbling at high speed and skidding along the ground on his beak in his frantic efforts. Little Albert was pure clown. After watching him day after day running into disaster, losing his mates because his little legs would not go fast enough, Eleanor said: "Now there's one duck I shall never be able to eat." But the ducklings graduated to the water and other interests crowded them out of our minds except for an occasional count. Keeping track of all the additions to our family was like trying to take in all the acts in a three-ring circus. By late fall Albert was just another duck; in fact, we could no longer positively identify him.

Spring made us think also of visitors. There had been no time for such amenities last summer, although we had been able to show a little hospitality to a few friends. Hutch had been out on a flying visit one Sunday to inspect the layout, the Wizard had shared the doubtful comforts of the crowded cabin in an attempt to straighten out our problems, and the good priest, who had put heart into me during the lowest ebb of our fortunes, had come out for a few days to help with the haying as he had promised. Eddie and Edna Goodfellow, who had given us such a big boost at Manyberries, dropped in late in the fall to see how we were making out. We had just moved into the house and were ashamed of our inadequately furnished home. Now that we were getting settled it would be fun having old friends inspect the place.

We hadn't long to wait. Before the roads had dried two cars came churning up through the mud bearing the faithful Harry Hargrave, two men from the Livestock Insect Laboratory in Lethbridge and a business man from Calgary. We decided to start a guest book. It was a great joy to be able to let off steam telling Harry about our experiences. They were all amused at the trial and error methods we had adopted during calving and at the machinery we had obtained, and while Eleanor produced a memorable meal we had a lot of laughs.

During my last visit with Mr. Miller in Lethbridge he had asked if he could send a reporter out to take some pictures and get a story for the veterans' paper. When I talked the proposition over with Eleanor she reasoned that if there was a story here I should write it myself and try to sell the article. Perhaps it would make some mad money for us. While Harold was ploughing I sneaked into the cabin and battled it out. When it was finished we didn't know what to do with it except use it for starting the fires. Eleanor said she was sure she had read worse stuff but I didn't ask her to remember when. That reminded me that one time I asked George Mowat which farm paper he would recommend us to take. "It depends upon how many stoves you have," said George. "If there are two fires to start you need to subscribe to a couple of them." Anyway, we borrowed a stack of Mowat's magazines and after some debate we sent the article to *MacLean's Magazine* in Toronto. Of course they didn't buy it but the article editor was nice enough to take the trouble to write a long letter in reply. He pointed out why it would not suit them in its present form and that they might be interested if we found time to do it over on the lines he suggested.

This was almost as exciting and as good for the morale as the thrilling letter from the silent partners when they sent us the big cheque. I put in some nervous hours on the typewriter and wrote the thing again. It didn't give us any big ideas, but on the strength of the encouragement we made a deal with Bill to buy his cream separator for $20. Up to that time Eleanor had been taking the cream off by letting the milk stand in cans. So with a few magic words, that considerate article editor, who was Scott Young, now a high-profile writer, unwittingly increased the butter production of the ranch.

Chapter Fifteen

WHEN THE Community Auction Sales started up for the summer we didn't have the time to follow the trend. These sales, held at Lundbreck, Pincher Creek and other points, were run by the same committee and attracted all the main buyers to one focal point where the cattle were gathered. The committee generally chose a good loading point for rail or truck hauling and organized each sale so efficiently that most of the producers preferred this type of marketing as it produced strong competitive bidding among the buyers for all classes of cattle. A grower got the same break whether he had only one head to sell—a cow, an old bull, a small calf—or a carload lot of even steers or heifers.

Toward the middle of August we had two cows ready to market. They were dry—that is, they had not produced calves— and the ranch could not afford to run boarders. As Bill was driving a bunch in to the sale at Pincher Creek on August 13 we entered our two in the same sale. It meant an early start the day before and driving the cattle some 20 miles, or less if the river could be forded. Bill knew our crowd was busy with the haying and offered to take ours in with his bunch.

I went in to the sale wondering just what those cows would bring. This was a trial run for us. Mr. Beaumont had tried to cheer us last summer by comparing life to the Grand National. You come to a big jump—a stone wall or brush—you check the horse's stride, tighten the grip and estimate the distance to the take-off point. Then you gird your loins for the big moment, give your horse some rein and leg him over. If you have everything right and the horse is in form you clear nicely and land safely. A long stretch of smooth running lies ahead while you concentrate on the next type of jump. It is important to know the course. In our Grand National we were approaching the first obstacle, which Mr. Beaumont might have called the water jump. I thought of the genial Irishman that day and the faithful bank manager as well as the silent partners. Mr. Beaumont had written us about gathering strength for the "lep" and I wondered if we had done all we could. Just two cows were entered, but we only had a total of 30 plus the Jersey from Dingreville and the shorthorn from Angus, none of them paid for. We had to make every jump count.

The yards were full of cattle. The buyers were sitting in an enclosed stand and I imagined they were all tough, hardboiled characters. On two other sides were rising tiers of seats for spectators, generally filled with farmers and ranchers who could, if the price was not right, bid their cattle in and take them home again. Across from the buyers, in a small stand on the other side of the sale ring, were the auctioneers and clerks.

The sale was in progress. I found it hard to estimate the weights of the animals as they entered the ring, and as the bid kept changing found it impossible in my excitement to work out in my head the total value of the animals in question. If we didn't get a good price for ours how could I know quickly enough to bid them in? We had bought the cows with calves at foot for $125. How much did the calf weigh at the time, and how much the cow? Let's make it easier. Say the cow would be worth $100 and the calf $25. No, that wasn't enough for the calf. Then what were the cows really worth?

I wished I had remained at home like Bill. He took his cattle in to the sale and then stayed away. He didn't even try to find out how they were selling and in due time the Association mailed him a cheque. Bill always said: "If you're going to sell 'em, take 'em in to the sale and fergit it. There's no sense hanging around trying to figger against those guys."

I turned to the man sitting next to me. "How is the sale going?"

"Fine," he said. "Just fine. It's a dandy sale."

"Are you buying or selling?"

"Me? I got a little bunch entered in this sale."

"How about prices, are they good today?"

"What do you mean good? Haven't you heard the news? Hell, man, they opened the American market yesterday and there's a bunch of buyers from across the line sitting right there in the stand. The Canadian buyers are mostly keeping quiet, all but Hymie Cohen and he's sure making them pay for the cattle all right. That Cohen, he sure is a good man and he's sparking this sale."

"How good are the prices?" I asked weakly.

"Just listen to the bidding, neighbour. It's getting stronger all the time."

That beautiful water jump. I looked over toward the Rockies and the friendly foothills. My, but the buyers were a fine-looking crowd of men, so intelligent and kind! Everyone looked nice but I wished someone would smile to break the tension. Such poker faces—you could hardly catch them bidding. Good old Cohen.

When our two cows came into the ring I sat on my hands in case the auctioneer might think I was bidding. My nose was suddenly very itchy and I fixed my eyes on the back of one of the cows and kept them there until they bored holes in the hide. Bidding opened at 12¢. If the cow weighed only a thousand pounds that made it $120. Don't think about it anymore. Don't look at anyone. Keep your eyes on the back of that cow. Now the bid is at 14¢. Holy cats! as Bill would say. Why didn't I make Eleanor come in with me? Now it's 16¢. When are they going to stop? Seventeen now and they are tapering off—and a quarter—. Now it's 18¢—18—now a quarter. It's got to stop some time. Keep your eyes on that cow. What a beautiful old girl! Gosh! they got past the quarter. It's 18½. Sold to Swifts. I wonder which one of those fine fellows bought them.

"Two cows. Put them in pen six."

I fell off the stand and walked around behind. Should I find the buyer and shake hands with him? Pull yourself together, chum. Look at all those other guys with poker faces. These are big operators. Try to behave like a cowman. All this excitement for two lousy cows. What would Bill or Fred Hewitt think of you now? Hang on to the old cow's tail, boy, and she'll pull you through. I wonder if there's a telephone out here? Must call Eleanor—and won't Hutch be pleased! But how about the cheque? I should get a receipt or something. The animals aren't mine now.

"Pardon me, but do you go to the office or something when you sell cattle here?"

"That shack over there is the place. They hand you a slip."

"Thanks."

I waited in line for my ticket. It read: "Weight 2500—2 head—cows branded 7C—. Price per cwt. $18.50—Total $462.50." I didn't stop driving until I came to our village and telephoned Eleanor from there. I kept taking out the ticket and looking at it. Then I drove home with a present for the boys.

Before I knew it I had the sharp pencil out trying to figure out future profits. Cattle had almost doubled in price. It didn't seem likely the price would drop as quickly as it had risen. Professor Ewen had it figured for a strong three-year market. No one had really believed the price could jump like that in a few days. If it would just remain strong we had the problem licked. Those calves we had bought would be all profit. We didn't think of the gruelling days of plodding work now, the storms of winter and the bitterness at losing a calf in the spring. If those prices could only hold up we couldn't help but make it. The calves we bought with the original cows might pay for the whole works. They were in the mountains and would come out in October as long yearlings. And how about the 15 head I had bought from Augie at $40 apiece? Augie's steers, too. Eleanor talked me into putting the pencil away. It was all guess work.

Augie left the steers on the ranch until the end of August. We stayed away from town and kept hitting the ball by putting up feed, building fences and riding regularly through the herd on the summer range. At the end of August the big Dane drove up to the ranch. He had telephoned Calgary and decided we should ship by rail from Cowley direct to the packers. He bought another few carloads of cattle from Bill and the Dumont brothers, so there were plenty of riders to make the 12-mile drive. Augie spent two days with us. In the air now was a different kind of excitement. He had a good look at the ranges, and the type of grass, and admired the cattle. When he returned to the house he said to us: "I can tell by the look of the place and the animals that you and Eleanor love it here and are putting your heart into it."

After the drive to the loading point the cattle were weighed and Augie cleared the shipment with the railway and the stock inspector. I was disappointed with the weights of our steers and Augie admitted they might have been heavier. But he added:

"Don't worry about that. Weight isn't everything. It's the price that counts. We are both going to make money on this deal."

On our return to the ranch Augie wanted to know how much hay we had fed the steers. I didn't want to charge the hay against the deal as without it we could both show more profit. But he insisted, marking down $600 to be paid us for the hay.

"Okay, Augie. You want to pay us $600 for the feed. I owe you $600 for those 15 calves. Do you want to call it quits?"

He put down his pencil and looked straight at me.

"I was only kidding about those calves. They are a present. You weren't going to pay me for them anyway. I should have told you when you sent the note but I just tore it up and threw it away."

"Now look, Augie. I came to you for a business deal, not charity. You can't do that sort of thing. It isn't fair to Ethel and Pat. It isn't that we need it either. And by doing something like this you are going to stop us from coming to you for any more business. Please, Augie, think of us. You've done too much as it is."

The big fellow was obstinate and I could hardly face him. The tension of the previous summer seemed to well up inside and break again as I remembered Augie and Tip fighting to hold our dreams together. There were strangers present, talking quietly in a corner of the kitchen, and I didn't like it. I was choking back emotion and fighting the tears. There wasn't a reason on earth why he should do this.

"Now listen, Gray. And you come here too, Eleanor. While you were flying bombers over Germany helping to win the war I was home here making money with a lot of others. I felt pretty badly when I couldn't help you better last summer. Ethel and I want to do this for you and this is the first chance we've had. Use your head for a change. I'm making enough money on the big steers."

"I can't do it, Augie. It will spoil everything."

"Listen to him," he boomed. "So it will spoil everything. You mean it will make Ethel and me both feel good. What's the matter with you, man? If you can't take the calves you can't stop me making a present of them to Eleanor. The business is finished. You get $600 for the feed. I'll take out the cost of a young bull for you and mail you a statement on the steers when I get the prices from the packers. Don't try to talk about it any more. I wish I could give you a statement now but I'm kind of slow at the pencil work."

Augie and his party got in their car to drive away. Eleanor and
I were so overwhelmed we just stood dumbly by the back door to
wave, feeling helpless that we could not thank him properly.
Then Davey Gibb, retired sheep herder and rancher from
Medicine Hat, turned to us and in his soft Scottish accent said:
"Good luck to you both and take a tip from me. I have known
the big fellow a long time and we always travel together. Don't
try to thank him. Mon, he's awful embarrassed right noo."

About September 11 we had a cheery letter from Augie. We
had both done well on the steers. Our share was over $2,000 and
for two heifers and two more dry cows we had shipped to Burns
at the same time there was another $850. We sent the cheque in
to Hutch at the bank and advised him we still had our yearlings
in the mountains. When we brought them out in the middle of
October we were going to try and market the steers if the price
was still high. We also had to find another deal for cattle the
coming winter. We had plenty of feed. The field Harold had
ploughed made a pretty sight. One of the best crops of oats in
the country. If we cut and stacked it all for green feed we should
be in a position to bargain with anyone. Augie had told us to
write him when we knew what the picture would be but we were
shy about bothering him again. If he really wanted to put cattle
up here he could do it any time but, as I wrote to Hutch, it might
be better for us to make our own deal with a stranger.

The North Fork Stock Association, to which we belonged, ran
our cattle through the summer in the mountains behind the
Livingstone Range. The Association was organized by arrangement with the Department of Lands and Mines. We had a rider
up there all summer and with extra men to help he began gathering the cattle toward the middle of October. On the 15th the
members collected at Maycroft, some 25 miles from the ranch, to
cut out their cattle. I rode over the hill to Mowat's place and we
eased our horses around through the hills to the Walronde flats
in the North Fork valley, across the large open range to the
bridge, where we joined strings of riders converging on Poverty
Flats, the site of the annual round-up.

It was a colourful scene with many groups of riders on their
best horses, gaily dressed, winding up the road towards
Maycroft. This annual affair brought together friends who might
not have met once during the summer, and on recognizing a
friend a rider would rein in and wait to exchange the latest
gossip. Often entire families would turn up in a dashing group—

parents, sons and daughters together. Generally it was a sparkling fall day in the beginning but later it too often turned suddenly wet and cold. Chaps, spare sweaters or jackets and a ground sheet were standard equipment. As this was one of the oldest stock association round-ups in the country many cars also gathered, passing in continual procession from the towns round about. Occasionally when a larger outfit employing half a dozen riders roared by on the road in a large stock truck with saddle horses aboard, someone would say ironically: "Dudes."

At Maycroft Hall the ladies of the neighbouring ranches were assembled and had a hot noon meal waiting for us. The saddle horses were turned loose to stand with drooping reins inside the hall yard. Everyone sat down to a good meal on a table running the length of the hall. From 10:30 in the morning until one in the afternoon the long line of cattle filed by on their way to the flats. At the end of the meal the Association rider and officials who had been detailed to help in the count reported their tally to the president. Generally the tally was about a thousand head.

After the meal we all gathered in the yard to yarn a bit and twist smokes. Groups tightened cinches and arranged their holding points outside the main herd. The president and secretary or an appointed round-up boss decided which outfits should cut first. They usually sent five men in at a time to cut for five outfits, then changed after a couple of hours. At this stage I noticed two ranchers with brand-new saddles. I hoped no one was paying any attention to the plug I was riding or the ancient saddle I had borrowed. As everyone crowded around to admire these fine examples of the saddle-maker's craft it was amusing to watch the faces of the two proud owners, each trying to judge the other man's saddle without being too obvious about it. They looked like a couple of ladies in church at Easter wearing the same exclusive piece of millinery.

When we moved out for the cutting and holding of cattle I found our place and learned we were putting four outfits together. Tom Heap, the vice-president, would cut for himself, Baillie, Mowat and me. Burles and Lank were together and they had four riders. Noel Cox was by himself, with Mrs. Cox riding to hold the cut. Lynch-Staunton, the president, had the whole family out. And there was the former polo star, Harry Gunn, 74 years old, doing the cutting for the Elton ranch in an old pair of sheepskin chaps. He could still ride hell-for-leather and put younger men to shame. The round-up went on for hours, changing outfits, holding cattle, chasing dogies back into the main bunch. About four o'clock it began to snow and the brands became hard to read. I thought we would never get finished before dark.

When the herd had been narrowed down to a half-dozen unidentified dogies and no one could see the brands, the ropers came into the picture. Sometimes the young bloods tried their hand at roping the big ones, eager to test their horses. Some years you could watch a master at work such as Frank MacDonald, one time world champion cowboy, who had a ranch at Maycroft. His rope, horse and technique were thrilling to watch.

With the round-up finished we trailed our herd to the Jack Baillie ranch, trying to light a smoke for comfort against the wet, the cold and the misery. I didn't know what to expect next but followed along, turning the cattle into pasture for the night, stabling the horse with the others after helping to feed and water.

Coming into the large, warm kitchen like drowned rats we were met by Jack Baillie who stood by a cupboard at the other end of the room firing dry clothing at us—jeans, shirts, sweaters and socks.

"Here, boys, try these for size and get into something dry," he called. "And I suppose you would be mad as hell if I poured you a hot rum."

Sitting in the living room before a roaring fire it sure felt good to be a rancher. And from the kitchen came the aroma of good cooking. Baillie was the perfect host, with a fund of stories about the old days and witty asides for any remarks we could make. Bob Burles, the Lank boys and Tom Heap rounded out the good company that evening and none were spared Baillie's playful barbs.

What a business, this ranching! The entire trip was like a convention. We had a good evening and a fine sleep. In the morning after a bang-up breakfast we were away for the long drag home. The cattle poked along, giving a man plenty of time to think to himself or talk shop with his neighbour. He could play his horse around if he wanted to school it or just amble along. If the weather was bad you could always find shelter for the stop to eat your sandwiches, and we generally made Mowat's in time for dinner.

On this trip we were three head short on the total but until we made the cut at Mowat's we would not know whether one or both of us was short. It was too dark to cut when we arrived, so I proceeded on the last two miles over Cabin Hill for home, both horse and rider feeling stiff and sore. I could tell how my horse felt by the way his eagerness for his home pasture fought against a shorter, choppier stride. There was no doubt about my own stiffness when I had to climb off and on at the gates. Mrs. Mowat had telephoned ahead, so Eleanor had a bath ready with lots of hot water. And after a meal I collapsed in bed.

Next morning when I returned for the cattle we cut on foot from Mowat's corral and found we were short the three head. Everyone tried to cheer us up. "Don't worry," they said. "The betting is that they will show up on the second drive." One man even offered to buy the three missing head, he was so sure we would recover them. Another told us the grass had been too good in the mountains that year and a lot of the animals had worked so far back on the ranges they were difficult to round up. But still we worried about them.

George felt badly at this loss in our first year, and when he attended an auction sale at Lundbreck the following week made a point to look up the rider for the Association. The chap told him he had definitely located two head of ours and would be bringing them out soon. George rushed to a telephone and called Eleanor. We accepted the fact that we would lose one head our first year in the mountains.

Another week went by. Finally the rider had a telephone message relayed that our cattle would be coming to Poverty Flats where we could pick them up Sunday. It was an unexpected surprise to find three animals instead of two, all in good flesh, and we trucked them home jubilantly to join the others on our best grass. When the oats had been cut and stacked we turned them into the stubble to pick up loose grain and they had weeks of splendid grazing.

There were 20 steers in the lot. We wanted to keep the heifers to build up our breeding stock, but if we could sell the steers at a good price we would be over the hump our first year. We didn't know whether to ride our luck through the auction ring or sell at private treaty. Only two more sales were listed for the year. I tried to get buyers to come out and make an offer but no one showed. Perhaps they figured that we intended to invite competitive bidding, which was correct, or perhaps they wanted to delay coming out until the auction sales had finished and we would not have so many alternatives.

The truth is we did not know which way to play it. One day I was convinced it would be safer to sell them by private treaty. A few days later I thought the auction-sale method would obtain the highest price, providing there was a good turnout of buyers. But here we were at the mercy of the elements because a bitter, raw day would keep them away. Some very cheap buys had been made in the past under these conditions. And this time we weren't selling a couple of head. Twenty of our own steers, representing a year of work, would be in the ring at once, and there had to be the right kind of buyers. Not all of them would be bidding for a lot of 20. They weren't fat enough for the packer. A steer man might buy them for stockers or a feeder might see a quick turnover in them. On the other hand they might just look at them and consider the steers were carrying too much flesh for the big gain they desired.

So we argued it out at meal times, the little boys probably unconsciously picking up the business, and vacillated from day to day. When no buyers showed I decided to take a chance on the last sale of the year at Pincher Station and entered the lot.

We didn't have much time to brood over it. We had to sell them to pay Mr. Rhodes the first instalment, square our running expenses, taxes, payment to the V.L.A. and all the rest of our commitments. Hutch had kindly refrained from sending us monthly statements reminding us of the mounting figures. I had only a vague idea how bad or good the picture might be.

Some of the neighbours thought we should keep the steers another year and with their gains make about $75 more a head. Even Gus Dingreville asked me if I had thought of that. I told him we had, but it was a good axiom of business to take a profit when you could and keep up with the payments. He liked the answer and said: "Now you should think like that." Then he told me about two ranchers living side by side on almost identical places. One fellow sold his beef every fall, "Never mind the price," Gus said, and paid his bills. The other fellow used to hold them over, carry a note at the bank and speculate. The former was still there, comfortable and prosperous. The other chap went broke and quit the country.

Then we received a fateful telephone call. It was Hutch. "Did you take on any more cattle?" he asked.

"Haven't had time to scout around," I replied.

"I've got a natural for you then. A new customer has been in the bank. A business man from a small town out here about 40 miles. He took in some two-year-old steers on a debt and doesn't know what to do with them. He can't sell them right away and feed lot charges are too high. I recommended your place and you better not waste time looking him up. I told him the bank would guarantee your integrity but you have to make your own deal. What? Go ahead and ask him for all the gain. He wants to get them off his mind and you can take them for a year without putting him to any expense. Let me know how you make out."

I lost no time driving down to look at the steers. They weren't as good as Augie's bunch but they would start us out with prospects for the second year. I saw the man and made arrangements to meet him in Lethbridge. We would weigh them there, sign a contract and I would take over the shipping charges from there to the ranch. Yes, I could have all the gain. He would set down their weights and the price at which he took them over. If the selling price next year was greater he stood to make the difference at the weights when I took them. I could have all the rest. We could also brand them as ours.

Back home I barely had time to figure that one out and type a sample contract when there was a telephone call to meet the train with the shipment in Lethbridge. There were 31 head, averaging 890 pounds. I billed them out to our station, raced for the ranch and arrived about midnight. Of course I had to lose an hour of sleep to tell Eleanor about the excitement.

Harold and I were up before daylight doing chores. I borrowed an extra saddle horse from Angus and trotted for town. The train arrived about 10:30 that morning. After giving the cattle a short rest we started for home. It was dark when we arrived at the calf pasture and turned them loose. And tomorrow our 20 steers had to be in the yards.

Next morning we had to make the same kind of early start with the steers for Pincher Station and the last auction sale. We were galloping to the next big jump in our Grand National. It was crowding things too closely but it was exciting. I had not had time to think about the market trend or prices. I didn't know if we were doing the right thing leaving the new steers without supervision and not branded. We concentrated on the drive. By road it was 21 miles, but by cutting across country and fording the river we might cut off six miles of the journey. Taking them to market you don't try to make a quick trip. You let them ooze along, grazing as they go, trying to hold their weight.

When we arrived at the river after the noon stop a thin layer of ice held us up. The cattle would take to the water, cross the ford to the ice, try to climb on it, break through, then turn back on us. After having them mill around in the river and slip by the horses to return to the starting side, we gave it up. We found a shoal of gravel on a bend farther down and headed them for it. They finally made it. After a slow climb out of the river valley to the flat prairie on top we had to bear a cold east wind. The last hours of the drag were most unpleasant, and when we arrived at the sale yards stiff and cold we had to hold our bunch for an hour to take our turn. Bands of cattle were converging from all directions. Everyone seemed to have waited for the last sale.

I dreaded the thought of riding all the way home again in the dark, but fortunately Bill arrived in his truck with a load of cows and offered to haul our ponies back into the hills for the return trip. I was so grateful I didn't even try to climb into the cab, which was crowded, but rode with the horses. It was cold out there, and slippery because the cows had been painting the floor. If I had been a horse with a preference I should have chosen to leg it home.

I was in early next day for the sale. I compared our steers with others in the yards, watched the buyers arrive and talked to ranchers about prices. You can't tell how a sale is going to go. Sales on succeeding days at two points 15 miles apart vary widely. The prices at the beginning and end of a sale often show a marked difference. One reason they tag off at the end is that no buyer wants to be left with part of a carload and they often sit back rather than risk it. Most ranchers, therefore, like to have their cattle come into the ring at the beginning. I found that ours would not be entering until near the end. A bad sign. This time I wasn't going to be caught in a whirl of excitement at the mounting bids. At the ranch we had agreed to be satisfied with 20¢ a pound. If the bidding didn't make that I would take them home. I told Hutch we would get 22 but he said we should be well satisfied if we got 20.

The sale started off fine, but the afternoon wore on and I watched them bringing in cattle from pens at the other end of the yards. It looked as if they would never get around to ours. I caught one of the officials at the sale and told him I had to get a good price as it was our one big chance to get through the year ahead of the game and our steers were first class. "Why don't you get the auctioneers to announce it as a special bunch?" he said. At a recess he called them over and I talked to them. Warren Cooper and Don Ball took my name and location, saying: "Sure, we don't mind making an announcement like that when we're asked."

Then I walked in among the buyers in their special stand. Bobby Dogterom, who knew I was trying to create interest, said in a loud voice: "I hear you've got some nice stuff entered today?" and winked at me.

"They sure are," I replied. "Twenty head of the best yearling steers in the sale." I wondered if it was ethical to act like this and thought of my neighbours and friends in the stands. But what the hell, we had to sell them and every cent would count. We hadn't taken all those chances last year to let it slip through our fingers now for lack of nerve.

"Hello there, Mr. Cohen, I hope you're bidding on yearling steers today."

"You got some in, Mr. Campbell? Sorry I'm not buying that class but I'll speak to Mr. Neufeld. He might be interested."

Mr. Neufeld came up to say, "Are these steers you entered out of the original Rhodes cows? I know that class of stuff and I may try to buy them. Twenty head eh? I'll think about it."

Bobby and I stood by the small door leading into the buyers' stand. We let buyers in, but when one tried to leave before the end of the sale Bobby turned him back. "You don't want to leave yet," he said. "Those good steers haven't come in."

I thought they would never get around to ours. Then I could see them. Bobby was now down in front, bang in the middle of the stand. He turned to look at me and I pointed and held up two fingers. They would come in after the next lot. When the gate finally opened Bobby turned and in a loud voice called: "Are these your cattle, Gray? Boy, they sure look classy." They did indeed, and I was proud of them filling the ring. A nice even bunch.

Booming out over the loudspeaker came the voice of Don Ball. "Now, gentlemen, we have a nice carload lot of special long yearling steers from the ranch of Gray Campbell in the Porcupine Hills." Golly, I thought, they are all we have and these guys must think they are hand picked from a hundred.

"What ranch did you say?" called Bobby.

"The Campbell ranch," said Warren Cooper, while I stood there, rigid, breaking out in a cold sweat. I could hardly take a breath. What a pressure play this was, and perhaps in bad taste.

"What will you start with this classy bunch?" called Don.

And away they went, like a horse race when you have put all your money on one nag to win. They opened at 20, and I could breathe again. The bidding went up slowly by quarters to 21. Now there were only two buyers left trying for them, but they were stubborn. I dug the nails of my right hand into the palm of my left. Twenty-one and a quarter,—and a half. It slowed down. Now 21.50—75. Twenty-two. It made 22. And a quarter. It's going to stop there. No, it isn't—it's a half. Twenty-two and a half. Is that it? The auctioneer faltered, was about to knock it down at the half when someone must have given him a secret signal. It went to 22.75, and stopped there. My heart picked up the beats it had missed. Yippee! What a price! We made it.

"Sold to Mr. Neufeld for 22.75—next lot."

Bobby walked by and gave me a pat on the back. He was in a hurry to return to Lethbridge and he was late. Cohen walked past me and gave me a big wink. Everyone seemed happy. I put my hands over my head and clasped them like a boxer towards the auctioneers. Mr. Neufeld came up and shook hands. He was a neighbour with a big ranch on our east border, and I thanked him. Someone mentioned it was the top price of the day.

There was no point in hanging around. I picked up the slip, asked Mr. Ryan to mail my cheque to the bank and crossed the railroad tracks to Cook's Trading Company store. We had been running groceries on the cuff there for months. So I asked for our bill. I added $200 to the amount owing, wrote a cheque with a flourish, told Gladys it was her turn to owe us and hoped it would carry us through until next summer. Then I went to the station and sent a wire to Hutch at the bank before racing home. I was tired from all the riding and the tension during the build-up of uncertainty. It was all over now and I was going to have a real night's sleep.

Our first full year on our own ranch was drawing to a close. We could look back and count our blessings. What a Christmas this one would be. Harold was going to be married and would be leaving us in the New Year. But we were confident enough now to carry on alone. And best of all, Harold would be paid off to the satisfaction of everyone. Whatever the future held, our Grand National could be summed up by thinking of the next two years as the same race with the same set of jumps. We had taken them all cleanly in the first round. We knew what to expect.

There was a letter dated December 1, 1948, from Hutch in Lethbridge. Here is what he wrote:

"Please be advised that we have today received a cheque from Pincher Creek for the sum of $3,076.67 which we have placed to your credit. We were very pleased to get your telegram and were very proud of your effort. The only thing is don't think Santa Claus is going to come around every day in the week. I have seen some lucky guys in my day, but I think you rate the top of the list. More power to you, and let us hope that they keep coming. You had better see Rhodes and give him a cheque for your payment."

Maybe Santa doesn't come every day but in our case he was around when we needed him. Maybe it was luck and I won't deny we needed it. But if it takes that much worry and tension to have that luck I would rather trade it for a few more cows and look for excitement elsewhere.

Chapter Sixteen

IF YOU live high up in the Porcupine Hills of southern Alberta and your wife wants to have another baby, you think twice about the idea. In fact you think about it a long time, considering all the angles—especially if you are a greenhorn starting out on the cattle ranch you have always wanted and have gone through anxious days and long, sleepless nights to get it. You don't want any doubtful incident to crop up that might throw out of balance the delicate scales weighing the odds of success or failure.

Eleanor's arguments can be convincing, especially when she has a long string of victories behind her. She has the happy faculty of making everything work out the way she wants it to. But her only argument was based on one female proposition, viz: we had the perfect spread for bringing up children; we were happy and busy doing the things we always wanted to do and it would be extremely selfish not to share the fun with another little papoose. So goes the argument of a woman! She did not elaborate, but the theme of being selfish rankled. She thought the work would not suffer too much; in fact we would hardly notice another baby in the set-up with two active little cowboys, and she insisted there was enough love to go around.

I had to think of the economic side first. A baby would certainly set us back financially. We had sacrificed personal comfort to getting a start with stock and equipment. The roof needed shingling and the living room was still unfurnished.

Plans for a set of harness for the team and for a second saddle horse would have to be shelved. How much more could I afford to disrupt our program in order to avoid being accused of self-ishness? I kept thinking over the idea while riding the hills working cattle and tried to avoid discussing the subject.

Eleanor had not included an obvious clincher to her argument. Our home was in Alberta, a province which encour-aged babies by paying the hospital bill in maternity cases. That meant we wouldn't have to worry the first two weeks! Then we heard about the Health Society in Pincher Creek where the nearest hospital was located. We could join as a family for $40. That plan would see us through sickness, accidents, and opera-tions up to a certain amount for one year. The secretary, Mr. Graham, who ran a barber shop in Pincher Creek, said the society would also take care of part of the doctor's bill for a maternity case.

It began to look possible on the economic side. But the second consideration, and the most important one, was Eleanor. She said it was all nonsense about having a baby being hard on a woman and ageing her. She pointed to classic examples in the district and said she would just have to be sensible about not overworking. Besides, she thought a family of five would be perfect. She wanted to have her family around her while she was still young enough to be included in their play and schemes. Dane was born during the war so she could have something permanent from a war-time marriage. Timmy was born because she wanted a playmate for Dane and was apprehensive that an only child would be spoiled. Now she thought that another one would be good for Timmy and remove him from the danger of being the youngest in the family. But where were we going to draw the line?

While still at the discussion stage I saddled Pete one day and jogged down the valley to visit my good friend Gus. Gus was by way of being an expert on these matters. He had come out from France about 40 years ago to work as a miner in the Blairmore district. After getting a stake in the mines, where he turned out more coal on contract than most men twice his size, he had turned his hand to farming in the Porcupines. From the start Gus had kept a fatherly eye upon our ranching venture, his sound advice and material help easing us over many a rough spot. We seemed to be his particular charges. He consistently tried to shield us from the reverses he had suffered.

"Sometimes," he said, "I no got 25¢ in the pocket. I work hard and we eat and when I get the chance to buy some land I go to the lawyer and say, 'You fix the paper, I get the crop and pay for the land,' and the lawyer, he say: 'Gus, I fix.' "

Gus had a good spread now. If you think hard work shows on a man, you should have seen him at 62 put in an ordinary day. In spite of his own busy season he always had time to run up to us. If he noticed we were going to take ten days to get our green feed stacked with snow threatening to pin it down in the fields, he would arrive at daybreak next morning with two teams and racks and a son in tow. And we would slap the stacks up in a couple of days.

"How much is that, Gus?"

"No matter how much. You should be have the feed up, and it's done. You no pay me for that. Some day I get stuck and you help me." And so it goes. We didn't keep a record except in our hearts and it made for a happy community. You share the good and the bad. But I am glad to say that we tried to keep the score balanced. The hills were full of neighbours like Gus.

He was the expert for the current problem, surrounded by children large and small, seven of them, ranging from 25 years to a baby of two. As I rode into the yard I noticed Gus wading through kids to feed his pigs. He waved a greeting and we went to the corral to talk. I told him that Eleanor wanted another baby but I thought it wise to wait until we had a few more years behind us.

Gus looked indignant. "You should not be worry about having kids on the farm, you know. I tell you that is easy. Maybe you milk another cow, raise a few more chickens, put some more potatoes in the garden, grow more vegetables. I tell you that. No, you don't worry about the kids. That is easy. You only worry when they grow up."

It sounded simple enough, so I had another talk with Eleanor. In the city you decide which hospital you wish to patronize and which doctor you would like, always on tap at the other end of the telephone. You have the corner drugstore to supply your needs, friends to pamper you and help to be obtained. In our country you wondered if you were going to be able to get to a doctor or hospital when the chips were down, whether you could make two or three trips out before the event. You also took into account how you were going to meet the emergency if you could not span the 21 miles.

The first thing to decide was when to have the baby. Eleanor's idea was to rule out spring because the gardening, chicks and ducklings were her special department and the calves' arriving would conflict with her own event. In the summer there was branding, haying and threshing with extra help around and she couldn't imagine taking time off. In the fall there were cattle drives, the movement to winter range and the activity in throwing a diamond hitch around the place before winter storms could strike. We agreed that March would be best; that would give us a fighting chance of the weather breaking and enough time to recover for spring. So we ordered a baby for March delivery, 1949 model.

Until September we were much too busy to think about the matter. We didn't even get in to see the doctor. The weeks raced along in pleasant weather and healthy activity. After the first snow we fitted two sets of chains on the jeep, filled up with anti-freeze and hauled out a 45-gallon drum of gasoline. Our main worry was the lack of a road from the ranch buildings to the Snake Trail leading to Cowley, which was on the main highway. The old bridge crossing the coulee a mile below the house had been taken down before we bought the place and our councillor was trying to get equipment to put in a culvert and fill. Temporarily we were driving through a field that had been ploughed and worked to give us feed. The long stubble was sure to hold the snow. The neighbours telephoned one day to say the graders were working this way and we became quite excited when they repaired the road to our gate. But the "cat" was somewhere else, broken down. The culvert was used on another job, and then the weather closed in with a vengeance. We realized there was no use hoping for a miracle; the coulee would not be bridged during 1948. We were now on our own in planning an avenue of escape.

After each heavy fall of snow I would rush through chores, warm up the jeep, and with shovels aboard break another trail out through the stubble. Angus, our closest neighbour a mile and a half below, would join me in the trail breaking and we began to find out what the jeep could do under adverse conditions. At this stage we were quite confident the little vehicle would see us through unless the weather worsened. But, just in case, we talked about relays of teams for a dash by sleigh to cover the 12 miles to Cowley. I brought a team in off the range and began hardening them. The Bourdiers and Lapointes, farther down the trail, offered to stand by with fresh horses.

The ranch in winter: the cabin on the left, main house on the right.

My sister Betty in Ottawa was getting ready to come out in March to look after Timmy and Dane. She planned to stay long enough to help Eleanor over the first few weeks back at the ranch. Excitement mounted as January blew itself out. The snow deepened in the hills and the drifts increased. The party-line telephone was busy after every storm. Neighbours riding out to look at their cattle would check bad drift points. A few days after every blow someone would dash to Cowley for mail and supplies—by sleigh from higher up, by car or truck from lower down. Thus we got up-to-date reports on road conditions.

On January 31 I managed to drive to Angus' place where he and George Mowat persuaded me to go in with them by sleigh. It was a cold trip but took the horses little more than two hours. At the beginning we joked about the diggable drifts along the way but farther down the sight was depressing. The trail was plugged solid on the straight stretches, the snow covering fence posts and reaching into the fields where there was a chance of a detour. The snow was hard, but not hard enough to carry a jeep on top, and the wind had formed wave-like crests and hollows that tipped the sleigh over on one occasion. We had to find an alternative way out quickly.

We began to make up routes. There was only one outlet, through the stubble field, but to get into the field we had to by-pass the dam, and the trail winding below the dam would fill up with snow after every wind. East, west and north were steep hills which blew clear on the west slopes but on the east lay deep under drifted snow through the winter. By ruling out the trail to Cowley and concentrating on a straight run to Pincher Creek, 21 miles away, one was faced with the same problem—how to cross the coulees and how to get out of our alpine bowl around the worst drifts in order to find a coulee crossing. The greatest obstacle was the Tennessee Coulee. One road crossed it linking up with the road to Cowley. We had to try and get a way out on this road.

It didn't take long for neighbours to rally in an emergency. That spirit seemed to be the essence of life in the hills. On February 3, Louis and family arrived by sleigh. While the children played and the women gossiped we set out with the jeep. We spent hours digging drifts and had some breathless moments riding over the top of deep spots on hard, crusted snow. By the time we were ready to eat shoe leather we reached Tennessee. It was plugged solid on the east slope and we estimated it would take a day, possibly two the way we were feeling, to dig it out. Louis suggested turning north, if I thought the jeep could climb through untracked snow, to follow the ridges higher up the coulee. By trial and error we broke a trail to Buck Baldwin's corrals. Buck had watched our progress and had managed to get in a team to come to our aid by the time we reached his camp. We found a way across the coulee by his buildings where the cattle had packed the snow, and after checking the latest report on the road, returned home at 4:30 in the afternoon to demolish a good roast.

February 4 brought light snow and cold. This was to be the last visit to the doctor before the event. We were all up before daylight. Louis rode up to Angus' place and George Mowat came over the hills by team. We left Dane and Timmy with Angus' good wife, and with the extra men for emergency ran to town on the trail we had opened the previous day. The news was good. Eleanor was fit and the doctor thought she should come in by the 14th to remain in town. Eleanor dashed off a note to Betty who was waiting in Ottawa. We thought we had the situation licked.

The next few days Eleanor worked hard getting the room ready for Betty and trying to have the house organized. By the 7th we had more light snow and the temperature dropped to 20 below. I removed the battery from the jeep and placed it behind the stove in the kitchen to keep it alive. We listened to every weather forecast on the radio. On the 8th when I took the team and sleigh to see Angus it began to dawn on me that the by-pass around the dam as well as through the stubble field was just about impassable. But we could hope to pull the jeep through there with the horses. I kept the news from Eleanor.

Each day I had grown more apprehensive and hesitant to call on the neighbours for further assistance. The morning of the 9th, with five days to go, I remembered how Louis had figured to cross Tennessee Coulee by going north, and taking a saddle horse I rode over our steepest hill east to look at the country from the top of the ridge. From there the country fell sharply to farmland a few miles away and undulated gently to the valley where lay Pincher Creek. Thinking there might be a chance of climbing up to this ridge, I tested the cattle trail which led down the other side to our east boundary fence and into the Neufeld ranch where the graded road started. Here also was the beginning of Tennessee Coulee, at this point only a small creek. The horse began to sink into the drift until I wondered if I was looking at the tops of bushes or trees. When the horse was shoulder deep and beginning to struggle I pulled him out. No way around at that point and the drift was a couple of hundred yards long. But if I could dig it out in a day the rest might be possible. By cutting around where no vehicle could go I rode across to the Neufeld buildings. Henry said they were keeping the road open and a jeep could get through with four chains. He offered his jeep if we had to get over there by sleigh and I told him we had to figure it out by the 14th, five days away. Riding back I checked the big drift again and decided digging it out was worth a try.

The weather was bright and warm on the 10th. No word from Betty yet. As the telephone line was out of order from the strong winds, we hoped there was a telegram waiting in Cowley. Little did we realize at this time that before we were through having our Porcupine Hill baby everyone would be in on the act.

I kept the calves in the corral and after watering and feeding went up to the house. I told Eleanor I was riding over the hill to dig out the drift, that it would only take a few hours. I didn't tell her that on the flat and up the hill were 12 to 14 inches of loose snow. Eleanor suggested a cup of coffee first and while I was warming up in the kitchen she went to the bedroom to lie down. Piles of dirty clothing were sorted out all over the kitchen floor, tubs of hot water waited on the stove. This was to be the last big wash and then Eleanor was going to clean the house once more before sitting back to wait. Betty was to find everything in order. All I had to do before leaving was to drink the coffee, start the little engine for the washing machine and leave Eleanor to it. That's what I thought.

There was a plaintive call from the bedroom. Would I go in there and leave the children in the kitchen? One minute I was young, determined and healthy. In the next ten minutes I was ageing far too quickly. Eleanor whispered in dismay that it was too late to get out. What were we going to do? I thought about jeeps and hills, snow and more snow, team and cold sleighs, the long miles between us and safety, the awful penalty of a wrong decision.

I tried to rush from one room to another, over and around piles of dirty clothing and little people always in the way, talking about the chance of getting somewhere in a couple of hours. Eleanor called out it was too late. If the telephone was working between here and town perhaps I could get hold of a woman. I made three local calls but everyone was out. I spoke to one woman but her man had gone to town with the team.

That did it. I turned back to Eleanor and told her we would just have to get over the hill to Neufeld's where there were three men and a housekeeper. I could make it in 40 minutes. She would have a woman with her and a fighting chance of getting the doctor to come out.

"But what if we get stuck in the drift half way?"

I told her we wouldn't get stuck and hoped it sounded convincing.

"How about the children?"

I told her they would be better off over there.

Then she couldn't hold back the tears at the thought of Betty coming out to this confusion, with the laundry all over the place and the house not ready after all her planning.

But I wasn't thinking of these things. I was throwing clothes at Dane and Timmy, aged five and two, telling them to get into their snowsuits as best they could. I tried to help Eleanor get her things ready, rushed for the jeep, then remembered the battery behind the stove. Somehow I thought the time it would take to get team and sleigh would not compensate for an immediate start. If we did get stuck Henry could drive his jeep up to meet us and we would effect a transfer downhill. The battery went into place but the connections would not fit. In the panic of the moment I tied the loose one with binder twine, hammered the tight one on. She started. I backed out and put the kids in while the engine was warming up. Back in the house again I fetched Eleanor's suitcases and tried to find a spare garment for Timmy. Both boys looked like tramps, but this wasn't a social call. Eleanor still had misgivings about trying to leave but I managed to get her into the jeep. It wasn't a happy or carefree moment.

In four-wheel drive and tractor gear we started out. It wasn't encouraging to find we could barely crawl over the flat, pushing the snow up over the radiator, with chains on all four wheels, for there was a big climb ahead. We couldn't get on the grass slope to start the climb until we had backed and shovelled the deepest snow away. Once committed to the climb we had to give the little engine everything, but we struggled to the top. I had been reasonably certain we would get there but now we had to make the decision that would spell success or failure. Should we try our luck and roll down the steepest part of the descent, hoping the vehicle would remain on top of the deep drift?

If the jeep broke through and high-centred we would be pinned down for many hours. Time was the factor, so I decided against it, swung south on top of the ridge to keep going. Here the snow was not too deep and we picked our way through the evergreens, over hard little short drifts, around deadfall timber, over stumps and rocks, down a dip and up on to the ridge again. But we kept going. We worked south and east again until we were on an east-west ridge giving us a clear view south to our target. Directly below we could also see the Neufeld buildings. There was only one way down, a very steep vertical drop that in summer was marked by a single cattle trail. I remembered asking why this track was worn in such an impossible place for the brutes to climb and had been told that in the toughest winters it was the only way out of the pocket.

I left the jeep and walked part way down to look, noticing the heads of wild hay sticking through the snow, trying to judge the slope for "sidling". If the vehicle could only track straight down without slewing we might make it. But if she changed direction anywhere during the descent we could roll over and over . . . . I had looked at this spot the other day when it was bare of snow and it reminded me of the landing hill below a ski jump.

I asked Eleanor if she was game to try, said it would be all over in a few minutes, then she would be safe in the house. She braced herself and said: "Let's go." I put the jeep in low gear, told the kids in the back to hang on . . . and we crept over the lip.

When the little vehicle tipped forward the boys were thrown off their seats and remained piled up against the back of ours, howling their heads off. We held our breath. I talked to myself on the way down, hardly daring to use brakes and handling the wheel as gingerly as possible.

We made the bottom after an eternity, stopped to get our breath and right the kids. Then we broke out of the valley to Neufeld's and the open road. When I pulled up at the house Eleanor decided to remain where she was until I had telephoned the doctor. If the road report was still good she thought we might keep going. Henry followed in his jeep and we made the dash in record time. It took two and a half hours from start to finish and it was a real family affair with Tippy, our collie, managing to stay with us all the way to Pincher Station. At the hospital a very tired old man, who that morning had been young and reasonably gay, handed his wife over to the cool competence of the staff. The relief was temporary for I had two apprehensive children on my hands and a ranch full of livestock back in the hills.

It is funny the things a chap does between crises. I took the jeep to a garage for servicing. The mechanic was amused to find the battery in backward. The gauge had registered discharge all the way to town! I bought the boys some candy and then we wandered into Mr. Graham's barber shop. It seemed to be something to do until the next problem was solved, so Dane had a haircut and Timmy talked to lots of people.

Then the two little boys were left in the care of a very kind couple we had met only recently. They offered to look after them until Betty should arrive. Now where was Betty? I telephoned to Cowley and learned that she would be arriving Saturday. This was Thursday. After a few hours of sleep I drove back to the ranch to look after the animals. Taking the same route I tried the steep slope in the same tracks while the Neufeld hands watched from a sleigh on the valley floor, betting on my chances. I figured if the jeep should stick I could back down and walk home, but she climbed steadily, like an old elevator.

I had assured Eleanor that I would do the washing somehow and put the finishing touches to the house. Just as I finished a meal and was deciding where to start in this domestic wilderness,

Angus rode up on his sorrel. We moved furniture around and I swept the floor, moaning about the big wash. Angus decided he would come up with a sleigh and take it down to his wife. We threw all the neat little piles into one awful-looking mound in the shed at the back.

The telephone began to work and I called Pincher Creek. Dr. Collins said Eleanor had presented the ranch with another cowboy. Both were fine. Holy cow! Another boy, and she had really wanted a girl! I opened a bottle of brandy. In our relief at the news Angus and I shook hands for a good five minutes. I began to telephone the neighbours asking if they wanted another hand. All the work waiting to be done around the house suddenly became very unimportant and I made plans to break out once again. Gus and his family were standing by and it didn't take long to arrange for his son Marcel to come up and take over. I don't remember this second trip, so it must have been made in a daze of thankfulness that all was well. Eleanor looked wonderful and the boy was a winner.

It seemed as if our troubles were over. All I had to do was meet Betty, take her out to the ranch with the boys and relax while Eleanor had a good rest in hospital. It was a fitting climax after such an upset to our carefully laid plans. I thought of Robert Burns' "The best laid schemes o' mice and men gang aft agley". Plan how you might, you cannot force your will on weather, nature and their effect on railway timetables.

I'll never know just how our wonderful telephone operator at Cowley kept in touch with events. When I arrived at Pincher Station to meet Betty on Saturday there she was on the tele-phone, speaking from Lethbridge. She was stranded because her train had arrived four hours late and missed the connection. I told her to take a ten o'clock train that would arrive at midnight. Before that time a first-class blizzard struck the country—the daddy of all the winter storms. Her train was now expected at three A.M. Sunday. I crawled out from Pincher Creek to the station, a distance of two miles, with visibility sometimes nil, sometimes a few feet, reaching from one telephone pole to the next and stopping to determine if I was still on the road. Mine was the last vehicle to travel that road before the storm blew itself out. From 3:30 A.M. on, the station filled up with train crews looking like embattled warriors. The drifting snow, which quickly filled the jeep and hid it from view, was immobilizing the great mountain locomotives. Crews in relays kept trying to dig the engines out to get them started while the operator hugged the telegraph key. Betty's train arrived at 7:30 A.M., after engines had gone down to bring it up the grade by the Piegan Indian Reserve at Brocket. They had to split the train in two sections.

Mr. and Mrs. Bundy at the station had stayed up all night keeping the wires open and serving coffee and sandwiches to the crews. They took Betty into the fold. They were old hands at this and to them it was a very natural thing to do. After a breakfast that raised our spirits they put me to bed. The blizzard persisted without slackening all Sunday; it wasn't until Monday noon that snowploughs were able to open the two miles to Pincher Creek. I made the trip in a sleigh to get a wrecking truck for the jeep. Betty joined the children while I set out for the ranch.

There was no sign of the emergency route we had taken, but it kept luring me on like a challenge. I kept trying to find a way through the coulees, working north to the top of them, and got to within five miles of the Neufeld ranch before turning back. Driving to Cowley on the highway I traded the jeep for a team and got home at midnight with relays of horses. On Wednesday I returned to Cowley by sleigh and picked up the jeep. A snow plough had been out and we managed to get the children home by way of Neufeld's.

I wanted to settle down for a good long stretch of peaceful routine but by Sunday Eleanor was clamouring to be home. Why on earth couldn't she leave the hospital and visit in town until the weather improved? All winter she had been talking about the rest she was going to enjoy, the lazy life in town. But here she was just aching to be back on the ranch, whatever the weather. So I had to do the trip again over the hill east and that steep slope provided the same thrill. But three times without a crack-up was enough! With the baby along I wasn't going to tempt the fates again. We returned from Neufeld's in a sleigh, baby Ian, nine days old, having his first sleigh ride. The team couldn't pull the hill, and in attempting to traverse, the sleigh nearly upset with two men hanging to the topside. Eleanor voted to get off and climb to the top on foot, carrying the baby. She wanted to get home in the worst way, and she did. With the driver and me hanging on to the sleigh we made the top but we wouldn't have tried it a second time on a bet.

The blizzards and snow and blocked roads faded into memory—something to talk about in later years. Life in the hills can dish up a mess of winter weather that hits with the fury of pent-up vengeance. Then spring comes and strokes the land with a gentle touch of magic. Everything turns green, melting snow swells the little streams, the water gurgles down from the heights. You awaken to a new world of buds, the cawing of crows, the bright flash of bluebirds. And you forgive nature for her pranks.

We were thankful to be back to normal again, but it was a busier normal. There was a little bundle of lovable, cooing humanity to share it with us. Dane and Timmy were fascinated.

And Eleanor? She took everything in her stride. During the winter she swore she wouldn't have time that year for a big garden or baby chicks but I didn't notice any difference when I sent off the seed order. I knew she wouldn't be able to waste a single broody hen and I caught her tucking turkey eggs under them when they weren't looking.

One evening she said the baby-bonus cheque was going to help a lot. It had been increased to 15 whole dollars a month to be spent at her discretion.

"Why," she said brightly, "just think what I could do with 20!"

* * *

PART THREE

PART THREE

GRAY'S PUBLISHING:
NOT SO PEACEFUL

Chapter One

IN 1953 *We Found Peace* was published, a gestation from the seed of many articles I had produced in an attempt to master the craft of writing. It picked up some dangerously flattering reviews and made us a lot of friends. Many kept in touch over the passing years. When we moved into new country and other adventures these early associates followed us with letters and surprise visits. Our old R.A.F. guest book had quickly filled on the ranch, to be replaced by a distinctive, proper one stamped with our old ranch brand, 7C—. And then it became downright embarrassing when the request for "When are you going to tell us what happened after?" kept popping up.

If variety is the spice of life, we have never had time to be bored. I spent 12 years learning to become a cowboy and, with Eleanor, raising three boys and a girl on a cattle ranch. Family cattle ranches were going through a transition, with horses being replaced by jeeps and expensive machinery which demanded larger acreage. The country schools our children rode to, where we held community concerts and dances, were disappearing. Roads into the foothills were upgraded and the children were carted off to town by school bus. We had found the peace we sought and had written about it in the book, but the dream was fading. Then disaster struck.

When Eleanor suddenly fell ill we rushed her to hospital 30 miles away and when she failed to rally she was transferred to the

Branding party, May 1958. Front row, l. to r.: Ian, Dane and Tim Campbell, two MacDonald boys. Back row, l. to r.: Eleanor holding Cathy, Gray, Mabel MacDonald, Frank MacDonald, Annora Brown, Claude Hammond. (PHOTO BY GORDON CRICHTON)

big hospital in Lethbridge. She suffered through months with a ruptured appendix and when we brought her back home into the foothills, it was obvious she could never be as active again. We had to put that lifestyle aside and seek another.

With temporary help on the domestic side and our eldest son, Dane, handling the animals and machinery, we took our first holiday. No one in the foothills had heard of Sidney, British Columbia, in 1959 but I had the address of Jim Eaton, a retired Mountie, who had been my room-mate in the barracks at Banff where he taught me the finer points of horsemanship. He and his wife, Edna, operated the Craigmyle Motel in Sidney and we had a standing invitation. Eleanor had visited them on detachment when I was flying out of Calgary in 1942; she was comfortable with Edna and could do with her support.

Sidney was reached by ferry from Anacortes, Washington, in those days before the B.C. fleet came into existence. We fell in love with the pace of the village and with Vancouver Island. It did not take us long to decide to move in this direction if we could manage to sell the ranch. Another important consideration was our feeling that our children needed the chance of a broader education unless they were going to spend their lives in the foothills.

We made one trip with the children in a station wagon and tent. Sidney was an unspoiled village, with no traffic lights and a winding country road linking it to Victoria. We camped in a vacant lot behind the Craigmyle, which was on Sidney's main avenue. Across the road from the Craigmyle Motel, where the Safeway mall stands today, was an open field. Sidney had one bank, three well-known citizens selling real estate and two doctors. A dentist came out from Victoria one day a week as well as a lawyer. Pretty nearly everyone had a nodding acquaintance up and down the streets and the main excitement was generated by the arrival of the ferry from Anacortes. We left the boys camped and raced back to Alberta to try and sell the ranch. Details of this and the hectic move are too boring to spoil a good story, but we found a very nice waterfront home on Curteis Point which we rented for a year while we looked around.

It was an interesting neighbourhood, with people who had made names for themselves in many fields but were not too remote to extend us a generous welcome. From our ranching background there was R.M. Patterson, who had had the Buffalo Head ranch in the Alberta foothills north of our Porcupine Hills spread. Already famous for his epic book *The Dangerous River*, he was on his way to a writing career. Just two houses away on the waterfront was the home of Donald MacLaren, D.S.O., M.C. & Bar, D.F.C., Chevalier of the Legion of Honour, Croix de Guerre, Canada's fourth-ranking air ace in World War One. He had recently retired from Trans Canada Airlines. Next door on the other side lived Guy Pearce, an old Mountie, ex-Royal Flying Corps pilot in W.W.I and retired from a Hollywood career as a make-up artist; his recent guest had been Charles Laughton.

The four of us travelled regularly to air force veterans' meetings and the Royal United Services Institute gatherings in Victoria. A bonding developed with my acceptance as junior boy, listening to Patterson recounting amusing anecdotes from his time as a German prisoner of war, Don MacLaren talking about Billy Bishop and the future of air travel, while Guy told entertaining incidents from his Hollywood days. When he carefully created one character to look like a repulsive villain, the result on screen bore such a striking resemblance to the studio head that Zanuck fired him. I started to file away ideas for articles and as we settled in to the community we began to discover an amazing collection of very colourful citizens.

Living modestly and quietly close by were salty types like Captain J.D. Prentice who had commanded the corvette *Chambly*, the first Royal Canadian Navy ship to sink a German submarine in World War Two. If you wanted to know about India there was Arthur Connell, a commercial fisherman who had been a British officer serving before the war with the legendary Gurkhas and was the colonel who commanded the riverboats in the book *Elephant Bill*. At the end of the point, living alone, was a quiet, reserved little lady who became a very close friend. Capi Blanchet went on to write the classic *The Curve of Time* which continues, after 30 years, to find its place on the best-seller lists.

For our first year, we did little but savour the discovery of so many interesting, talented people. The sensation was head-spinning after 12 lonely years struggling on the ranch, fighting weather and other challenges of nature in the foothills. We spent the summer months indulging ourselves with the children, exploring the Gulf Islands in the old ferry *Cy Peck* when it was commanded by Captain Maude of Fulford Harbour. Then we acquired a small motor sailer and cruised around on our own. I began writing articles about the characters we discovered, tucked away in remote places, carving out original projects, following their bliss. It was a time when the myriad dream islands were uncrowded, many awaiting a first inhabitant. One was David Conover who came from California to build his paradise on Wallace Island. After our visit and a sketchy article, he settled down to write the popular adventure book *Once Upon An Island*, which was published in New York in 1967.

Our boat, the *Lady Mine*, was kept at a small marina in Canoe Cove, a short distance from the house, and when we were not sailing I typed articles in the cabin, then tried to write a sequel to *We Found Peace*. In the slip next to ours was *Caprice*, the little vessel that Capi Blanchet would make famous with her book. When Capi came around to check on her boat and pump out the bilge, she would find me tapping away at the small portable typewriter and after she had finished her chores, she would perch on the transom of *Lady Mine*, read the pages of my first draft and urge me to keep going. I don't recall any comments of criticism or advice but I couldn't seem to get it on the right tack and was easily diverted.

Gray aboard the Lady Mine. *(PHOTO BY GORDON CRICHTON)*

Capi would often stop on her way into Sidney to see if we had something to mail, or needed anything. One day she arrived unexpectedly with an urgent air and a letter addressed to her from Blackwood & Sons, Edinburgh. They had decided to publish her book *The Curve of Time* and she asked if we would read the contract and try to figure out the legal nuances. Only then did we realize just how successful a writer she had been. Not only had *Blackwoods Magazine* been publishing her articles, she had sold pieces to yachting publications and had made it into the *Atlantic Monthly*. We discussed her contract at length and then were so caught up in the excitement of her first book I offered to help organize press and radio interviews. My enthusiasm fairly bubbled along, stressing the importance of publicity without thinking of her innate shyness, until Capi turned to Eleanor in dismay.

"He isn't serious, is he? If he is, you must stop him."

Her book was published in 1961 and we shared her frustration in its slow start. Before she had a chance to realize that she had indeed written a classic, her heart stopped on September 30, 1961, while she was at her typewriter in her bright and cheerful kitchen, working on a sequel.

Donald MacLaren came to tell us, for we had by then moved into our own home, a cottage in Deep Cove in an acre of beautiful garden that had been created by the Sparlings. Sidney had two real estate firms in those uncrowded days and Donald Sparling was the head of one. Our first home had a cabin in the woods where I established a study in one room while Dane took over the other.

Our main house was quite small but we managed to have Capi's children, the MacLarens and a few of her closest friends in for tea after the memorial service at St. Andrew's Church in Sidney and we had a chance to meet them all for the first time. From this casual, solemn beginning an event of singular importance for us all would later unfold.

We were busy getting settled and arranging the schools the children would attend from this unorganized North Saanich district with its winding country lanes threading through forest, farm and cottage areas. No one wanted to see developers. Descendants of pioneers were still living in the area and their names graced the roads and country lanes. There were two small general stores and a school within cycling distance before the peninsula fell prey to progress: the ferry fleet and city-type malls which began to fill the empty fields in Sidney.

In the meantime the new university in Victoria, in its formative years, was giving a series of lectures by Dr. Douglas Leechman in the old Victoria College building. It was a chance to learn the mysteries of creative writing and I applied when I learned that a few of our new North Saanich neighbours were going. Rosemary Owen, who lived in Ardmore, had been picking up and driving a blind war veteran from Brentwood and after the first couple of lectures she asked if I could do this. That's when I met John Windsor, a graduate of the Royal Military College and a career officer with Lord Strathcona's Horse who had been blinded at the Melfa River in Italy in a tank battle. With his career at an end, his immediate future endless days undergoing plastic surgery and learning to be blind, John Windsor and his English bride, Pam, had come to Canada.

It did not take us long to establish that we had many mutual friends, both in the services and in Alberta, where John had spent his boyhood. We began to open up to each other, sharing our private concerns as veterans who had been out of touch with Canada and left at the end of the war with uncertainty in our future. And we exchanged a few choked-back confidences. John, with Pam's help, had taken a course at Queen's University in business administration which he passed successfully. After a few false starts, trials and tribulations, they had moved west and were living in Brentwood Bay with three children. John kept busy writing magazine articles with fair success and taking part in local politics. One thing led to another and as we shared our dreams it was obvious to me that here was one gutsy, obstinate young man in his thirties who wasn't going to let depressing handicaps get him down or restrain his lively sense of humour.

One evening I switched off the engine of our old Rover in front of his house and we had a fateful few words. There was a pause, an awkward moment, until John brought up something that had been bothering him.

"You wrote a book that was published, didn't you?"

"Yes, but it was a lucky break at the right time."

"I wish I had enough guts to try it."

"Just think of the chapters as a series of connected articles. You could handle that."

"Wish I had the nerve—good night and thanks again."

When I reached our cottage I told Eleanor about it and said I had a mind to urge him to try.

"Oh, but what if he devoted a year to it and failed?"

"It would be good for him just trying," I replied.

"Let's sleep on it," she decided.

Next morning we talked at length over coffee, and after going through the pros and cons we felt it would give him a worthwhile project even if the outcome was in the lap of the gods. I picked up the telephone and called him.

"Get cracking on that book," I said. "I want to pick up the first chapter in a week."

"How will I start?" He sounded panicky.

"What's your first problem in the morning?"

"Finding my second sock."

"Start there." And I rang off.

That was the beginning of a new adventure.

Chapter Two

THE PROJECT got off to a faltering start which was not helped by our writing course. Dr. Leechman had sharply criticized the work of several elderly lady pupils. This left both John and me with less confidence in our ability so we did not submit any of our work for the class to see. But as we got down to planning John's project, we began to shake off the doubts and assure ourselves it was possible to produce a book, as others had done biographies with somewhat similar backgrounds.

For a start, I suggested that John describe his two worlds; youth with all his faculties, then the tragedy, and the long process of learning to be blind. He went to work with his terrific memory, sharp brain, a healthy sense of humour and the drive to see it through. Pam would feed the paper into his typewriter and set the margins and spaces. Then John would patiently type paragraphs, dialogue and chapters with some sentences unfortunately running off the paper. When it reached me I was distressed at the amount of work involved until a visitor suggested I seek the help of Mary Gibbs. She lived close by, through the woods from our cabin, had a typewriter and wrote articles. Mary cheerfully volunteered to take on the job of retyping and quickly became a part of the team.

Eleanor and I now had something interesting to add to our letters and quite innocently began to involve our friends. Peter and Catharine Whyte in Banff, both prominent artists, contributed more than enthusiasm. Pete offered to do sketches for chapter headings, and topped it with a splendid portrait of John as a cadet at the Royal Military College and one of Pam and John when they met, both in uniform. The portrait was exactly what we needed for the frontispiece and the drawing graced the introduction by Lord Fraser of Lonsdale. He had created world-famous St. Dunstan's School which took in the war-blinded for training after "what seems to be one of life's greatest tragedies" as he had written for the book. Lord Fraser had been blinded in World War One.

When Catharine wrote to tell us that Pete would like to do the illustrations, she added that her contribution would be paying for the plates. This added to John's incentive, increased our priorities on the project, and we lost no time sending copies of chapters to Banff and spreading the word as the manuscript neared completion. At the same time we became absolutely convinced that we had a successful product to market.

Finally, I got in touch with Dud Allen who had published *We Found Peace* and with almost arrogant confidence sent him the manuscript. Eleanor had given it the title "Blind Date" and with Peter Whyte's sketches to boost it along there was no doubt about the theme of war-time. I could hardly believe it when the package was returned with Dud's note which said it was a very nice story, but he couldn't see it selling 10,000 copies at three dollars apiece. It was my turn to hit a new low after what John had been through and I avoided him for a few days until I could handle it. If a good friend in the publishing world could not see the possibility of this work, what chance would we have with strangers? Finally I talked to John about it and Pam decided to send it off to one of the larger firms in Toronto. It was returned quickly without even a note, just a coldly printed rejection slip. So now we were left in the deepest sort of depression, to which I had to add a feeling of guilt for having put the Windsor family through so much work and hope.

We could only go up out of this pit of despair and as I began to recover, still convinced it was an inspiring story, I wondered what could be done to get the reader's attention and draw him into book. It began with John's boyhood in Calgary and his acceptance to the Royal Military College. Obviously that wasn't enough to make a casual reader turn the page; the very first page had to be a grabber. I drove down to Brentwood once again and told John what I thought was needed; he went to work. On the first page John describes the scene as the tanks went into battle to reach the Melfa River in Italy. Then the direct hit, and the disaster which had abruptly finished his career was followed by a flash-back to his childhood.

Our spirits picked up but I did not know where to turn next and I was afraid a third refusal as cold as the last could douse the fire of ambition. I went to talk about this to an old friend from my days in the R.C.M.P. In the early 1930s Clair Rivers had been a reporter for the *Lethbridge Herald* who used to call regularly at the barracks for any news. Now he was the publisher of the *Sidney Review*, a lively weekly. He knew John, was acquainted with the story and shared my conviction that we had the possibility of a book to publish.

"We can't afford another rejection," I said, "so what do we do if we can't convince these guys in Toronto?"

"You'll just have to make up your mind to publish it yourself."

When I told him the bit about the Toronto attitude, not being able to sell 10,000 copies at the going rate in those days, he pulled me up short.

Cathy, Gray and Eleanor, with Clair and Helen Rivers, picnicking on the Saanich Peninsula.

"Why 10,000? Why not two or three thousand?"

"The cost per copy could be too much for the market."

He picked up a sheet of newsprint and started putting down his estimates for paper and typesetting costs, a ball-park figure for press time and binding, added it up and divided it by two and three thousand to arrive at a rough cost per copy. Clair had served his war in the artillery and was just as anxious for the project to succeed. However, I didn't have any capital: the final sale of the ranch had not been completed, our bank credit was tied up and I needed time to think.

At home I related all this to Eleanor, who was just as anxious to pull off some kind of miracle, and we started searching for ideas. She noticed that a C.B.C. producer was coming to Victoria to interview applicants for a new quiz show on television. It was the predecessor of the hugely successful "Front Page Challenge".

"Live a Borrowed Life" challenged the applicant to impersonate some well-known Canadian in history and if one could stump the panel, and then successfully answer tough questions about the subject, there was a cash award. Eleanor suggested I give it a try and send in my name for the interview. I could do Don MacLaren, for in addition to knowing and admiring the man, I had a copy of George Drew's book, *Canada's Fighting Airmen*, published in 1931, so his life up to the war was a piece of cake. I mailed the idea to the C.B.C. in Vancouver.

On a fateful day I was summoned to meet the official at Victoria's Strathcona Hotel and was interviewed by Philip Keatley at some length. In a few days I was advised that my application had been accepted for an appearance on a program to be recorded in a few weeks at a Victoria high school. Now I had to ask Don MacLaren if it would be with his blessing. He didn't exactly show any pleasure in the idea. Friendship was one thing; publicity did not sit well with him. But when I explained the reason, to be able to publish the great story of John Windsor, he reluctantly gave his consent.

The next thing I did was get in touch with an official of Trans Canada Airlines who also happened to be an old friend from my R.C.M.P. years and he sent me a large file of T.C.A. archival records concerning MacLaren's career with the airline. There was so much detail I started to worry about the type of questions the panel might throw at me, to prevent my winning the big cash; I would prefer just to talk about Don's war. About a week before the show Don got in touch, in his direct way.

"If you're going ahead with this, you'd better get it right. Come around this evening and we can find out what you know." We sat in his den for a couple of hours and touched all the points I might need. It was a memorable evening but it did not lessen my doubts in my ability to carry it off, and my fear of the consequences if I failed. There was too much riding on the outcome and we had too many people involved.

I drove alone to the auditorium of Oak Bay High School, found a scarce parking spot and mixed with the crowd filing in. I was placed in a small room with a mixture of contestants for the two shows to be taped. I found myself seated beside James K. Nesbitt, Victoria's well-known historian-journalist who was going to impersonate the coal baron, Robert Dunsmuir. He was just as nervous as I was, probably more so, for the guest on the panel was his boss, Stu Keate, publisher of *The Victoria Times*, and his questions could really test Nesbitt's reputation.

The auditorium was packed as the contestants marched out to their fate and we could hear voices, laughter and sometimes applause. Jim Nesbitt went ahead of me and returned crushed. Probably Stu Keate had easily guessed his identity on one of the first questions, because Nesbitt was famous for leading the drive to preserve Dunsmuir's Craigdarroch Castle. Although Jim had crashed and retired in confusion, I remember hearing his boss loyally pointing out that Nesbitt was Victoria's expert on local history.

It was my turn for the inquisition and I faced the hot, bright lights while Charles Templeton waved me to a seat beside him and tried to put me at ease. Then the grilling started and I got through the first part of the ordeal without a mistake. When they got to their list of questions I don't recall any details except that Stu Keate nearly tripped me up and I'm not sure that I answered fairly or from ignorance. It was the big win; not only had I stumped the panel, but I had answered all the questions to hit the jackpot for, I think, the immense sum of $225.

A few days later, when the cheque arrived, I drove into Sidney to make an important call at the *Review*. Clair Rivers was putting on his morning show—opening the mail, tossing obvious junk into a large basket, looking sharply for treasures. He pointed to a chair and settled back, expectantly. I think he had been in that crowd at the TV show. I broke the ice. Timidly.

"How much would it take for a down payment to start printing?"

"How much have you got?"

"Two hundred and twenty-five dollars," I blurted.

"That's exactly what it takes," he said, and started calling for dear old Jim Wakefield, on the verge of retirement, who had been a printer since he fought as a boy at Ypres in World War One.

My problems had just started.

Chapter Three

AT THE *Review* they dusted off an old, unused, flat-bed press that had been idle in storage and could print four pages at a time. They moved it to a clear space while Jim Wakefield and Al McCormick started setting type. The spirit of the enterprise caught the entire staff, which included Esther Berry, the publisher's gal Friday, and I could see that Jim Wakefield at least had read the manuscript and was caught up in the story. The mood was contagious.

Meanwhile, I had to hustle because I needed advice for the next step. When the *Review* had finished printing and binding I would have a few thousand copies of a book by an author no one had heard about. The only person in the book trade that I knew was Bill Duthie who had recently opened his store on Robson Street in Vancouver. We had met years ago in Calgary when he was making his annual trip west for Macmillan in Toronto.

As a well-known publisher's representative, Bill would travel by train with trunks full of the Macmillan list. At each city he would rent the sample room in a prominent hotel, set up his display and invite bookstore owners, buyers and librarians. Louise Riley, an old friend, a noted author and Calgary librarian, had taken us to meet Bill after we had launched *We Found Peace* at Eaton's in 1953.

Bill was both a sound bookman and a booster of Canadian talent. His new store was cunningly nestled beside the Vancouver

Public Library, a busy place that collected a constant flow of bibliophiles who all seemed to want a word with Bill. Always warmly friendly, he took time to hear about our involvement with John Windsor and our first attempts to find a publisher. Bill had also fought in tanks and I had heard he had been through some sticky situations.

"Give me the manuscript, and I'll send it to Macmillan," he said.

"Too late," I replied. "They're setting type in Sidney."

"That's a mistake. Too bad. But when you're ready, I'll help."

Then he started listing some of the finer points in book publishing, the times in the year for Easter or Christmas sales, what discounts were expected by the trade and the libraries, getting the right people to review the book and interview the author. He had me meet his paperback manager, Binkie Marks, an interesting character who wasn't too friendly at first until he had made up his mind that for an ex-Mountie I wasn't too bad. Apparently when he was a student at the University of Toronto he hadn't seen eye-to-eye with the gendarmes. Binkie was another real asset in getting out the word, and shared the popularity that Bill Duthie was building with his customers. Anyone visiting the paperback department in the basement invariably went to Binkie for advice.

There was a good story at the time that spread the Duthie name and reputation: regular customers would telephone Bill and ask him to select a few titles for them to take for week-end reading; he would put an order together and send it off. If they were puzzled by the choice, or could not enjoy or understand something, they figured it was their own ignorance, not the selection. Bill's reputation was never in doubt.

He had me meet several "reps" for the big publishers and I was particularly taken with Jim Douglas, who was western agent for McClelland and Stewart. He took me around to meet bookstore owners where I on my own might have had trouble getting in the door. There were several occasions when owners and chain managers had made up their minds that Canadian titles had to be published in and ordered from Toronto. Jim admitted he had been seriously considering starting up his own firm in Vancouver and understood the obstacles to be overcome. He was helpful, enthusiastic and kind. He did eventually start up in Vancouver and developed the growing firm of Douglas & McIntyre.

I returned from Vancouver wiser and a bit chastened by the job ahead, but determined to see it through. We needed all the help we could get, and after I talked with Clair while the old flat-bed antique was still whomping out the pages of *Blind Date*, we thought that though Lord Fraser's introduction would give the work an international appeal, we could use a foreword as well. It had to be a prominent Canadian, which meant that the first name on our list was our own Lieutenant-Governor, Major-General George Pearkes, whose personal popularity was as high as anyone's. Lord Fraser had mentioned the tragedy of the blinding and John's recovery through training at St. Dunstan's in Britain. We felt it would help if General Pearkes could cover his popularity as a cadet at the Royal Military College and his once-promising future as a professional soldier. Clair Rivers suggested that I telephone for an appointment and take along an outline of what we thought was required.

One morning I drove to Government House in Victoria and the general saw me in his study. He had known John and was pleased to help. When I mentioned a foreword he got up and walked toward his bookshelves.

"Let's see what the foreword says about Monty's war memoirs," as he picked out the autobiography. There was a pause followed by a deep chuckle. "Wouldn't you know it—Monty wrote his own." He sat at his desk and produced exactly what we required.

I returned to the *Review* and Clair gave it his professional eye. In addition to being an outstanding journalist and voracious reader of history, biography and politics, he was a first-class editor. I don't think Clair Rivers ever read a book without a pencil in his hand to mark any typos, cliches or spelling errors. In his office I remember a fairly large printed sign that said "We never make MISTEAKS" and he had a wonderful anecdote about his experience in reading Winston Churchill's five volumes on the history of World War Two. He was so pleased to find one typo in all the five volumes that he sat down to write the publisher in London, who replied with a graceful letter thanking him but saying they had also picked it up and had corrected it.

We now had everything but a cover for the book. We had agreed on Eleanor's title of *Blind Date* and that book titles were less awkward to buy or sell if they were kept to two or three words. Flos Williams, a retired novelist living in Deep Cove, told us the sad story of a potential best seller that had such a tongue-twister of a clever title that people who wanted it were afraid of mispronouncing the word. They would enter a bookstore and if they could not spot it they would purchase something else. It was Bill Duthie who suggested I drop around to the Vancouver Art College and offer the senior class an honorarium for the best cover sketch. Every pupil submitted at least one design ranging from crowded battle scenes to close-ups of tanks and warriors in battle dress. Their instructor, a Mr. Reid, arranged a day when the winner would be announced and Fletcher Bennett, an old friend from our ranching days, offered to fly me to Vancouver in time for the event.

His seaplane took off from St. Mary's Lake on Salt Spring Island to pick me up at Deep Cove. I had dressed up for the occasion with regimental tie and blazer. Unfortunately, I slipped on the float when climbing aboard the little Cessna, which ruined the sharp crease in my grey flannels, and at the Vancouver dock I squelched ashore in dismay, hoping to hide behind a desk for the ceremony.

Reid knew we needed all the ink we could get from the media and had telephoned the newspapers but they probably figured it was a ho-hum item and did not turn up. He took me around the display of interesting results and I was pleased that I did not have to make the final decision. I had left that to Reid who, in Duthie's opinion, rated highly as a book designer. He passed up the gorgeous battle scenes but stopped at a plain white sheet with two black ink smears surrounding the stark words *Blind Date*. It was a surprise, yet I felt drawn to it, fascinated as to its meaning, as if it were a Rorschach test. It certainly dispelled any idea that the story involved adolescent romance, and it provoked curiosity. I handed over a modest cheque and congratulated the young lady, Rita Taylor, thinking it was a pity that we could not have a photograph of her, as she was a most attractive person. Apparently, she had spent most of her time doing a formal military scene for her contribution, and when she had finished she had taken a last sheet and pressed ink to paper with this startling result.

It wasn't much of an event but I brightened up when Reid said this pupil lived in Victoria and I could try the papers there with the item. Fletcher and I walked the few blocks to the harbour, took off and flew across to Sidney right on the deck, just lifting up to clear the masts of fishing vessels.

Next morning I went to Victoria, called at the *Times* and told Lloyd Baker, the city editor, about yesterday's incident, stressing how a Victoria student had won, and he might like to break this pleasant news with a photograph of the girl who was even better looking than her art. He said he would look into it, and perhaps send a photographer, but as I was leaving he grabbed my arm.

"Don't you dare go across to the *Colonist* or I'll break your neck."

The threat taught me another lesson; don't mess around with the press. I went straight home and tried to be patient. On Saturday, June 2, 1962, just above Frank Ritter's column from the legislature, there was a large photograph of the 20-year-old Rita Taylor, top student of the Vancouver Art College and a two-column-wide announcement that she had won first prize in design for the cover of *Blind Date* by John Windsor of Brentwood Bay. The publisher, it said, had put up the prize money with a cheque for $35!

The book was bound and packaged in boxes by the end of May 1962 and then my work was kicked into high gear. It was a case of getting review copies out to the right people and then hustling to get copies into the stores in time. Apart from Bill Duthie, and Molly Charles at Eaton's in Victoria, the booksellers were merely curious, with an attitude of trying a few copies to see what happened before they would show any enthusiasm.

The press at all levels could not have been more helpful and unexpectedly, fate stepped in with an assist from C.B.C. Television. They ran a film of Canadians in action just before the Melfa River battle where John Windsor met his tragic fate and there was John with a group of fellow officers. This caused members of the faculty at the University of Victoria to telephone the news. Then Peter Bruton's "Notebook" in the *Colonist* had the following, timed perfectly for the launching in 1962:

> Local man in scenes from the Melfa River battle in Italy, shown on the C.B.C.'s television program Canada at War the other night was John Windsor. John couldn't see the program — he's blind as the result of being hit in the tank battle. His book dealing with his experiences since then — *Blind Date* — will be on city bookstore shelves Monday.

How lucky could we get? These were generous, forgiving days before the "Me" generation, when the public had time to understand nervous, uncertain war veterans. Glowing reviews appeared in many prominent papers for as well as the ones I

Gray and Eleanor with John Windsor.

covered, undoubtedly ex-cadets from the Royal Military College were working behind the scenes. The *R.C.M.P. Quarterly* and the *United Church Observer* also gave it wide coverage.

When the first edition, a printing of 3,000 bound in softcover, sold out in less than a year, we printed up the same number. I took the uncut sheets to Vancouver in a borrowed station wagon and there Evergreen Press produced a hardcover, second edition with Peter Whyte's drawings on the dust jacket. There was a photograph of John on the back holding a copy of the first edition with the unusual first cover. Three thousand copies sold in less than 12 months from a standing start wasn't bad. This was my first contact with Evergreen Press, who had experience in book binding, and it was the start of an interesting relationship.

John and I were on a roll and we took full advantage of it, turning up at stores to autograph books and giving interviews on radio and television. The media never lost its friendly interest. I will never forget one incident that brought home, more than anything, the effect of the passing of time on the sightless. John had remarked once that he had difficulty remembering certain colours; then at one autographing session when he was asked to write a particular message he turned to me and whispered, "I've forgotten how to make that capital letter."

While we were travelling to bookstores on Vancouver Island and the mainland, manuscripts began to turn up in the mail and that is when we turned to another old friend, Flos Jewell Williams, who lived on the waterfront a few houses away. Drawing on years of experience as a successful author of fiction, Flos soon became the main reason we could consider hanging onto the tail of this tiger. As a retired novelist, she had the ability to size up a writer's potential by reading a few pages. With amused interest in our attempt to get John Windsor in print, and the consequent follow-up of queries and manuscripts, she volunteered to be our back-stop.

One day she had a gleam in her eye. She had cautioned us many times that we had to be extremely careful, that any second attempt at regional publishing had to be both unusual and well written. She thought she had found it, an adventure by a school-teacher in Doukhobor country, and she urged us to give it several readings. If we had the same opinion, then we could talk about it. I took it away to share with Eleanor.

Meanwhile, John Windsor and I continued to share many light-hearted and rewarding adventures. The C.B.C. decided to dramatize *Blind Date* on radio. The Windsors' social life enlarged and John was approached to enter politics as well as to write a regular column for the *Review* which he called "Wit's End". Many ideas for articles also kept him busy. By October the *Colonist* again gave his book some ink with Ted Shackleford's "Notebook" which started off with "*Blind Date* takes publisher down the aisle to success" and announced that we were going ahead with a second title. It was the first mention in print of our decision to follow the Windsor story with the hilarious *Doukhobor Daze*, the second of Eleanor's catchy titles. It was the school-teacher's manuscript that had caught the critical eye of Flos.

We went back to Clair Rivers for a second work-out on the old flat-bed press to turn out the same format in December 1962. The action, risky adventure and, yes, fun were starting all over again.

Chapter Four

LOOKING BACK at those exciting, exuberant days I am sure we would never have gone ahead, or progressed as we did, had it not been for Flos. We had got away with it the first time to prove a point. I had enjoyed taking the initial risk without the responsibility of a reputation to lose. Once we had achieved that, it was time to escape to another interest. This was the prevailing mood with many veterans who had survived the war and still felt they were living on borrowed time. I was no exception. We had the little motor sailer at Tom Sauvary's Deep Cove dock practically across the road, and I could slip away on the slightest pretext any time. After the responsibility and hard work on the ranch, this was paradise. The ranch had not been sold but there had been a down payment. I was still selling articles but, as Barry Broadfoot put it, recalling those days, "You were running on air."

Flos Williams was a wise old owl, living alone in her charming cottage, always surrounded by friends of all ages. She had raised two sons in Calgary and while Dave, her husband, was on the road as a travelling salesman she had turned to writing short stories and poetry. Between the 1920s and the '50s, four of her novels had been published. She was a witty raconteur, very much in tune with current literature and state affairs. Dave's travelling partner over the years was Stephen Leacock's brother, which had resulted in a fund of anecdotes about the famous humourist.

We had many mutual friends from the old days in Calgary and Banff and it was always a good day when we could drop in on Flos for a drink and a chat. She generously let our children range freely with their pets and friends on her beach so that when our post office box began to fill with letters and manuscripts, she was more than eager to help sort out the chaff from the wheat.

However, it took Hazel O'Neail's neatly typewritten tale of danger among the Doukhobors to kick-start the idea of our risking a second title. The characters and settings were so outrageously funny, yet the situations she got into so dangerous with bombings and burnings, that we felt it was important to check out the author. We wondered just what kind of person could have written about this so delightfully when the average young teacher would have been scared out of her wits. We had to find out before taking a chance. So Flos, Eleanor and I set out during a July heat wave to drive into the Slocan Valley in our old Rover.

When we stopped at a motel near Grand Forks we knew that we were in Doukhobor country, because the rooms were full of framed cartoons, by many of our best-known newspaper artists, highlighting the antics of the Sons of Freedom. It put us in the right mood to meet the author next day in Slocan, a tiny settlement with a sawmill and a school where Hazel's husband taught. There wasn't a soul in sight when we stopped at a nice-looking house that might belong to the teacher, climbed out stiffly and knocked.

The fine-looking, decorous lady who stood there rather shyly fit the description of a successful, retired schoolteacher. It was Hazel, dignified and poised, surprisingly not the type I had expected as the author. She seemed nervous at the confrontation with an imposing, authentic author who had given her a good report and a book publisher with another assistant. We were ushered into a cool, comfortable room and tried to get through the preliminaries, not knowing just how to start. We had tea and made light talk and I didn't know what to say, but I think Flos asked all the right questions. We didn't have time to waste as Flos was due in Calgary for a visit with her son, while Eleanor and I had to hurry home.

There was not a minute to lose if we were going to get the book out in time to catch the Christmas spirit. I knew we were already too late, according to Bill Duthie's dictum for timing to catch Easter or Christmas sales. Flos had agreed to write the foreword, but what the story really needed to put it over was an illustrator who could draw Doukhobors, and caricature the high spots in some of the almost unbelievable situations.

By now I had a nice relationship with our daily papers. Neither the *Colonist* nor the *Times* were the quiet morgues they are today in the computer age. The rattle of noisy Underwoods clashed with jangling telephones and the intermittent squawk of the police and fire radio. Photographers and reporters were coming and going; at the *Colonist* freelancers were lined up outside the door of John Shaw's cubbyhole where he produced *The Islander* magazine in its heyday. The atmosphere was stimulating, competitive and exciting.

Some reporters waved the usual hello when I hurried in, others looked inquiringly and I stopped someone heading out on assignment.

"I'm looking for an illustrator to draw characters with humour."

"Try Ed. He's always fooling around with sketches."

He pointed to a young chap who was attacking his typewriter with fair good spirit and I interrupted Ed Cosgrove, who stopped with a ready smile to let his machine cool down. He was in a hurry to reach the courthouse so there was no time for small talk.

"Would you like to try illustrating a book?"

"I'll give it a shot."

"Can you draw Doukhobors?"

His reply was the same. I quickly outlined the story and in a few days he showed me some fine examples. I had him read the manuscript and he came up with serious and funny scenes that appealed to him. As a police reporter he spent boring hours in court listening to petty crimes, and instead of doodling he began to sketch figures he could use; prisoners, lawyers, and anyone on the bench were subjects for the drawings that enhanced the book. Ed soon went on to Toronto where he became an illustrator in the big time and also an author in his own right. In 1994 he was an established anchor man on the B.C.T.V. network doing news features in Vancouver.

Again I turned to Bill Duthie for advice, which led to organizing appearances on radio and television for John Windsor and Hazel O'Neail and having them meet the friendly press.

When Hazel came to visit, her comic story was in sharp contrast with the mood of the radical Doukhobors who were on their way to Victoria. Camped outside Hope, their intention was to march on the Legislative Buildings. With two competing newspapers and reporters scrambling, one wag wondered in print if we had organized the march to publicize *Doukhobor Daze!* It didn't hurt the sales but one sensitive store owner, feeling it poked fun at these people, refused to sell the book at first. Then when publicity mounted, and demand increased, they started selling it under the counter! At the same time I had a letter from an ambitious young Doukhobor storekeeper around Grand Forks who wanted to be the exclusive agent to sell it to his people.

Doukhobor Daze set us off on another publicity spin. The actions of the radical Sons of Freedom appeared in the press every day, with details of where they camped on their trek to Victoria, their daily progress and speculations as to how the politicians would react. The main event fizzled out when the plan to camp on the legislative grounds was dampened: someone turned on the sprinklers and forgot to turn them off. This gave us easy access to television and radio exposure and Hazel came through with flying colours. She could re-create the accent of her pupils and during one memorable appearance on CHEK-TV she fairly surprised Andy Stephen and left Ida Clarkson almost speechless with the account of how "Neecky Stoochnoff ees een de toilet," a wonderful chapter on her early days of teaching.

Unfortunately, perhaps, we were picking up more publicity than we needed to make a success of book publishing. Early in the year I had a telephone call from a deputy minister in the provincial government who asked if he could charter *Lady Mine* for a day of local cruising. I could afford a day off if it meant making an extra few bucks so I agreed. Then I was asked not to discuss this with anyone, but he would bring a V.I.P. to our dock about ten next morning; I asked Ian, 13 years old, to come along as crew.

We were ready and curious at the appointed time when a car drove into the parking lot at Deep Cove and who should come aboard but the premier, W.A.C. Bennett himself. We enjoyed the privacy of the seldom-used government dock. Mr. Bennett and his companion, Ron Worley, disappeared into the tiny cabin while Ian and I lost no time clearing the cove. Worley had told me "to just cruise anywhere, Maple Bay would do" and as we set our course we could hear them chuckling, and sometimes exploding with laughter, over something that was happening.

They did not surface to enjoy the scenery and fine weather until they had got it out of their systems and they could emerge composed.

We had a lovely day with a picnic on board and a stroll around Mill Bay, a curiously incognito foursome. Only once or twice a native did a double-take and we pretended not to notice. Then a smooth, relaxed sail home. Ian will never forget it for at the friendly parting, Mr. Bennett gave him a warm handshake and left him clutching a crisp, five-dollar bill, the first one he had ever received.

Next day we found out why this trip was laid on, and possibly why we were chartered, for politically we were strictly from out-of-town. It was announced that the Social Credit government had taken over B.C. Hydro.

When I think back and try to sort out the events that shaped our lives, I see that 1962 included a twist or two that made it a turning point. Early in the year Victoria started cranking up communities and organizations to celebrate its centennial. Committees were formed to gather individual citizens, small business firms and corporations, putting them to work with politicians to make a success of the occasion. I was much too busy launching our first books and getting our share of publicity to realize the extent of this effort until one day I had a call from an advertising executive in a large department store. He asked me to meet him at a Victoria high school one evening, which I found puzzling, but agreed to do.

At the school gymnasium groups of volunteers were being sorted out and instructed while my cigar-smoking friend took me aside to explain his problem. The organizers felt they weren't getting through to the press, though they had tried several approaches. Somebody on one of the dailies suggested they should hire me as I was on good terms with both newsrooms. His plan was for the city to hire me to help organize the publicity and act as liaison to present it to the press. I felt there wasn't enough time in my days but he assured me that it would only tie me down part-time, and only for a few weeks. I went home to think about it and decided I would give it a try if they hired John Windsor too, to help get out the press releases.

City Hall agreed and I briefed John who stood by at home near the telephone with his tape recorder and typewriter. I was given a cubbyhole in the airless basement of an empty building on Douglas Street. The main room on the ground floor had telephones, secretaries, typewriters and growing files. The organizers were kept busy with volunteers sent in from charitable organizations, churches and clubs. The city had hired an outfit from the United States to put together a pageant. This firm specialized in such events with a standard plot line; all they had to do was fill the adaptable script with characters from local history. Bebe Eversfield, a local choreographer, had a prominent position drilling amateur actors, and as local citizens volunteered, they were selected to play various parts, and sent off with assistant directors to go over their lines. These groups would often spill down into the basement to fill the large room beside my cell and I could not help wondering how on earth they would manage to be sorted out on time.

When someone came to me with a request for a notice intended for radio or press, I would phone John and he would ask for 20 minutes or more. When he was ready I called for a secretary who took down his words in shorthand. As we moved closer to the start of the pageant, the requests increased and more often they wanted it in a hurry. John never let us down. One call from City Hall was an address of welcome for the R.C.M.P. Musical Ride who were to parade down Douglas Street and would be featured in the performance certain evenings. It was an exciting challenge, sometimes nail-biting, but Windsor never failed to cut the mustard.

When I asked him, 30 years later, what he remembered as a highlight in the summer of 1962, he said it was the time he was called upon to write something momentous to be buried in the time capsule and he sweated over it. Finally, he calmed down with a reasonable attitude. "Whatever goes in," he said, "isn't all that important for there won't be anyone around to criticize when they dig it up."

Our job, which started out as part-time, began to stretch into full days as we approached the deadline and we would both be very glad to see it behind us. A few days before the pageant opened I started for home after a busy day, joining the five o'clock rush out the old narrow road that led to Sidney before the Pat Bay highway was built. Around Royal Oak I stopped and called home.

"Do we need anything for supper?"

"Where are you? There's a flap on. They want you back at the office."

I did not relish threading back through the evening rush, finding a place to park and having to handle another crisis. The office upstairs was full of strangers, reporters, photographers and the curious milling around three figures pinned in the centre of the room. A huge, wide male figure overflowing the largest chair was flanked by a lady and a small girl. The man looked surprisingly familiar.

I was introduced to Sebastian Cabot, English actor of stage and screen who was currently starring in a long-running, popular TV series, "Checkmate", made in Hollywood. He was civil but not particularly happy at being confined for no apparent reason while his equally puzzled wife, Kay, and their daughter, Yvonne, were beginning to feel restless.

They had been attending the World's Fair in Seattle, and had ventured to Victoria for the day on the Anacortes ferry, leaving their car and luggage at a motel in Anacortes. They had been having a lovely time taking in the atmosphere, which was like their home in London, and when they saw the fish-and-chip shop near City Hall they were captivated. Someone spotted them, recognized Sebastian and called the papers. This brought reporters and photographers to catch the big actor devouring the food that any Londoner would miss in the States.

Fortunately for the centennial, a committee member turned up and persuaded the little family to take refuge in our office. I was summoned to help work out a plan to keep this celebrity around so he could help open the pageant every evening during the week it ran. We got them into the Imperial Inn as guests of the city and sent one of the volunteers on the ferry to pick up their car and luggage.

Now it was my turn to ride herd on the Cabots, picking them up each morning and trying to keep them entertained. I was also responsible for delivering the star in a good mood in time for the curtain raiser each evening. By the second or third day I was running out of ideas and took them to our home in Deep Cove. They were fascinated by the rural setting, with our country lanes and neighbours, which reminded them of England and this, together with the relaxed pace of country living, helped turn their experience into a real holiday. Sebastian also loved sailing so we made full use of our *Lady Mine*; they also had interesting days with John and Pam Windsor who helped enlarge their growing circle of friends.

Kay Cabot, Gray, Sebastian Cabot and Eleanor.

As the responsibility of the Cabot assignment began to ease for me, you may imagine what it had been doing to Eleanor's routine. Looking after the children plus an acre of garden, she was also being invaded at unpredictable times by odd groups and could never plan a day on her own. I would go off sailing with guests on trips which she helped provision and she was never sure when we would show up. If she tried to arrange something on her own, I might be called out. It was beginning to put a strain on our marriage, with Eleanor missing the fun, the telephone ringing at all hours and strangers turning up.

Things began to settle down as the Cabots eased into our Deep Cove community and Sebastian started making noises about finding property near by. Kay and Yvonne Cabot were comfortable sharing activities and interests with Eleanor and our Cathy. At first we did not take Sebastian seriously when he talked about wanting to live in Deep Cove, assuming it was merely polite tourist manners. But as we found out much later, he was serious.

Then, just as I thought we had the situation under control, and the centennial program was running calmly, we had another live one on our hands. When I saw the wire, I thought in despair, "Oh boy, here we go again." Here is part of the press release we issued:

> Burt Reynolds, 26-year-old Hollywood star, arrives in
> Victoria Thursday, July 6 on loan to Victoria Centennial by
> CBS TV. He will take part in the week-long celebration as
> guest...

The rest was a fill-in of his film credits, which indicated that
he was about to emerge as a celebrity. When he joined our
little circle, to sail and picnic through the day before each
evening appearance with Sebastian, he was popular with
everyone. We judged him a very nice young man who showed
respect and consideration and played up to the older actor so
that the two never failed to warm up the crowd each evening
before the pageant.

Again, it wasn't the easiest of times for our little household,
but Eleanor and the children went along with amused tolerance,
knowing the end of the ordeal was in sight. After it was over, and
only memories remained, Sebastian kept returning for short
visits alone until we helped him find his dream home in a lovely,
private part of the cove just a short walk through the woods from
our acre. He and Kay eventually retired there.

The coming together of Cabots, Windsors, Flos Williams and
all the others concerned with the publishing venture, had
combined to make 1962 remain in memory as a very bizarre
year.

Chapter Five

WHILE ALL this was going on I had to handle a few other problems which fussed me. The surprising success of *Blind Date* had brought more mail and telephone calls than I could handle. I was still trying to work in the cabin in the woods while the telephone was in the house, and I was constantly having to run back and forth. Trying to package orders on one table, type invoices on another and keep track without a proper system showed that I had never intended to continue.

For the first book I had a large sheet of cardboard pinned on the wall with the title at the top and lines drawn to separate date, customer and number of copies shipped, which would be deducted from the total printed. I had a three-part invoice form of which two copies went with the shipment and our copy went into a top drawer on my desk. When the order had been paid for it was marked and moved into a second drawer. It was so simple: one glance at the cardboard told us what had been sold and what was left in stock; the top drawer had accounts receivable. But pressure was building with mail and telephone requests asking for sympathy or help, and I became testy.

And that was when one of our dearest and closest neighbours, Laura Baker, arrived with her project. She had a positive, no-nonsense, direct manner. There was no question but that I had a duty to pick up and publish Dr. Coleman's poetry.

Gray running from the cabin to the house for a phone call.

"I can't do poetry, Mrs. Baker, I don't understand it."

"Of course you can. It will be good for him, confined to his bed."

Then I blew a fuse. "It's all very well for you to talk. But I have enough trouble and responsibilities with four kids in school and not enough capital to gamble."

She took it well and went into the garden to visit with Eleanor. I began to feel sorry that I had spoken to her like that but I did know that poetry wasn't a very good bet at the best of times.

A few days later the bank called. Allan Spooner, the manager, would like to see me and the tension returned. One of the printers might have asked him to bear down on our payments while we were struggling along with the attitude that a book should pay its own way on sales. Negotiations were still going on over the sale of the ranch and we were in the habit of running on short-term loans. So I called at the bank with something less than a light heart. The news was not what I had expected. Allan had the smile of a cherub instead of the banker's poker mask.

"A sum of money has been deposited to your credit by Mrs. Baker, your neighbour, so that you may publish Dr. Coleman's poems."

"How would she know what the job would cost?"

"She paid a visit at the *Review* and showed the material to Clair Rivers."

"Holy cow, I don't want to handle it. What if I can't sell enough copies to pay her back?"

"I don't think she's concerned about that and it's not your worry. For your private information, when she was a little girl in Montreal, one of the first things her Daddy taught her was how to clip coupons."

When I told Eleanor, she agreed that since Mrs. Baker was such a very determined person, we had better go through with it. I walked to the corner and down the short lane to meet Dr. Coleman, a charming recluse, 90 years old with a bright, young mind. Almost a quarter of a century before he had been head of the department of philosophy and psychology at the University of British Columbia. He had been writing poetry since his childhood, and had published four small works and one epic, *Education in Upper Canada* in 1908.

The collection we were to publish had been written to assist teachers in holding the attention of children, to begin their appreciation of poetry through the theme that mother love is universal. He also hoped the poems would have a greater effect than any number of lectures in fostering kindness to animals. He achieved this by devoting poems to babies in the animal kingdom and how each mother handled and taught her offspring in the furry, feathered and domestic world. The last poem was about the human baby which is the only one that can laugh.

There was nothing to stop us going ahead and with Mrs. Baker's son doing the cover and delightful illustrations for each animal, we brought out a first edition in January 1963 in soft-cover. *Doukhobor Daze* had been successfully launched late in 1962 and we just included copies of *All About Babies* with our orders, hoping it would catch on and we could repay Mrs. Baker. It did so well it was followed by a hardcover printing the next November. I couldn't believe how well known and respected Dr. Coleman's name and reputation were after all those years in retirement. Teachers, pupils and the press remembered him with great affection and it seemed most of the bookstores in the province wanted the book in stock. It was a perfect example how word of mouth could help sales. There were telephone calls from old pupils, and columnists who wanted to remember this revered teacher.

I had to tack up another sheet of cardboard to keep visual track of inventory and sales, then find two more drawers or boxes for the invoices. We were surprised and delighted to be able to repay Mrs. Baker in less than three months.

If I had a handle on inventory and sales I cannot say the same for my banking. At the Bank of Montreal I had accounts for *Blind Date* and *All About Babies* but now *Doukhobor Daze* was moving ahead full steam so I opened an account for it in the Toronto Dominion Bank which had just established a branch in Sidney. No one had considered the need for contracts; with John Windsor we had had a gentleman's agreement which simply meant we got his book out, made enough sales to pay the printer and then we would split whatever remained. I had figured on doing the same with Hazel O'Neail.

The business had reached a point where, in reality, I had bitten off more than I could chew. It meant the carefree days of innocent experimentation were fading and my personal freedom was curtailed. It wasn't so easy to slip away in the *Lady Mine* for a sail down Satellite Channel. I was stressed and tired and did not know how to ease the pressure.

One morning at the post office in Sidney I was scooping letters of all sizes out of Box 718 which I had foolishly included with our name on the title pages. Some envelopes slipped to the floor and I muttered something unprintable as I picked them up. And that is when I ran into another lucky break. I bumped into John Barclay, an old friend from our first days at Curteis Point. We had both been involved with the Boy Scouts with our sons, and since we were self-employed, we had been handed jobs like bottle collecting and disposal. John helped me to my feet.

"What's the matter?" he asked. "You don't look too well."

"Nothing really, but at the moment I've got too much on my plate."

"Could I help?" he asked and I admitted I could use some advice.

"I'll drop around this afternoon."

It was an important turning point when Commander J.W.C. Barclay, R.C.N. retd., turned up with his navy training in accounting, was appalled to find the confusion in the cabin, rolled up his sleeves and went to work

When he arrived he found me sorting out the mail. He is a big man and the two of us had little room to manoeuvre. Against one wall was a packing table with boxes of books and packing material. My desk with the portable typewriter was beside the large window. John filled the space left. He took it all in at a glance.

"Let's see your ledger," he said. "Inventory, sales, accounts receivable."

I pointed to the cardboard tacked to the wall behind the packing table.

"It's all there at a glance. Title, number printed, each line gives the date, customer, and copies shipped. Subtracting that from the total gives you a perpetual inventory."

"But where's your accounts receivable?"

I opened the top drawer and explained how the invoices worked their way down into the second drawer and pulled out the bank books to show how I had kept the accounts neatly separated. When he asked how I handled accounts payable I had printers' bills with payments and amounts owing clipped together and explained how, without contracts, I simply shared with the authors whatever was left in each account.

"I'm not sure you're operating legally without proper contracts. I think you need to see an accountant and set up a better system."

John Barclay only intended to help me catch up, I feel sure, but he gradually got drawn into the momentum that was devel-

John Barclay and Gray in the cabin-office.

oping. Unknown to me, people like R.M. Patterson were keeping a curious eye on this strangely developing list of subjects. He was at the time living in Spain, researching and writing a monumental study of Napoleon's cavalry. He wrote with an idea I might like to consider: publishing a collection of his western Canadian articles which had appeared in English and Canadian magazines. He referred to the fact we had shared a common interest in cattle ranching. John Barclay had been raised in the same environment so we were able to consider the current interest in such a book.

I could not resist the temptation of adding an international author to our list. We would be the first regional, western Canadian "firm" to publish a talent that had publishers in London and New York and a firmly established following. After an exchange of letters, R.M. returned to his home in Victoria, where he had moved from Curteis Point, and we got to work seriously. He has written an amusing account of this in his introduction to *Far Pastures*, which we originally published in 1963. This was a step I could not have taken without the moral support of our friend and neighbour, John Barclay.

Now we were moving out of the amateur league, easing into a professional mode, and we needed better equipment playing at this level. R.M. expected a proper contract and he handed me examples of his contracts with his publishers in New York and London. That certainly opened my eyes and I hurried to Victoria for legal advice. Pearlman & Lindholm, a legal firm, became interested, probably for the reason that a book publisher's contract was not in their repertoire. Louis Lindholm studied these examples and drew up the sort of contract we could use and apply generally. I did not know at the time that Lindholm happened to be Mr. Patterson's lawyer as well, which seemed to please R.M.

Now I needed John Barclay more than ever and his own interest grew with the possibilities that a Patterson title would generate. John's name and connections would help raise my own local status, understandably suspect in the developing world of western literature. With an accountant setting up a proper system and a legal firm to help with advice, we had one more change to make. In a cheerful letter, Frank Jacobs, editor of *Canadian Cattlemen*, chided me on the presumptuous name we had selected for the first three titles. "Gray's Publishing Canada", he intimated, was trying to take in too much territory.

So we changed it to "Gray's Publishing Ltd." Campbell Publishing sounded both awkward and pretentious, copying houses like Macmillan or Collins. A short first name like Gray kept the image on a personal, first-name basis.

While John was busy sorting out the accounting confusion and mastering the stock control, getting cost analysis, mark-up and discounts in line, I began to relax. We started to see more of Flos and our neighbours, and had Tom Sauvary for meals to the delight of the boys, who needed another boyhood hero with the same qualities as Bill Lagarde, the mountain man they had left behind in the foothills. Eleanor and I had many a happy-hour in Tom's quarters over the boathouse where a select few old-timers used to gather and reminisce about the rum-running days. They were always careful only to mention names of participants who were no longer in the area and we were careful not to ask for details that might connect with anyone present.

We had also been enjoying the swimming from Flos Williams' beach every warm afternoon and a regular visit with Flos, which always resulted in a spirited discussion on a variety of subjects. I shall never forget one beautiful summer's night with a full moon that inspired us to summer madness. Just before bedtime, Eleanor thought we should go for a swim in the moonlight. Saanich Inlet was dead calm and the entire waterfront was dark. We crept down the path quietly so as not to awaken Flos or cause any dogs to bark, parked our clothes on a large, warm rock and waded in over the sand. It was so stimulating, stroking through the silvery sea, that I felt the urge to let out a cowboy whoop and holler. We splashed at each other and rushed out farther away from the sleeping houses, marvelling at the phosphorescent drops of salt water, until we were far enough out to talk. It was a very precious moment, floating easily on our backs, taking in a star-filled universe and reverting to the carefree days of youth. The sea was not only peacefully calm, it was the warmest of the year. Skinny-dipping at its most glorious, the world to ourselves while the rest were asleep.

Our reverie was shattered by the sound of engines. Several cars turned in to the driveway of the mansion which had recently been built next to the Williams' cottage and their headlights flashed over the peaceful scene, only to be dimmed when house lights, and then the floodlights on the deck, diminished the moonlight. The occupants of the cars settled on the patio to continue their party as we trod water and whispered about how to get out of this undetected. We felt like sneaks in the night, veritably caught with our pants down, a couple of middle-aged nuts. We began to swim without stirring up the phosphorescence, making waves or attracting attention until we were clear of the lights. Then we headed for the far end of the beach, dressed quickly and stole up the bank on the far side of the house and I cannot remember if we ever told anyone about this except to confess to Flos.

With *Blind Date* at its peak and *Doukhobor Daze* ready to face an unsuspecting public in December of 1962, we sent Dane into the heart of Doukhobor country and as far into southern Alberta as he could go with as many boxes of books as the bus people would tolerate. He was just 20 years of age with energy to burn. Whenever the Greyhound made a stop he would nip out looking for any business that could sell a few copies. He had a good quantity of both books and was taking orders for *All About Babies*. If there was no bookstore or stationer, he sold to drugstores. One order came in from Joe's Confectionery near Kingsgate, B.C., and I think that Ed Cosgrove's captivating cover had a lot to do with these places giving it a try. I remember taking a collect call from Dane at this time asking us to ship ahead boxes of both titles before he reached Alberta.

Nelson proved to be a learning experience. Hazel and her husband met him at the depot and took him around to meet the owner of Oliver's Books who wanted to take a hundred copies of *Doukhobor Daze* on consignment. This was a new idea for Dane and before deciding he called on the owner of Mann's Drugs who was afraid to order if Oliver was prepared to corner the market. Dane resolved it by persuading Oliver to start with 30 copies, then Mann bought 20. He also took an order from Oliver for ten *All About Babies* while Mann's Drugs wanted more information about the new poetry book.

It wasn't *all* hard work, for a detailed letter in January 1963 described Dane's unforgettable experience arriving in Cowley, on the doorstep of the foothills ranching country. This is how the letter started:

> Never! Never! have I had so much fun. Last night was a
> panic. I went to Cowley's New Year dance and met everyone
> in the district. The dance ended at 2 AM then everyone
> dropped over to Bourdier and I didn't get to bed till 6 this
> morning. I will tell you all about it later.

He was reminding us of a highlight during our salad days on the ranch, when families in that part of the foothills gathered at the single-room country school.

While Dane was on the road I was pushing out the orders and answering the mail; John had the accounting well in hand. R.M. Patterson had been working harder than he expected but had put together, in four sections, the entire range of his pioneering adventures in Canada between 1924 and 1955. *Far Pastures* was a wonderfully well-balanced narrative that drew fine reviews, pleased his fans with word pictures of the true north and caused his Nahanni partner, Gordon Mathews, to tell him it was the best book he had written. R.M. and I had great fun working on this volume, choosing and arranging the articles, with an additional flow of narrative, and I think we both came up with the idea that this title was the right one for the work.

It had also put me in an embarrassing position. An author of this stature expected a hardcover book. With our first three titles we had undertaken the job of introducing unknown authors and their books the cheapest and easiest way we could, by getting people involved, donating time and talent, and binding the books at the cheapest rate we could find.

A Patterson had to have a proper frame for his life portrait and again I went to Vancouver for advice. Bill Duthie suggested Evergreen Press so I drove out there and fortunately met Glen Hyatt, the head of a growing concern. I showed him the manuscript and photographs and asked for a quotation. Glen was a bookman, eager to see another book by R.M. Patterson, and his quotation seemed right for 5,000 copies. I came back to discuss it with John Barclay and Eleanor and we agreed that if our luck held, and the momentum that had carried us this far did not lose steam, risking a hardcover was less of a gamble with a known writer who had a following. I ordered the first printing.

It was just as delightful working with the designers, printers and Glen Hyatt himself at Evergreen as it had been with the old-timers like Jim Wakefield at the *Review* in Sidney. Glen himself shared our confidence and enthusiasm. But there was a difference when the order got into the hands of their accountants. All the excitement of this new venture took on a chill when I opened a letter from them enclosing a demand note for me to sign before the order went ahead. It caught me completely by surprise and I went off by myself to spend a few hours sorting out the implications. The figure frozen on that note I have

R.M. Patterson. (PHOTO BY DANE CAMPBELL)

managed to forget. It was, I think, $5,000 but the exact amount was incidental. If I slipped, it would be putting the cottage, even the car, in jeopardy. The final payment on the sale of the ranch had not been made. Dane had written from Cowley that the new owners were still negotiating the backing of a government loan.

The good old days of flying by the seat of our pants, relying on good will, fine weather and unlimited visibility had suddenly turned bleak. This was the real world we had finally entered, which rewards only success, with no marks for good intentions. I had gone too far, too quickly, to try and change course. Mr. Patterson held our signed contract. It never entered my head that we might have talked it over with Glen, to see if he knew what was happening. I don't think that I dared share any of this with family or friends, even Eleanor, probably figuring I had to face this alone.

Next day I signed the demand note and mailed it to Vancouver. The die had been cast.

Chapter Six

WHEN WORD leaked out that we had a book by an established author, our first carefree attempts to dip a timid toe into the cool pool of book publishing took a more serious turn. Things began to move at a faster pace and I began to feel like the Leacock character who mounted his horse and "galloped off in all directions." We really had to hustle because I started to imagine we were dealing with hard-nosed strangers who had no time for sentiment or sympathy. That meant rushed trips to the mainland to increase sales of the existing titles and pre-sell the coming Patterson epic.

Until the fall of 1963 we had not taken ourselves too seriously. I had not signed that demand note; the books were selling, accounts increasing and cash flow growing. We were intent on just paying the printers and sharing the profit with the authors as a secondary consideration. We took no salary; I worked with a contingency fund to pay for such items as rent, telephone, freight and postage. For a short time John Barclay accepted a modest salary for the long hours he devoted to the cause, but he turned it back to the firm so we could hire our son Tim on a regular basis. It was none too soon for with *Far Pastures* coming on stream, we had to ship out a lot of books quickly. We had been counting on the good will of the printers to store the stock until we needed it, but our presumption was wearing thin and we were facing the day when we had to find our own storage space.

We had only survived this far with practically no overhead because local printers wanted to be in on the action. To help delay things I began looking for more printers who might be interested and fastened on the sales staff of Colonist Printers who had a ground-floor office in the *Colonist* building.

Victoria had a popular entertainer in Jerry Gosley who had created a bright and cheeky production called the "Smile Show" which played in summer to tourists and local fans. The humour was vintage English music-hall and the revue each season offered nostalgia to British Victoria and puzzled amusement to American visitors. I had approached Jerry, another R.A.F. veteran, with an idea to do an article about him and out of that came Jerry's suggestion that we publish a small book on the show's origins, with good photographs, to be sold at bookstores and the theatre. We turned the idea over to John Windsor who worked with Jerry through the off-season to produce a charming little book titled *Nowhere Else To Go*. This kept John busy at his home with regular visits from Jerry, and the new printers in our list of eager helpers did a nice job. The book was a modest success and brought us many attractive, interesting friends.

After the theatrical diversions of 1962, we settled down to the real job of promoting and selling our small but growing list of four titles. We were confident we had a winner coming with the Patterson book and Evergreen Press in Vancouver certainly proved they could design and package a literary work with the best in the business. *Far Pastures* was published in the fall of 1963 and I think a great deal of our energy through that year was spent in promotion. We turned Dane and Tim loose to make sure that every outlet, stores and libraries, had stock to meet the demand. While our boys were travelling through the province, R.M. Patterson and I were appearing at stores and for interviews on radio and television in Victoria, Vancouver and Calgary. That Evergreen note was hanging over my head so menacingly that I don't think I ever let anyone know about my feeling of guilt. I was running so scared we managed to pay it off in less than six months. Which of course proved that R.M. Patterson had great appeal and bounced me back safely into the ring, ready for the next round.

About this time Eleanor and I had been invited to the annual banquet of the Canadian Authors Association in Victoria. Among the interesting group was Art Willis, formerly from Edmonton, who had, after graduation from university, drifted into the

Yukon as a young adventurer after gold. It was at the height of the Great Depression in the 1930s and out of those years he had written a novel, and some 60 short stories. He wanted to talk about something entirely different, which was not my cup of tea. He had written a book for west-coast gardeners, based on his experience with his West Saanich nursery. Here he was, trying to interest a publisher who could not be trusted in our own garden without supervision. But Eleanor heard us talking and she wanted to see his manuscript. She mentioned it enthusiastically to John Barclay, also an avid and knowledgeable gardener, who agreed with her. I was outvoted and sent to consult with printers about the format.

The Colonist Printers suggested a book with ring binding so that the pages would lie flat while a gardener was studying diagrams and directions in the field. The cover was coated so a damp cloth could wipe it clean after a session in the garden. While we were at Chesterman's Beach near Tofino, Eleanor drew a cover design for it in the sand with a stick of driftwood. Her creation was the figure of a typical, full-blown Oak Bay matron bending over to admire an emerging flower. She copied the figure on a sketch pad but when *The Pacific Gardener* was produced, the designer had changed the figure to a man.

I was reminded of this when a yellowing clipping fell out of a file. Dated 1966, Candide Temple had written a column with the heading, "Gardeners Take Heart—Help Is On The Way", and she said, in part:

> The first edition, out in time for the snowdrops in 1964, sold 5,000 copies. Now an additional 3,000 in a second edition are being printed for local garden fans to put on their bookshelves. The ironical part of the book's success is that it was originally turned down by large publishing companies back east. "The eastern publishers thought it was well put together," recalls author Willis, "but it was too regional for them to take a chance on."

By the time we had published the ninth edition in 1975, about 70,000 copies had been printed and the last time I looked, over 100,000 copies were in print. It is now published by Whitecap Books in North Vancouver.

Art and Blanche Willis became close friends, We seldom made a run to Victoria without dropping in at the "Home of Happy

Plants" and they would often come out to our place where Eleanor loved to pick Art's brains for gardening nuggets. The four of us went on a Caribbean cruise together in 1970 and later we helped them celebrate their fiftieth anniversary. May 10, 1983, was a sad day when Art left us after 76 years of a rich, eventful life, a gentle man who would be missed by many friends in all walks of life.

The next challenge came in an interesting letter from an elderly nurse who was working in Calgary. She had had an unusual adventure in the Yukon which, unknown to me, had been featured in a spectacular article in *Time* magazine. The article had been critical of the way government had handled the native emergencies which this nurse and her partner had fought to overcome. Becoming local heroines, their publicity embarrassing to officialdom, they were rewarded by the termination of their contracts.

Amy Wilson, R.N., then went to Calgary to find a job in the health field and took time to write about her adventures in the Yukon. After submitting the manuscript to publishers in Toronto, which resulted in rejection slips, she wrote for advice to Doris Anderson, then editor of *Chatelaine*. She was convinced she had a real story to tell, and she must have impressed this legendary editor. Her reply to Amy was to try this new publisher out on Vancouver Island, which naturally piqued my curiosity.

When Eleanor and I agreed it was an interesting and satisfying tale, we had to see what Flos Williams would think. We were faced with the fact that our publishing future depended upon the next title being strong enough to stand beside the Patterson epic on our list. This first effort of Amy Wilson's just might fill the bill, but if we thought so, why had they turned it down in Toronto?

The story started in a straightforward manner. Amy's parents, with four children, had migrated from Missouri to Alberta to start a different life on a homestead. There she was born and after the birth of her younger sister, their mother died, leaving the father to bring up six children on a farm near Didsbury. Amy went on to tell how she trained as a nurse, graduated in the middle of the Depression, and found work as a district nurse in northern Alberta.

The second chapter was an eye-popper. An emaciated Indian had stumbled into the shack of a radio operator at Hudson Hope, mumbled "bad sickness" and collapsed. He had snow-shoed 60 miles over an unbroken trail to get help for his people.

Four natives were already dead, the rest too sick to leave camp. The radio crackled out its "Mayday" until there was an answer from Fort St. John and Amy was on her way to fight the dreaded diphtheria epidemic.

Although 1963 kept us scrambling with sales and promotion, I sat down and wrote a careful letter to Miss Wilson, saying we thought her story was well worth publishing, but could be greatly improved with a few changes to catch the interest of the reader sooner. If she could start it with the drama of the diphtheria epidemic, then flash back to her childhood and how she found herself in this situation, the book would have a better chance in the marketplace. She complied cheerfully and we went back to our friends at the *Review* for another estimate.

The story needed illustrations and a map. Here we were in luck again for an old friend from the Alberta foothills had moved to Deep Cove and lived close by. Annora Brown, author and artist, had her paintings in permanent collections in Canada and the United States. Her subjects included landscapes, Indians and wildflowers.

Annora Brown with a design for Amy Wilson's No Man Stands Alone. *(PHOTO BY GORDON CRICHTON)*

Amy Wilson came to visit us, to meet Annora and work over the manuscript. She quickly became part of our community on two short visits, making friends with Flos and Annora and launching her book quietly at our home in April 1964. Later in Calgary she had another celebration, surrounded by relatives and friends at Carmen Moore's bookstore. We had been friends with Carmen since 1953 when she was manager of the book department at Eaton's, where *We Found Peace* had been launched, and Carmen pulled out all the stops to make Amy's debut a success. Privately, Carmen expressed disappointment in the fact that we had produced a quality paperback instead of a hardcover, but dear Amy passed it off lightly. She never knew what a success her book was to become for death claimed her in October 1965, when her overworked heart gave up. (Her Yukon partner, Aileen Bond, R.N., who had flown in as back-up for the diphtheria emergency, had discovered on their first trip together that Amy had a heart condition.)

In 1965 we had a hardcover edition with our title, *No Man Stands Alone*, printed in England and co-published with Hodder & Stoughton Ltd., who covered the United Kingdom and British Commonwealth. In 1966 the story took on new life when Dodd, Mead & Company, in New York, published a lovely edition, titled *A Nurse In The Yukon*, with photographs, map and a touching postscript by Aileen Bond.

Working with Dodd, Mead's editor was a tremendous learning experience for me in the art of good publishing. She questioned many small details that I had either taken for granted or over-looked. And of course Aileen Bond's postscript, taken from her letters to me, added a new dimension to a wonderful person. Amy's humanity, generosity and sense of humour were illumi-nated, and it included this tribute:

> Amy was gullible, sympathetic and generous to a fault, with a deep sense of religion and a true appreciation of music. She collected friends from every walk of life, and it always amazed me to see how pleased people were when she showed up.

1965 ended on this sad note, but members of Amy's family kept in touch with us over the years by mail and occasional visits.

In 1966 Eleanor and I were inclined to reduce the tension and we did so with escapes to remote hideaways like Long Beach on the west coast before the highway was built. In the mood to relax, I was in no condition to get excited over future publishing risks and started depending on Tim to pick up and handle the mail. I was quite ready to let 1966 slip by and it might have done so without incident except for three names; Patterson, Bowman and Marriott.

R.M. Patterson had been delighted, and probably surprised, that we had done so well with *Far Pastures*. He came up with another idea, wondering if we would be interested in republishing his famous classic, *The Dangerous River*, as his publisher in London thought it had reached its market potential. I replied that we would consider taking it on if he could get clearances from the American and English firms. London figured they had exhausted the market with translations in Spanish and Dutch. Sloane in New York said they would not mind if a Canadian firm did a local edition but they reserved the right to publish a deluxe edition if it suited them.

We had attracted more attention through the Patterson connection and after *Far Pastures* appeared, word came through that Charlie Morriss, an outstanding printer and book designer in Victoria, would like to do a book for us. He turned out special jobs for universities and societies, loved good paper, fine print, generous margins and excellent binding, and was a master craftsman. I took him a copy of *The Dangerous River* and he went to work on it personally. By the time he had finished, we had our own deluxe edition. It was the start of a long and rewarding friendship.

Charles A. Bowman, retired and living near Nanaimo, got in touch with a letter asking if we would be interested in his autobiography. He was a famed editor of *The Ottawa Citizen* through two world wars, the confidant of prime ministers and others in power throughout the world. I was in awe, and felt the responsibility of undertaking this man's memoirs. One exciting day he called at our house, having been driven by his daughter, Nancy Heath, from their home at Departure Bay. The four of us had tea in the garden and great fun discovering mutual friends in the Ottawa scene. Growing up in Ottawa between the wars, I had been at school with the sons of his contemporaries. Our son, Dane, now a photographer, took a most affectionate portrait of the author in our garden, which graced the book. From then on, through visits to his home, the friendship grew until Charles Bowman became, in the eyes of our family, like a favourite uncle.

I took this important work to the Colonist Printers, feeling that their close connection to both local papers might help stir up interest in the story of an influential editor who was not directly connected with the west coast. They did a fine job, with an eye-catching jacket design by a young artist, Robert Wilson, who surrounded the red letters *Ottawa Editor* with a portrait of the author composed in news type. The name of the paper was prominent, and the Peace Tower which indicated the setting certainly invited one to pick it up. This clever young man also designed a logo for Gray's Publishing which we adopted for future use. Dr. Hugh Keenleyside, retired Ambassador to Japan who was featured in the book, contributed a foreword that revealed the gentle simplicity of Mr. Bowman and the young men he had assisted in their careers with fatherly advice.

GRAY'S PUBLISHING LIMITED

Nancy brought her father to us for the launching in July and we took over the Deep Cove Chalet for a tea party where his Nanaimo and Victoria friends gathered. At 84, he enjoyed every second and the Chalet was a perfect setting. It was then still operated by a local family, before it passed into the realm of international fame. Nancy did not remain long in the background, for a few months later she received a telephone call. It was the Prime Minister, Pierre Trudeau, asking her to become a senator; she accepted and worked diligently to uphold the stature of that chamber.

Harry Marriott came to us obliquely through Mary Squire, a Victoria schoolteacher who discovered him on Big Bar Lake Ranch, near Clinton in the Cariboo. His wife, Peg, ran tourist cabins and Harry entertained the dudes with his stories of early days in the Cariboo. Mary was instrumental in getting him to write about the cowboy adventures he had had since he arrived at Ashcroft in 1912 and landed his first job on the Gang Ranch. She helped him type his story but, bless her heart, she never changed his language or tried to lessen the colour of his dialogue. When the manuscript was ready for a publisher, Mary brought it to us on the recommendation of

Dr. Hartmanshenn, a professor at the University of Victoria who also lived in Deep Cove. We just had to publish this little classic, so packed with original characters, and asked Mary if we could meet the author.

She brought Harry and Peg to our house for a get-together. He proved to be genuine and then we simply had to see his spread and get the feel of his country. John and Elizabeth Barclay came with us, to spend a couple of days with the Marriotts and visit the various ranches Harry had written about. Then we drove to the Jones Lake Ranch, near 150 Mile House, to visit John's cousins, Hugh and Sonia Cornwall, both descendants of pioneer Cariboo ranchers. We felt Harry's book needed good illustrations and Sonia had a studio where she painted ranch and landscape scenes in oils and water colours. Sonia agreed to do the assignment and Hugh filled us in with anecdotes about Harry. These had been gleaned from cattle association meetings where Harry had been known as a witty but prickly critic of government regulations and any interference with the way he preferred to run the Cariboo. We all agreed that the title of this gem would be *Cariboo Cowboy*.

We returned to civilization reluctantly and had another session with Charlie Morriss who was anxious to design this one. We told him about Sonia and he asked us to suggest that when doing chapter headings, she draw some scenes so they would bleed down the outer margin of the page instead of the regular format.

While this was going on we were looking for larger quarters. We needed to handle the stock we had been failing to pick up from various printers because their good will was wearing thin. The village of Sidney allowed us to use the tourist office in the off-season so we had this as a temporary convenience. We settled in and everything seemed to be going along smoothly. *Ottawa Editor* was taking shape at the printers, *The Dangerous River* was well on its way with Morriss Printing and Charlie was giving full attention to *Cariboo Cowboy*. One peaceful, sunny day I shall never forget; our temporary office across from the Sidney Hotel was in sight of the sea, and John and I were happy as clams with the way things were going.

Then the roof fell in! Word came out of the Cariboo that Harry Marriott was not going to sign the contract we had mailed to him. We looked at each other in dismay as we realized it was too late to stop the press. We had failed to take into account

Harry's background and character. He just wasn't going to sign any legal document made up by any "rangydang" big-city lawyer. No sirree, he was too smart for that.

We telephoned Mary Squire with the news. She felt partly responsible for having brought us together, and Harry had dedicated the book to her. She hung up the phone and took off. About 36 hours later she turned up with a signed contract. Mary had driven to Big Bar non-stop, explained with her teaching skills the protection the contract gave Harry, had him sign it and had driven back without losing a moment.

We now had added three intriguing, widely different titles to our small but growing list. It was hardly enough for a catalogue, but strong enough to justify five years of a roller-coaster venture. In addition to all this, Eleanor and I had taken another tremendous gamble in moving from our small cottage with its huge garden to larger quarters on Cromar Road which gave us nearly two acres. The older buildings were part of the original Downey Farm and afforded enough room for our growing sons to stretch out in. We made the move in November 1966.

John Barclay, Gray and Tim in the new office in the former chicken barn.
(PHOTO BY DANE CAMPBELL)

We had not been able to find accommodation in Sidney large enough for all the stock we had been accumulating after the printers insisted we take delivery from their impatient warehouse people. Tim and a friend had beefed up the floor of the double-car garage attached to the chicken barn to take up the tonnage while the long, narrow barn had space for packing, an order desk, Barclay's account books, files and calculator and enough space for lighter loads of stock in open boxes or shelves.

John had a quiet corner while I managed to squeeze into a miniature office space at the entrance with a telephone and type-writer, shut off from the big room. There I had manuscripts and correspondence to handle, where I would sort out the mail, hand John bills and cheques, complete the necessary phone calls and type out the orders. On the other side of the big room across from John, Tim and I would cut up cardboard to make boxes, line up the books and pack the orders for the post office or Sidney Freight. One copy of the invoice went to John who now handled the inventory in a more professional manner.

We braced ourselves for 1967.

Chapter Seven

THE PACE never slowed in the New Year. We just had time to relish good reviews for *Ottawa Editor* from Victoria to Ottawa when *The Vancouver Sun* ran a brilliant review by Barry Broadfoot which elevated *Cariboo Cowboy* to its proper level. He started with:

> Ma Murray remarked recently that Harry Marriott 'can't swing that old rack of bones of his'n into the stirrups anymore, so he took to writing.' As I said he has his own writing style, like Ma Murray, he just lets things run till they pile up at the bottom of the hill — but he's straight, honest, sincere and his philosophy is his own.

This was the sort of encouragement that kept us going, that helped move our books and pay the bills even if we could not find the means to pay more than one salary. Barry had given the book half a page, with Harry's photograph by Dane, and two of Sonia Cornwall's delightful sketches.

We were coasting along in a mild state of euphoria when a letter arrived on February 6 from Port Hope, Ontario. The Reverend Hugh McKervill, a United Church minister, had a problem. His early ministry had been at Bella Bella, on the central B.C. coast, and he had written the story of an earlier missionary, published in 1964 by Ryerson as *Darby of Bella Bella*.

Now he had written a history of the British Columbia salmon-fishing industry. He had received an award to assist in his research, and I understood payment depended on its being published during this centennial year, 1967. To McKervill's dismay, Ryerson decided it was not their kind of book and someone in Ontario had suggested I might be able to help. I replied cautiously on February 20 that we were attempting to slow down; if he wanted to send it along we would read it but he must allow us several months to consider it. The manuscript arrived in March and we were so caught up with the author's startling views that we decided to give it priority; I wrote McKervill on May 8 that we had decided to go ahead.

It was a lesson in how not to publish: every element in good publishing faced a race against the clock. Hasty editing, a scramble for photographs and maps, trusting the design to strangers at Evergreen Press in Vancouver, speedy turn-arounds of correspondence with a busy clergyman we had never met, all helped to increase the pressure. In retrospect, it really is a wonder that something did not give when we thought of nothing but the ability to meet a deadline in September.

Hugh McKervill did not realize that descendants of the characters he had mentioned in his history were prominent citizens. Some of his descriptions were less than flattering but they certainly gave the book colour. Dane knew a grandson of one individual the author had so treated, and I asked him to sound out the reaction. Dane's friend could not care less, but another member of the family telephoned with a threat to take legal action. I needed help in a hurry so I barged into the office of the *Times* at its busiest and took Arthur Mayse away from his column. Above the din I tried to explain the problem and this gentle author, scriptwriter and journalist patiently read the chapter. He took a pencil, shifted the dialogue and punctuation, said we would now be in the clear, and we went to print.

The Salmon People brought us reviews that were pleasantly satisfying until our confidence was shaken by *The Vancouver Sun*, with headlines and half a page devoted to a vicious attack on the entire work by a well-known critic whose name was Alan Morley. This reduced us to days of despair. Our confidence evaporating, we were almost in shock, until one old-time newsman relayed the information that the critic was about to launch his own manuscript dealing with the same subject. Still, we felt sure the damage would hit us hard.

Hugh McKervill and Tim. (PHOTO BY GARY WEBSTER)

The reviewer took exception to three of the book's conclusions: that the salmon was a fragile resource, under stress from over-fishing, pollution and human folly; that the relocation of the Japanese-Canadians during the war had more to do with racial bigotry than any threat to security; and that the right of Indians to catch fish from time immemorial was threatened and ought to be protected.

Fortunately, Hugh McKervill had a friend, then living in Port Hope, who helped teach me another lesson in publishing; there is nothing like controversy and publicity to help sell an unknown title. I snapped out of the doldrums when the mail brought a cheerful note from Stu Keate, now publisher of the *Sun*, with a copy of page six a few days later. He had given a catchy headline and equal space to Hugh's friend, Farley Mowat, never one to miss an opportunity to defend the underdog and the environment. Mowat had sharpened his editorial knife to carve a few strips off the critic in rebuttal and Stu Keate's cheer-up note said this should even the score.

The Salmon People not only went on to deserved success, but on its 25th anniversary, a new edition was published by Whitecap Books in North Vancouver with an added introduction by McKervill, now Atlantic Regional Director for the Human Rights

Commission. He expressed pleasure at being vindicated a quarter of a century later.

There never seemed to be a time when something new did not pop up to challenge us, which practically guaranteed we would never be stuck in a rut. Eleanor had a very dear elderly friend, Molly Paterson, who lived at the end of the trail in the woods behind us. They shared an interest in gardening and art but on one of her visits, she asked Eleanor if I would like to read about her son's military citations and clippings. I was surprised and thrilled to discover that Molly and Jock's boy, George, had been decorated with three Military Crosses working for British Intelligence in Italy.

An escaped prisoner of war after a parachute drop, he had volunteered to return into Italian territory from a safe haven in Switzerland and had worked underground with the Italian Partisans. His decorations were not for killing the enemy, but for saving the lives of British escapees. From his first parachute drop in 1941 until the end of the war when he saw the mob turn on Mussolini, George Paterson's life had been in constant danger.

When I met him, he was a partner in a firm of forest-management consultants in Vancouver whose job took him to many parts of the world. He knew there was a story to tell and though he had little time to spare, he wanted to please his mother. I took him to meet John Windsor and they decided to give it a try with John listening to George's story and putting it together. George would come over when he could get away and they worked together in fits and starts for the better part of a year.

As I realized this international war adventure was too important for a regional firm like ours to handle properly, I got in touch with an agent in London. Curtis Brown found that Hodder & Stoughton were interested and they arranged to design and print in the United Kingdom, running our edition with theirs. John advised Lord Fraser, head of St. Dunstan's, that the book was in progress and he arranged for John and Pam to visit Britain. John met Field Marshal Viscount Montgomery at the House of Lords where they were photographed for the dust jacket of the book and Monty wrote the introduction. They decided to call the book *The Mouth of The Wolf*.

The title was taken from a well-known saying of the Italian Partisans. When they slipped out of hiding to undertake a dangerous task, they said it was "Into the mouth of the wolf", a valiant gesture and phrase to those they were leaving behind. They all knew there was a price on their heads and they also knew, in grim detail, what the Gestapo did to those who were caught. In the worst cases it was known that they crucified their victims by hanging them on a meat hook where they were left to die.

The book was published in England and Canada simultaneously in 1967 and appeared in paperback, published by Collins, 11 years later. The story was a modest success in Canada but the experience left me disappointed with our general attitude toward our decorated veterans. Many who had done outstanding things on their own initiative, and had survived the war, remained unrecognized. I tried to arouse interest in Vancouver where the media might have been pleased to discover a man with these unusual accomplishments living in their midst. I had even entertained hopes that a film script might emerge to compete with the fiction that was appearing. Alas, though real-life heroes may be recognized in the United States and the United Kingdom, Canada must keep ours under cover.

Our greatest pleasure was to see the delight in the eyes of Jock and Molly when George and John appeared to autograph books in Sidney. George was also able to get in touch with the leader of the Partisan group he had been associated with, now a successful engineer, for an update on those who had survived. They were still referred to by their code names, because apparently George seldom knew who they really were, for the safety of their families.

While we seemed to be running along peacefully at cruising speed, it was merely a temporary slow-down in our surging momentum. Behind the scenes a heady brew, innocently stirred in the past, was fermenting. As we became known for publishing west-coast hopefuls, telephone calls and letters tried to draw our attention to others trying for that first break. Time and again I was told to watch for a Vancouver Island native, George Clutesi, who had an important message for those interested in our west-coast Indian culture. Every time he appeared to talk to non-native groups I would get another request to look him up. But I really had too much on my plate at the time and kept putting the idea on a back burner. Finally, it was a very positive letter from a schoolteacher in Ladysmith that left me feeling guilty and nudged me into action. She described the effect he had had on a group talking about his people, their legends and their moral standards. To nail it down she included his address on the reserve beside Sproat Lake, between Port Alberni and Long Beach.

When I made the next book-selling trip up-island, which I tried to do with each new title, travelling as far as Campbell River, I set out one afternoon in search of Clutesi. His house was at the end of a lane well back from the highway. I knocked at the door and a youngster said he was working on the roof. I walked around the substantial house, found the ladder and called to a figure with his back to me.

"What do you want?" he called in a flat tone.

"I want to ask about your stories. I'm a publisher."

"I'm busy," he said, and went on working.

I had a mind to scribble a note with my address and leave it at that, but on impulse I climbed the ladder and edged over to him. I had to talk quickly because it was getting dark and I started by asking if he remembered the teacher and the Ladysmith group. He nodded. I explained that I had only called because she thought I could help, and jotted my name, address and telephone number. He nodded again, took the note and I climbed down and drove away. I had completed my part of the commitment but as I reached the main road I was convinced the stop was a total loss. I did not learn until much later that George Clutesi had tried to interest publishers in eastern Canada, had been turned down brusquely on more than one occasion and had understandably lost all hope.

Weeks later there was a telephone call and when I answered, a flat, lifeless voice said, "This is George Clutesi."

"Where are you?"

"At the airport. Leaving for Montreal. EXPO. Got something for you."

"I'll be there in ten minutes."

When we met for the second time, he was less distant but still cool. He handed over a packet, saying he was on his way to paint a mural for the Indian Pavilion at EXPO '67. I thanked him, and said we would take good care of his material and let him know in a few weeks. He turned and left.

When I opened the parcel and riffled through the pages, the contents left me dismayed. I scanned uneven typing on tired paper, disconnected sentences which simply did not flow, and certainly failed to fit the lyric descriptions of his patrons. Only the illustrations held up. Thank goodness he was busy in

Montreal and I had time to figure out how to let him down gently. One day I went to see Mary Gibbs about this. She had always taken a personal interest in our Indian neighbours who lived on three reserves along our waterfront. She had played such an active part in their welfare that Chief Underwood of the Tsartlips had invited her as a guest to some of their longhouse ceremonies. Mary had been a tower of strength helping with *Blind Date* so I told her all about my encounter with Clutesi and how I felt about the manuscript.

Mary asked to have a look at it and began to sort out the meanings of the sentences. She understood and arranged the legends in sequence and began to type a crisp copy. She suggested a title, *Son of Raven Son of Deer*, which she felt suited the native rhythm with words. By the time George returned from his Montreal assignment we were ready for him with the good news. He brightened up and confessed to Mary that he had been trying to get these legends published for 22 years. It was the start of a long and fruitful friendship and bonding between Mary and George. Once we were committed to publish, they spent hours together, exploring Indian thoughts and ways of expression and putting them into understandable English for the average reader in a form that would also be acceptable to George.

His illustrations became clearer and sharper, opening the possibility of a new art form with economy of line. The enthusiasm of Mary and George began to spread and the suspicious personality of the author turned to one of charm and understanding. When all was ready and in order I gathered the legends and illustrations and took the problem to Charlie Morriss for production and design ideas. It was another turning point.

It did not take long for Morriss and his team to realize that here was an artistic challenge, to turn the 12 stories that had been handed down in the Clutesi family for hundreds of years into a visual classic. When Charlie saw the drawings he wanted George to help him select the right shades of colours for the title page and end papers, particularly the red. He produced these fables of the Tse-Shaht People in hardcover, with Ko-ishin-mit and his herring rake in red, black and a touch of blue on the yellow jacket. He used beautiful typefaces for the original poetry, giving a full page for the illustrations of each character, and achieving a mystical quality. Events began to happen with little warning.

The first indication was when Pat Bluett decided on an autograph party to introduce this newly discovered talent. She was another Deep Cove neighbour, a close friend of Mary Gibbs, who had recently opened the Book Nook in Centennial Square, Victoria, in the heart of town. It was a nice location if book people in Oak Bay, Royal Oak and the outskirts could be persuaded to attend. I took my time driving in, loaded with extra books just in case, but I was really not expecting anything unusual.

When I turned up I thought there had been an accident. People were milling about the square and starting to form a queue, and Pat's little store was packed with some important-looking citizens. Pat had volunteers directing traffic, with clerks handing out copies to people lined up for George to autograph. The cash register was singing a merry tune and the mood was like old-home week. Even Dr. Douglas Leechman, our creative-writing instructor, showed up with quite a few academics and writers. It was a heady moment for George, but if he felt slightly dazed by it all, he did not let on. However, to say it was just an unexpected surprise would be an understatement, because the first reporter on the scene called for someone else from his office to come and verify what he was witnessing. George, the centre of the scrum while everyone was trying to monopolize his attention, kept his cool. In fact he acted as if he had been expecting this to happen all his life.

Pat Bluett remembered the incident as the break her little store needed to put it on the map. She put modest notices of George Clutesi's appearance between 3:00 and 4:30 in the two Victoria dailies and because we were close neighbours, she had taken extra books on consignment and dressed her window with a display of 25 copies, opened to show the illustrations. She believed it was the advance publicity before the book was published, together with curiosity at seeing Indian legends actually in print, plus word of mouth for she noticed many visitors from out of town, including some important native leaders from Port Alberni.

She had engaged a waitress from the restaurant beside the McPherson Theatre to serve tea and cakes and when she noticed George perspiring in the press of people, trying to write names, answer questions and please several fans at once, she asked him if he would care to retire to the back room and have a quiet cup of tea.

"Oh no," he said, "I'm having too good a time."

The crowd did not leave until after 5:30. Pat sold all her stock and the extra boxes I had to carry in from the next block, through the crowds. Then she stripped her window display and sold the lot. In the buying frenzy she found that customers were returning to pick up extra copies when they realized the little volume had opened a window to the mystery of the legends. And in the midst of her busiest day she received a phone call from the manager of the Hudson's Bay who wanted to know what the book was all about. Their customers were calling to order copies on their charge accounts.

Later we went to Vancouver, George and I, where we discovered the Victoria experience was not a flash in the pan. We booked into the York Hotel, which was closest to Duthie Books, and most reasonable, where the friendly staff gave us first-class service. This was the first time George revealed any bitterness from his past.

"When I was working on the docks," he said, "they refused me a room here."

"Perhaps they were booked up."

George Clutesi and Gray. (PHOTO BY DANE CAMPBELL)

"I hung round the entrance and watched other people come in and get rooms."

In the restaurant, when I informed the waitress that she was serving a famous author, her surprise and George's delight at the special attention quickly changed his mood. After breakfast we walked the short block to call on Bill Duthie, who had arranged an autograph party which, I had cautioned George, might not be quite as busy as the Victoria one. Bill must have made some extra calls, in addition to a mailing, because many regulars, as well as the curious, turned up. The biggest surprise to me was an old friend from *The Victoria Times* who arrived with a columnist whose name would soon win acclaim. It was Stu Keate, publisher of the *Sun*, with Alan Fotheringham. Stu had a cottage at Sproat Lake and it appeared that he and George were old friends. They sat with George to chat and watch his graceful performance.

We spent several days calling at stores to autograph copies. George fully enjoyed making new friends with the buyers, but I distinctly recall beginning to feel my 55 years. While I left the author comfortably settled on the fourth floor of the Bay I was dashing for the parking lot, lugging 40-pound boxes of books to a spare elevator and delivering them to the person responsible for receiving. When the book department was on the ground floor I had to carry them through crowded aisles.

Bill Duthie had also arranged an important meeting for an evening radio interview with another popular personality who would soon rocket to international fame. Jack Webster (the sterling oatmeal savage) had a tiny cubicle in the basement of the old Georgia Hotel in those days. From there he entertained, informed and stimulated Vancouver families in the early evening. He wanted to meet us first in a quiet corner of the basement pub where the wall behind us had an enlargement of Stu Keate's headline announcing the death of Winston Churchill. I was the one who was nervous about how the soft-spoken George Clutesi would stand up to the fierce little public figure with the Glasgow accent. He was well known for puncturing the bubbles of egotists. If there was any sign of weakness or phoniness he was expected to go in for the kill.

George never took a drink so we ordered a pop and waited for Webster to sweep in. He was amiable, delighted with George's replies to his questions and interested in the book's illustrations of the mythical animal characters. He stopped at page 62, studied three stylized figures and read the description, "Son of Bear loved to swat salmon with his left hand." After a few more questions Jack told us how to find his cubbyhole and said he would expect us around seven. He left me still slightly nervous at the impending exposure.

Finally we were ushered through several doors into a quiet room; Webster waved us into a corner while he pushed buttons, and handled the telephone and mike as lights went off and on. This was a remote from the main studio and we were apparently standing by. After more intercom, Jack motioned to George to stand beside him and you could feel the tension of the moment. Then they were on.

"There's a guy here," rasped Webster, "who claims bears are left-handed."

George's face lit up in a beautiful smile, "That's right."

"If I came up to a bear with his back to me and tapped him on the shoulder, what would he do?" challenged Webster.

And they were off at a gallop in a delightful romp that must have had many a family chuckling and those homeward bound slowing for the next quip. When Webster finally turned it over to the public for questions, the calls came in thick and fast, building interest as host and guest played their parts. Voices came on the air from remote parts of the province calling to George, "Remember me?": buddies recalling incidents from logging, fishing and pile-driving days.

From then on Jack Webster never turned me down if I showed up with an author. Eleanor came along once to meet him and, watching one of his shows, summed him up neatly.

"He's just a lovable pussy-cat," she decided, "but he tries to hide it."

We lost no time riding the crest of this wave. George and I travelled up Vancouver Island visiting bookstores, staying in motels, and meeting librarians and the press. At Nanaimo I was left standing alone in a shop while the well-known mayor, Frank Ney, took the newsworthy author away for coffee and treats. It was a humbling lesson in the status of the publisher. When we stopped at Parksville for a meal, George told me that this was another place that had refused to serve him when he was logging or fishing.

When we went to Port Alberni for the autograph party there, it was almost as great a success as Pat Bluett's in Victoria. Charlie Morriss came along, and with him and the Barclays, Eleanor and

I celebrated with a hilarious dinner party. The little book and craft store in Port Alberni was crowded with officials and citizens from organizations anxious to celebrate their favourite native son's finally receiving recognition.

Another time, a bit more of George's darker side surfaced when we called at the book department of a large store. Some of the well-wishers had been connected with his early education. He recalled those days when Indian children were forbidden to speak their native tongue at school, and were not allowed to sing or dance in their traditional way.

On a later visit, my arrival in Port Alberni with more books coincided with a civic luncheon which the mayor and council had organized. There was consternation at the bookstore when I arrived with no knowledge of this event.

"Can you do something with George?" the owner asked.

"What's wrong?"

"They're all waiting for him and he won't leave home."

"Why wouldn't he jump at it?"

"They forgot to invite his wife, and he won't appear without her."

I left them to sort it out themselves and to this day I don't know how or if it was resolved.

I was too busy keeping up with orders, alternating quick sales trips with typing invoices, and packing books in the boxes we made with recycled cardboard. John Barclay had a job trying to keep us honest with his accounting skills and Tim was travelling farther afield into Alberta with a small van. I will never forget the Sidney post office in those days; they had a fine group of local citizens who worked flat out to help us along by expediting the increased flow of traffic. Sometimes late in the day we would drive in with a truck-load of parcels and someone had to volunteer extra time to get them away. It did help to raise their category as a post office, which pleased them, and we made a point to remember them at Christmas. The ladies received chocolates and the men a bottle of cheer.

We were sailing along on a tranquil sea of orders and cash flow when one day the telephone rang, and the message blew us off course. It started with a friendly enquiry about our progress and how we managed to discover the Indian author, George Clutesi. The caller was an official of the provincial Department of Education, speaking for a deputy minister, I suspect, and he tried to explain just how the department worked. They were

Tim setting off on a sales trip in the van, 1968.

having a serious discussion about getting *Son of Raven Son of Deer* into the schools. The friendly voice warned us to be prepared for an important letter, and advised us to seek advice before replying. He pointed out that we could lose this opportunity unless we clearly understood that a textbook order from the government is not in the same category as orders from either bookstore chains or libraries and it was most important to know the form. The voice wished us well, congratulated us on our progress, and signed off.

John Barclay and I both stopped work and tried to assess this unexpected hurdle. No one we knew had ever had to handle a textbook order. Local printers did not have either the machinery or space for large printings and the only firms that dealt in textbooks were on the other side of the mountains. But we did know one man who might be able to help. I called Glen Hyatt, whose Evergreen Press handled telephone directories and printed the bulk of the textbooks in B.C. schools. They had also done good jobs with *Far Pastures* and *The Salmon People* in hardcover. He sounded both enthusiastic and pleased, and suggested we let him make enquiries, handle the preliminaries and be ready to assist us make the right response. Apparently our quotation would have to include a price for the initial order and sufficient copies in the first printing to include back-up stock to meet future orders. We sat back, relieved, temporarily on course again.

The important, coldly efficient letter arrived and we replied with the figures and response that Glen Hyatt had recommended, based on an initial printing of 80,000 copies. There was another quiet spell and we were busy enough to put ambitious thoughts aside until there was another telephone call, still friendly, which asked us to get hold of George Clutesi and appear with him for a press conference at the Parliament Buildings.

We were taken in to meet the Honourable Leslie Peterson, and when the members of the press gallery filed in the big announcement was made. *Son of Raven Son of Deer* had been selected as a textbook. George Clutesi's years of struggle had received recognition at last with an official blessing. At the moment I was not sure he realized just what it meant for he showed no trace of excitement or pleasure. The press asked a few questions, but showed little reaction; the only ones with pleased smiles seemed to be the government officials. In today's context, with natives everywhere gaining long-overdue recognition, it is probably no big deal. But at the time, it was a milestone. *Son of Raven Son of Deer* had appeared in June 1967 and sold 4,000 copies in four weeks. A second printing of 5,000 was ordered and in ten months of its first year 80,000 copies were printed.

George went back to his home, but not to rest on his laurels. He was attracting boys and girls in all the bands within reach, teaching them the traditions and ceremonies that had been handed down from his father's generation and kept alive in story, song and dance. He brought a troop to Victoria where they performed at the McPherson Theatre.

He also took his ambitious ideas to Mary Gibbs again and told her about the almost-forgotten tales that he wanted to develop and preserve in print. She was concerned that he might be the last of the story-tellers to keep their traditions alive, to help the Tse-shaht clan hold on to their communion with nature and the environment. He brought his manuscript to her in a succession of visits and together, they made sure that his Indian thoughts and phrases could be understood by all races when they appeared in print. It was a task that would take several years to complete.

Meanwhile, the first large shipment of the textbook of *Son of Raven* was delivered from Evergreen straight to the government warehouse and all we had to do was send an invoice. When it was processed, the first big cheque we had ever received popped up in our mail; it caused John Barclay and me many interruptions for days, just looking at it, photographing it, and wondering how it had all come about.

When I finally took the cheque to the bank for deposit, wiping out the overdraft and our monthly payments of interest, the bank manager seemed on the verge of tears. He was losing a pretty good customer whose value had been increasing. He glanced at the very substantial figure, looked up and said wistfully, "I hope we can still be friends." We were foolish enough to believe the days of high risk were over.

The moccasin telegraph must have been working far and wide in the book world. Some time later we listened to a C.B.C. openline talk show discussing arts and The Canada Council. A voice from Montreal broke in with an indignant comment about an unknown publisher in British Columbia who had produced a book by an obscure Indian that had gone into the school system and was selling in astronomical numbers. He seemed to resent the fact it had been accomplished without an assist from The Canada Council. What on earth was the world coming to?

Eleanor and I were beginning to feel the stress. She had been fielding telephone calls, putting up with itinerant visitors and helping to decide on manuscripts as well as looking after the garden and the children. We had paid off the bank and, at John Barclay's suggestion, we had adjusted George Clutesi's royalty payment to include a hefty bonus. Aladdin Travel in Sidney had a bargain holiday package that included a charter flight to Portugal, a week of guided tours and a week on the island of Madeira. We booked it and let friends know that we were trying to slow down. The boys could look after themselves for a while and a close neighbour offered to take Cathy into her home. When we went to pick up our tickets, the agent said they had already been paid for, a gift from our fairy godmother in Banff.

It had been a very good year.

Chapter Eight

WHEN 1968 rolled around and we had put up a clean, unmarked calendar, we all felt it would be a good idea to try and keep it spotless. In other words, we agreed it would be wise to slow our pace and literally catch our breath.

In the meantime, of course, things continued to happen. Mary was working steadily with George Clutesi, trying to bring alive the subjects that until now had been bottled up. We continued to pass manuscripts on to Flos Williams for evaluation for we felt the authors deserved an intelligent response. There were several approaches from the academic world and an interesting bit of early western history from Edmonton. But we tried to persist in the idea of dampening the fires of ambition because we had proved our point. Our publishing endeavour could make its way, at least on a break-even level, but we weren't prepared to expand.

Only one thing kept gnawing at my conscience. Capi Blanchet had never had a fair shake with her little classic *The Curve of Time*. Back in 1961, when we had first become friends, we had shared her dismay when her book, published in the United Kingdom, had never reached its British Columbia, west-coast market.

Capi had received six copies of the first edition in March 1961, one for each of her children and one for herself. Eleanor had been able to get her hands on Capi's copy and probably was the first in our neck of the woods to realize that it was not only a superb account of coastal cruising but something uniquely more. Capi had combined history and the environment with word-pictures, connecting characters out of the past and the present with the mysteries and moods of the west coast.

However, there were no books available in Victoria or Vancouver for her many friends. Capi wrote to her publisher in Edinburgh who advised that 700 copies were shipped to a distributor in Toronto. To help get it into British Columbia, she made a loan so the small Cornish bookstore in Sidney could order stock. At the time, I sent off reviews as far east as *The Beaver* magazine in Winnipeg and caught the attention of C.B.C. producer Bob Orchard. He came to visit us and meet Capi, more than a little annoyed that he could not find the book in Vancouver. He shared our indignation and helped stir things up, but before Capi received full recognition for her work, other than the enthusiasm of friends, her heart decided to quit.

When we were struggling to get John Windsor's book published I remembered these details of Capi's frustration and disappointment. In six years we had proved quite a few times that there was merit in regional publishing. Now I got in touch with Capi's family, convinced that her work had a sustaining quality and could still make its way if we could produce it locally. The children agreed and wrote to Blackwood's for clearance.

We picked up the extra material that Capi had been working on and I took it to Mary Gibbs. She carefully stitched in two more chapters towards the end of the original edition, working with Eleanor's autographed copy. (We now have this Blackwood's copy marked in pencil with Mary's editorial notes.) I took this to Charlie Morriss who treated the work with great respect. With Gus Rueter designing the frontispiece and title page and Charlie the typography, this first Canadian edition consisted of 225 pages in hardcover, with a map and beautiful pencil sketches. The original had been 202 pages.

Now the reviews poured out in superlatives; the book went on to seven printings through 1990, 1991 and 1993, appearing in trade paperback and mass-market paperback editions. On the book's 30th anniversary, Whitecap Books in North Vancouver brought out their special edition which has helped keep it on many best-seller lists in the trade.

While 1968 appeared to sail along, John Barclay and I were lulled into thinking that our responsibilities and risks were behind us: we were finally clear at the bank, the printers had been paid and the royalty cheques had gone out on time. We were definitely not in the mood to look for more challenges. What we failed to realize was that the energy that had built up to get us this far was not going to dissipate.

In 1969 two forces were gathering to interrupt our peaceful, rural life-style. The mail continued to fill our large box at the post office with manuscripts that someone had to look at and comment upon. Also, every printer who had helped us along was eager to have a share in the next project that might interest us. Their confidence was not a good thing for it increased the temptation to gamble and weakened the practical side of business. That, and the euphoria caused by the large textbook cheque for the first Clutesi book!

One peaceful morning I took a call from around Campbell River. It was a man with an impediment in his speech trying to interest us in a strange-sounding topic and I asked him to repeat the subject of the book he had written with illustrations.

"Chinese brothels in British Columbia," he repeated.

"With illustrations?"

"Of course," he said. "Some in colour."

I asked him to hold on and called out to John in the other room.

"Want to look at an illustrated book on Chinese brothels?"

"Why not," he replied, so I told the voice to send it along and gave him our address. In due time a neat package arrived and we opened a tidy, serious study of artifacts and the history of last-century Chinatowns in old mining and railway camps with photographs of unusual medicine and nostrum *bottles*. We had to report regretfully that we did not think there would be a large enough market.

George Clutesi, working with Mary Gibbs, handed us another winner with the title *Potlatch*. We took it to Charlie Morriss who produced a book in hardcover, using the native red for the dust jacket and end papers, yellow and black on the title page and George's illustrations covering full pages. A first printing in May 1969 was quickly followed by a second in August and a third in May 1971. If I remember correctly, with George's name established, we did a first printing of 5,000, followed by print runs of 3,000. In 1973 a paperback edition followed.

When we started publishing we made every decision with a shortage of working capital and confidence. Our first books were in softcover with the cheapest binding. When they had sold enough copies and had attracted the attention of critics, we brought them out in hardcover with the pages properly stitched. After the gamble with *Far Pastures* in hardcover and dust jacket had paid off, we switched to hardcover initially and later turned out a softcover version so the books would be within reach of students who could ill afford the more deluxe edition. This became even more important when we got into the larger format art books.

Although we were determined to avoid more responsibility in 1968, creative ideas continued to pressure us. It was no longer just a case of trying to help an unknown get a start, but a feeling that something worthwhile might get lost unless we helped to save it. Iris Allan in Edmonton had caught my attention with her study of the life of James Morrow Walsh of the North-West Mounted Police. Mrs. Allan had been studying and writing western Canadian history, and for 15 years she had been producing radio dramas for school broadcasts in Alberta. Major Walsh was the remarkable Mountie who handled Sitting Bull and his warriors when they escaped across the border after the Custer Massacre. Walsh, almost single-handed, had shown such magnificent bravery in standing up to Sitting Bull's bluff that the chief had called him "White Sioux", which we had decided would make a fine selling title.

Things began to happen as though there was something mysterious manipulating puppet strings. Glen Hyatt of Evergreen Press, probably impressed with the surprising success of *Far Pastures* and *Son of Raven Son of Deer*, decided to pay us a visit, bringing with him a red-headed new Canadian from Germany who had a great sense of humour combined with Teutonic determination. Gerry Siebert had been a schoolboy when World War Two started and had been pitched into battle as a Hitler youth to try and stop the invading tide in the final year. He became a prisoner of the Americans. His family had lost their estate when the Russians swept through and he had come to the New World to start again from scratch.

Gerry gave us his full attention and helped us over many a hurdle, which meant that gradually he became a close friend of our family. It started when I showed him the Walsh manuscript and told him that I had actually met Major Walsh's Sergeant Bob McCutcheon who had played a prominent part in a dramatic arrest. The irrepressible Gerry took the manuscript away before

I realized what was happening and set to work designing a book. From then on he paid regular visits which we welcomed, for he had international experience in the book world.

By 1969 we had also attracted the attention of a few in the academic world. Two professors of history with attractive subjects wanted to discuss their projects. I was in awe of scholarship and still as naive as the day I told John Windsor he could be a success with his first book.

From the University of Victoria, S.W. (Toby) Jackman was in the process of writing a history of British Columbia based on the careers of its political leaders. The series of sketches could easily fit our list, but before I could summon the fortitude to go ahead, it seemed that Gerry Siebert came along from Vancouver and took it back to Evergreen. It became a book titled *Portraits of the Premiers*.

From Royal Roads Military College, William Rodney had written about Kootenai Brown, western Canada's most famous legend about whose achievements no fiction had to be spun. Rodney had spent 15 years in historical research to track this soldier of fortune, buffalo hunter, prospector, and wolfer who had once been captured by Sitting Bull. I had not only grown up with the legend of Kootenai during my seven young years in the R.C.M.P., but we knew someone who had known him and could add details about his life.

When Annora Brown, our old friend from the foothills ranching days, was a little girl at Fort Macleod, Kootenai used to call on her father on his trips to town from his cabin at Waterton Lakes. He had become the first superintendent of Waterton Lakes National Park and Canada's first conservationist. Annora's dad, an ex-Mountie, was one of the first magistrates in Fort Macleod and Kootenai (no relation) called him "Dr. Brown" because he had been able to relieve an upset stomach with some patent medicine. This one we had to publish and I took it to Charlie Morriss. So away we went again, on another wave of enthusiasm, supported by the printers' continuing interest and belief in us, and the bank manager's wanting us to be more than friends, to the extent of a temporary loan or two.

With both books, I discovered my limitations as a *bona fide* publisher; I took too much for granted, expecting the trained academics to accept responsibility for checking their own galleys. Then I began to detect a subtle difference in style between chapters and when I found spelling and punctuation changes and pointed them out, I was told that must have been the Japanese typist in the pool! I also suspected that there were parts of the manuscripts where dictating and plain old sitting down to the discipline of writing seemed to mix. But I did not feel sufficiently qualified to criticize.

Bill Rodney and I had both ridden over the Kootenai country and knew the hazards Kootenai had faced when traversing the untamed frontier, without trails or bridges, at certain times of the year. Annora had also mentioned that it was important to describe some of the famous tragedies when horse and rider had simply disappeared. When I suggested adding more colour, the author was adamant. No colour unless his research could prove it. Bill Rodney was not going to slip into fiction and I had to admire this principle.

We became close friends over this and we had another bond as well. He had also flown in Bomber Command, completed tours and had won the Distinguished Flying Cross and Bar. In his student days Bill had worked for the Waterton Lakes Park Service and that was when he began to track the famous fighter's past.

After I had taken the book to typesetting, Bill went off to Europe on a sabbatical, which left me responsible for doing all the proof-reading. The reward could not have been sweeter than his cable after I had airmailed a copy to London, hot off the press. It arrived when he was travelling on the continent. His silence left me in suspense until I received the following:

JUST RETURNED THRILLED WITH KOOTENAI DEEPEST
THANKS FOR SUPREME EFFORT AND WARMEST REGARDS BILL

It turned out that I had indeed made a mistake on the dustjacket blurb when I failed to capitalize the word Fellow. This is the way I had written it:

He holds degrees from the Universities of Alberta, Cambridge and London, is a fellow of the Royal Historical Society.

All was forgiven when the book went on to become a solid standard on our list, was awarded the University of British Columbia's Medal for Popular Biography and received a Certificate of Merit from the American Association for State and Local History.

The Daily Colonist in January 1970 had an article about the book by Bill Thomas who reported that Rodney told him, after submitting the manuscript to a Toronto publisher, "I was a bit shocked at what they said...it had great promise but should be fictionalized and made more romantic.... Here was Kootenai Brown and they wanted romantic fiction." So he brought it to us. In the end we were satisfied that the work by Dr. Rodney proved equally popular with students, the public and academics for its depth of research combined with a story-telling style.

With 1969 behind us, for all our good intentions to slow the pace, we found that we had added four big titles, all in hardcover, and at least two had appeared on our list through the energies of our new friend Gerry Siebert. One of them, *Portraits of the Premiers,* was in a pretty expensive-looking style, with gold lettering on a leathery cover. Gerry had wanted to try out an idea he had picked up when he had worked for *Reader's Digest* in Montreal, believing it had a better chance to promote sales. Jim Nesbitt in a review pointed out some careless editing, particularly when the name of one of the premiers was misspelled and that is when I realized my own responsibilities.

I don't recall by what miracle we managed to handle the financial end. I was too busy running to keep ahead, leaving that to Barclay, the solid citizen. But I do remember bringing my worries to Glen Hyatt, head of Evergreen.

"Glen, this fellow Siebert scares me. He bosses me into doing things before I'm ready."

"To be perfectly honest," he replied, "he frightens us too."

What we did not know was that Gerry Siebert was just warming up to give us all the roller-coaster ride of our lives. However, we were determined that 1970 would be a year of peace and quiet.

Chapter Nine

CALL IT fate, or pure chance, but we were not going to be let
off the hook as easily as we wanted. In the summer of 1969
Eleanor and I had taken a short break and escaped to the
Porcupine Hills in southern Alberta. We hoped that seeing the
old friends we had left, and the improvements the new owners
had made on our old ranch, would help to slow us down. On the
way we planned to stop at the Bar-S Ranch near Nanton to find
out what was causing Maxine Chattaway enough concern to
write us at length.

She was the wife of George Chattaway, a retired experimental
farm researcher, and the daughter of Rod McLay, a prominent
pioneer cattleman. On their visit to Vancouver Island in our
more carefree days, we had taken them sailing. Her letter a few
years later was a surprise, until I recalled that she had been
interested in our discovery of George Clutesi. Her letter told
about a visit to the spread of her sister, Dorothy Blades, where
she picked up an interesting wood carving and sketch. Where,
she asked Dorothy, had she found these?

A young Indian from the Eden Valley Reserve had called at
the kitchen door and offered them for sale, said Dorothy.
Maxine asked her sister to send the young man around to the
Bar-S the next time he appeared. And that is how she met Sarain
Stump, a tall, handsome youth of 24. She bought several pencil
sketches which were drawn on brown paper grocery bags.

Realizing that here was a talent that should be helped and encouraged, she had written us a forceful letter. Not a person to be diverted if she decided something was worthwhile, she asked us to engage him to illustrate a book, or find him a job doing art work for a magazine. She added that he had drifted into Alberta from Wyoming, and was living in a pretty bleak environment; someone had to do something. She judged him above average.

We had been itching to get away and visit our old stomping grounds and this was just the excuse we needed. On July 20, 1969, we arrived at the Bar-S, a very modern, efficient spread, to a warm welcome. Arrangements had been made for our visit to Eden Valley next day. After dinner we sat glued to the television set watching mankind's first landing on the moon, an eerie sensation from our lonely rangeland environment. We climbed the stairs to bed in a strange mood and looked out on a sparkling, clear night to stare at the moon and simply wonder at it all. What we had been watching on the screen was actually happening up there!

The contrast next day was also weird as after breakfast we set off to bounce over back trails, threading our way through one of the less-equipped reserves. We were, in fact, stepping into the past after a visit the night before into the stratosphere. There was no sign of life—no dogs, horses or children which are usually a part of the landscape—as we drove through the heat, turned into a deserted yard and found a lone person on a bench, whittling. There was Sarain.

We had a slow start with a diffident, very shy young man who responded only to Maxine's questions, answering ours with a nod. When I asked where everyone was he pointed with his knife over the hill behind him and muttered they were all at the church service. To our apology for keeping him from attending, he shrugged his shoulders and shook his head as if to indicate it didn't matter to him; as an outside influence it was a waste of time. Obviously he was in no hurry to open up until he could figure out our motives and it reminded me of my awkward first encounter with George Clutesi when I had to climb the ladder to his roof to get his attention. Finally Eleanor broke the ice by asking if we could see his drawings. Without a word or change of expression he put down his whittling, went into the shack and emerged with a parcel under his arm. He unrolled it and passed the work around. We stood there studying the figures sketched in pencil and I tried to decipher the words, some of which were in English. We suspected his art was a personal matter, not shared with the Eden Valley people who might consider it a waste of time, or ridicule it. I asked why he had not shown these particular drawings to anyone else.

"I think they're too strong for white man," he replied.

It was Eleanor who realized his potential, whispering to me that this young fellow did not have to illustrate the writing of others; he had a book inside him. She said he should use his own words to describe each sketch and tell us the meaning. He began to react with interest for the first time. How should he start?

I pointed around the yard to the shells of cars that had been cannibalized and left to rust. You should get that in, I told him and, pointing over the hill where the rest were at their Sunday meeting, that too.

Sarain gradually warmed to the plan. We told him about George Clutesi's west-coast fables and felt sure he had a message for us from the plains. Then Eleanor had a chat with Maxine, saying the boy should come to us for a visit as he needed better paper and equipment, and we could help him develop a theme. Possibly he could pick up encouragement from Clutesi. Maxine quickly agreed and said she would arrange it. There was nothing more to say, so after a more friendly parting, waving *au revoir*, we drove away leaving him standing there, a lonely figure.

We left the Bar-S knowing that Maxine was determined to lift the young man out of that depressing scene of poverty, indifference and neglect, and that we wanted to join her team. Then we drove the ridge in the back country south to our old range under Squaw Butte. It was a pleasant reunion with old friends but the scene we had left had undergone the changes we had predicted. The one-room country school had closed, and the old trails had been upgraded so the children could be taken to larger schools in Cowley and Lundbreck by bus. This was not entirely a good thing for it drew their interests away from home. When we called on former neighbours, the teenagers were all in town. We left before our feelings showed.

Some weeks later Maxine phoned to say that Sarain was coming by bus and would wait for us to pick him up at the ferry terminal. Our meeting was a big surprise as Maxine had taken him shopping in High River and we weren't sure that this was the young man we had met in the Eden Valley. He was decked out like a Texas millionaire, looking proud and confident in expensive cowboy boots, western jacket and string tie.

Eleanor had the cottage ready and had also been shopping for sketch pads, quality art paper and a variety of coloured felt pens. Sarain had never worked with colour and after we had showed him over the house and introduced the family, he wanted to practise with this new material. Eleanor set him up in our living-room with a large table looking over Saanich Inlet to the Malahat and we gave him some quiet time.

The next few mornings, right after breakfast, he asked if he could do some more work and we left him to it, taking him sight-seeing in the afternoons. Eleanor gathered up his practice lines and first tentative sketches, retrieving the ones he had tossed away and placing them all in a folder. Each drawing he completed was sending a message that cried for words to inter-pret it, a project he had to complete later. We could not have had a more perfect guest. He seemed most relaxed with Eleanor and mentioned that he had a son named Angus. Eleanor was intrigued to the point where she said, "Don't send me a photo of Angus, do a portrait." It is now a framed, treasured possession in our living room.

We showed him the sights and sounds of Victoria, including the world-class provincial museum with its Indian artifacts. He also had a visit in Port Alberni with George Clutesi whose second book, *Potlatch*, we had published in May 1969. Sarain was our guest from September 21 to 28 and Clutesi helped us send him back to Alberta with inspiration and enthusiasm.

Back at Eden Valley he went to work on sets of drawings with lines of spare verse that enlarged the meaning of each scene. He was creating a jolting, sharp, meaningful insight into a world on the other side of the ethnic curtain in North America. Intensive, it ranged through pent-up emotions from bitter to sweet. When the drawings were completed Maxine got them to us safely and we had in our possession a portfolio that stirred those who saw it for the first time and tried to understand. Stimulating, honest and strong, the words matched the scenes and we had a book in embryo.

Sarain had portrayed the shack with the hulks of cars, the missionary, the Indian agent and the booze. He had frozen the feelings that only an underprivileged minority can experience. He had put those feelings into words like the following:

And there is my people sleeping
Since a long time
But aren't just dreams
The old cars without engine
Parking in front of the house
Or angry words ordering peace of mind
Or who steals from you for your own good
And doesn't wanna remember what he owes you
Sometimes I'd like to fall asleep too,
But I can't
I can't

We began to handle the portfolio with reverence and we had a title. *There Is My People Sleeping* we felt, with the right cover, would make any bibliophile peek inside. I showed it to Charlie Morriss in Victoria. Charlie quickly realized the value of Sarain's work, and offered to design and print it. We knew that we were in good hands. He decided on a large format to display the art most advantageously, using coloured ink on the cover and end papers. Then he turned it over to a talented young designer, Bev Leech, who had just joined his staff. Bev went to work on the book and we knew Charlie was going overboard. All I could do was hold my breath. There was a problem in reproducing the drawings as Sarain had worked on a variety of paper using different pens and pencils. Once again we were in luck for Dick Morriss, Charlie's son who ran the firm later, did outstanding camera work and overcame the obstacles.

We kept in touch with Sarain who left the Eden Valley Reserve, and a "blanket marriage", (an arrangement without a ceremony) to start work on a cattle ranch for Albert McDonald. He was busy riding herd, helping with calving and feeding, generally doing the work of an all-round cowboy and living alone in a shack. When the book was in production we told him it would be 8½" by 9" and about an inch thick, and that everyone concerned was sure he would be pleased with the result. He replied that he was so excited at the news he had to tell someone about it and there wasn't a soul within miles. So he rode out on the range and talked to the cows. "I think they understood," he wrote.

The presses stopped finally in May 1970, and we picked up the first copies of *There Is My People Sleeping*, subtitled, *The Ethnic Poem-Drawings of Sarain Stump*. In our copy of the first printing he wrote the following:

MAY 1970

To MR. AND MRS. GRAY CAMPBELL
AS MOST OF MY PEOPLE, I GREATLY ADMIRE
SOMEBODY'S COURAGE. WHAT BROUGHT THIS
BOOK TO EXISTENCE IS, ABOVE ALL, YOUR
COURAGE. IF I WAS SITTING BULL, I'D CALLED
THE BOTH OF YOU "WHITE SIOUX", BEST WISHES
Sarain Stump

Tim hustled across British Columbia and Alberta in our camper, rationing copies to bookstores and selected publications for review, then headed for the McDonald ranch. Sarain was given time off and Tim drove him to Calgary where he was confronted by cameras, microphones and the press. The book quickly gained universal acceptance.

Back at the ranch, Sarain and Tim would unwind by saddling a couple of lively mounts and exuberantly dashing over the range. A warm and close friendship developed between them. When Sarain noticed that Tim was a southpaw he dubbed him the "Bear's Brother", for, as George Clutesi had said earlier, Indians generally believe all bears are left-handed, and they grew progressively as close as favourite cousins, sharing the hopes and dreams of youth.

After two printings, May and December, we realized that average students could not afford the beautiful Morriss edition so we produced a paperback which brought the price within reach, to sell at $2.95.

The book was just the start. At every step in our association Lady Luck was winging it for Sarain. Into the picture came our good friends and neighbours, the Garlands, from Ottawa, who had recently retired to Vancouver Island. Don had been office manager at the Indian Pavilion for EXPO '67 in Montreal. He had been most successful in handling the Indian artists who were selected to do the murals, shepherding our friend George Clutesi from the west coast, Gerald Tailfeathers, the Blackfoot from Alberta, Norval Morriseau, the Ojibway, and half a dozen others, all talented and temperamental, through the bureaucratic maze.

Don and Betty Garland had been quietly effective boosters behind the scenes for Clutesi's two books and when Don discovered Sarain emerging on the scene, he joined the fun. Don had the experience to draw out and promote all the young man's talents and he started to fire letters around and about, attracting more attention. Then he took Sarain to a lawyer and a chartered accountant, set himself up as an agent and began to stir up a campaign that kept Sarain busy turning out art work for exhibitions at Banff, Montreal and Ottawa.

Don treated him like a son leaving home for the first time. When he arranged to send Sarain to a prestigious show in Montreal, he included a careful letter of instructions with his air fare. It told him how to proceed from airport to hotel, what he would have to pay for a room, who would meet him from Indian Affairs and other timely tips. He enclosed $300, advising him to get money orders and only carry $50 in cash. And he was to call Don collect if he ran into any problem. Of course, most times Don forgot to charge for his services, well satisfied that he had an interesting hobby in retirement. His most treasured reward came in a stream of notes, sometimes cryptic, often funny, that flowed from his *protégé*.

Sarain wrote from the ranch after a trip to speak at Mount Royal College in Calgary. He tried to refuse a gratuity and wrote Don, "The teacher said that the college pays automatically lecturers and teachers of any kind." He added that he planned to take a trip to Mexico with a cousin, and ended abruptly: "Gotta stop now. It's time to go out with the lantern and see if any of the heifers had the bad idea to become mother tonight."

When Don sent him income tax forms to sign: "It's more taxes I ever paid in my whole life altogether. I must have been rich and didn't even know it."

As the sales of books and drawings escalated and his fame spread, Sarain was drawn out of the Eden Valley and the ranch job by a widening circle of friends. He moved around on both sides of the border until he settled on the staff of the Saskatchewan Indian Cultural College, teaching art. Amerindian cultures were being revitalized and Sarain found himself leading the rebirth that was taking place across the plains from his position in Saskatoon.

Then he met Linda Youens, a lovely, intelligent girl on the staff of the college in Saskatoon and they fell in love. As the first Indians of their generation who wanted a wedding in the old tradition, they had to find someone who could recall the rites. They discovered two elders, over 80, who could handle the day-long ceremony in their native tongue.

Only two non-native guests were invited. One was the well-known, respected and loved Catharine Whyte of Banff who had for years befriended the Stoney Indians at Morley, Alberta, and had opened doors for Sarain. The other was the "Bear's Brother", our son, Tim.

Sarain's career continued to prosper. The Department of Indian and Northern Affairs invited him to be guest editor and layout artist for the 1974 edition of *Tawow*, their slick, Indian cultural magazine. All contributors to that issue would be native people. Linda and Sarain threw themselves into the project with art, design, articles and poetry. The unexpected end of this saga is contained in a special insert in that edition by Mary E. Jamieson, the regular editor:

> Sarain Stump was a Cree-Shoshone from Wyoming. He was an artist, a poet, a philosopher and a spiritualist. He gained fame through the publishing of his book *There is My People Sleeping*, which contains some of Sarain's most sensitive words about his people.
>
> Sarain agreed to create one issue of *Tawow* and he called it "Immortality of Indian Art". I believe it to be a profoundly moving work of art. After he completed the magazine, he travelled to Mexico for a holiday.
>
> Sarain Stump drowned in the coastal waters on December 20, 1974.
>
> We will miss him, but his art and his humanity will truly make Sarain Stump immortal.

There is a photograph of Sarain with long braids and buckskin, beating a drum and chanting for the Round Dance with his own words:

> Don't break this circle
> Before the song is over
> Because all of our people
> Even the ones long gone
> Are holding hands

Maxine Chattaway was devastated when she telephoned us. Sarain had dedicated his book to her. He was on the threshold of a distinguished career, she cried, and had so much to offer.

Thus another chapter in our career came to a shattering end.

Chapter Ten

ONE FATEFUL day early in 1971 I was puzzled by a letter from New Brunswick whose content seemed strangely out of place yet was vaguely familiar. I had to read it twice before the penny dropped and blew me out of the present, forcing my mind back nearly half a century. It was a peculiar letter, written by F.G. Stanley, professor of history at Mount Allison University, but it triggered my recalling a strange experience in the early 1930s. It was an incident I had always hesitated to share with anyone.

In 1933, while serving in the R.C.M.P., I had been posted to Banff where I spent four interesting years. Then, it was an unspoiled, quiet mountain village in winter, while in summer tourists would pour in by special trains, cars and buses, and the villagers were happy to find seasonal work. When winter clamped down the community returned to its placid life with skiing in its infancy, curling, skating and parties.

One bitterly cold night in mid-winter I was alone on the main street on foot patrol, checking premises and looking for possible fires from overheated stoves. There wasn't another person in sight. Insulated by a heavy buffalo coat, moccasins and fur cap pulled well down over cheeks and ears, I still felt the wind chill. This least pleasant duty lasted one month on and two off. I was leaning into the wind on Banff Avenue when the silence was broken by the sound of a late car, driven quickly and heading south on the main street that stretched from Mount Norquay to the foot of Sulphur Mountain. I made sure the driver noticed that one of us was on duty. He slowed down, pulled into the curb and opened the passenger door.

"Jump in," he said, and I was grateful to get out of the wind.

As the car accelerated across the Bow River bridge with powder snow flying behind I recognized the driver; it was Norman Luxton who, with his brother Lou, operated the Sign of the Goat Trading Post in the log cabin at the end of the bridge. When we reached it, the volatile Norman, used to ordering people around, told me to follow him as he wrestled with his key, opened the door and disappeared into the darkened store. We made our way between display cases in this veritable museum to another door, leading to Norman's inner sanctum, where he switched on a light, checked his big heater and fired it up.

While we waited for the heat to build, Norman was in an expansive mood and wanted to talk. We settled comfortably in chairs and he reached into his roll-top desk, extracted a bottle and poured each of us a dram.

"You need this to fight that cold," he said with a smile and I felt the warmth before his heater started to pick up a glow.

Then he began to talk about a strange adventure he had had in his youth. I found it difficult to follow until he pulled out a journal, with photographs pasted in it, which was an account of a Pacific Ocean crossing by two men in a west-coast Indian canoe. Norman had bought this vessel and made a deal with a rather mysterious John Voss, a veteran seaman with unknown dark moods, to sail it into the Pacific with Norman as his mate. They had set sail from Victoria in May 1901. As he explained this he had me read descriptive bits here and there and pointed out the photographs. I began to understand the audacity of the enterprise and was impressed with the story.

"Why haven't you had it published?" I asked the man who had started Banff's weekly *Crag & Canyon*.

"It will never be published," he replied. "I said too much about Voss and others. I did this for my daughter."

"But surely, if it's true, it would make a great book."

Then he explained, briefly, the various dangers they had encountered with weather, and how each of them had reacted to emergencies. As he expanded, he described his suspicions about Voss and how he felt his life was in danger. Until the breaking point, when he locked Voss in the tiny cabin and sailed for days as if in a dream, with a loaded rifle across his knees. This tale, in the darkened, empty trading post in the middle of a brutal winter night, seemed slightly unreal. By the time the fire had picked up and was banked for the rest of the night, Luxton had got it out of his system. He drove me back across the bridge to my cold and lonely patrol. I was in a bit of a daze, scarcely believing it all, as if the ghostly half-light in the cabin had stirred both our imaginations.

Here I was, in 1970, wondering how to reply to this unexpected letter from Dr. Stanley, who had written on behalf of Eleanor Luxton. It had to be something related to the journal I recalled from that night. On October 26, 1962, Norman Kenny Luxton, newspaperman, hunter, trader, adventurer, sailor and early conservationist, had died in Calgary. He was buried in Banff among the pioneers while the Indians, in full ceremonial dress, held a special service. Of course, I was anxious to see the entire journal that Norman had talked about and displayed that weird night so many years ago, and curious to find out how his daughter, Eleanor, had managed to edit the remarkable story of Pacific adventure that he had left her.

After an exchange of letters with Dr. Stanley I got in touch with Eleanor Luxton, who flew out on a visit and left us the manuscript. Most of what I expected was there, with a great deal of additional background gleaned from family letters, her father's published works and details of his eventful life that he had revealed to her.

With Luxton family photographs and a selection from the British Columbia Provincial Archives, I went to visit with Charlie and Dick Morriss. We discussed how best to present this record. Luxton had said it was an answer to a book called *The Venturesome Voyages of Captain Voss*, by the man whose background and careers were shrouded in mystery.

Charlie handed the uneven photographs to Dick for processing and the design to that incomparable young man, Bev Leech, who turned *Tilikum / Luxton's Pacific Crossing* into a veritable art form. We had little trouble getting the book into major bookstores and enjoying fine reviews.

The year 1971 had been extremely busy and had also produced several surprises, one the result of a casual encounter on the Brentwood-Mill Bay ferry. In fine weather on the short run passengers mix as they walk about the small deck space, enjoying the scenery of Saanich Inlet. On one occasion we bumped into a friend whom I had met through John Shaw,

editor of the *Colonist's* magazine, *The Islander*. I introduced
Eleanor to Cecil (Nobby) Clark, retired deputy commissioner of
the fabled British Columbia Provincial Police. We were on our
way to the west coast and Nobby was on a short trip to Ladysmith
to check out a story he was interested in. For nearly a hundred
years, the B.C.P.P. had been North America's oldest territorial
constabulary; then it was taken over by the younger R.C.M.P. in
1950. Nobby Clark in his retirement had become the unofficial
historian of the outfit he had joined at the age of 17 and served
with distinction for 35 years.

Eleanor was intrigued by his anecdotes, ranging from mysterious geological discoveries to fascinating details about the
places we were going to visit. His personal knowledge of British
Columbia, combined with an ability to recall names and dates,
made him a master at weaving a good story. We were so
enthralled it was the shortest crossing we had ever made on that
ferry. At parting I thanked Nobby, said, "You should write a
book," and thought nothing more about it.

At least a year after this encounter John Barclay and I were
extremely busy getting out book orders and doing accounts
when a little Volkswagen stopped at the barn and who should
unwrap himself but Nobby Clark.

"Here's the book you told me to write," he said, handing me a
package, and it took me a moment to recall the incident on the
ferry. Another book at this time was a bit more than we had
anticipated or felt we could handle. We got through the visit by
showing Nobby our set-up.

As I read the manuscript, Nobby Clark's *Tales of the British
Columbia Provincial Police* had two things going for it. It was a
well-constructed and beautifully crafted series of true adventures
concerning this unique organization over the 93 years of its
history. Also, there was a ready audience of old-timers scattered
through the land with their own memories of rum runners,
smugglers, horse thieves and hold-ups, eager for more stories of
the "good old days." I managed to convince myself that we
couldn't miss and made another run into Victoria to have a chat
with Charlie. He took this on without batting an eye, for by now
we had a decent cash flow, a ready market and a bank manager
still on side.

As I was writing this in 1994, trying to explain the unique sort
of game we were playing, with no credit rating, but compliance
by printers who didn't demand cash up front, and a bank

"Our set-up", with Gray, John Barclay, Eleanor, Tim and dog Ketchup. (PHOTO BY DANE CAMPBELL)

willing to back our ideas, I had a chat with an old acquaintance, Alice Munro.

"When Jim and I started our first bookstore on Yates Street in 1963," she said, "you were a bit of a puzzle, the first B.C. publisher. We figured you must have had unlimited backing."

Jim Munro must have wondered at times why I was so anxious to collect our invoices so quickly. Only Bill Duthie knew or suspected that we were flying by the seat of our pants for I remember Binkie saying that Bill had instructed him to see that we were paid first. We had to play our cards mighty close to our chest because if the chill wind of suspicion had revealed the thin hand we were holding, our growing list of titles might have been in jeopardy. There were a few times when John Barclay, who knew our ticklish financial position, had to handle embarrassing telephone calls at home in the evening from printers who had started to worry about being paid. He had managed to buy us time and, bless his heart, to keep me in the dark.

242 BUTTER SIDE UP

Since those precarious years for us both, Jim Munro has slowly but firmly established himself as a leading bookman in one of the best literary areas of Canada, helping to fill the gap left by the death of Bill Duthie.

The threat of crashing failed to stop us or slow us down and I must have had a suicidal tendency, after the war years, to continue taking risks. When Alex Bulman wrote that he had put together a history of the Kamloops cattle industry from its beginning a hundred years ago, I felt that this son of a pioneer had something of value to say. He had lived through cattle ranching's greatest days.

After reading his manuscript I asked John Shaw, the eminent journalist, to look it over; he agreed that it was worthy of publishing but thought Alex needed to work on his draft.

"I won't write it for him," John said, "but I'm willing to show him where he should rewrite, and advise him."

They hit it off as I was confident they would and the book was published in 1972 with a collection of valuable photographs and a good press which received the work with respect.

It was a heady year, 1971, as each week brought mail and telephone calls with tempting ideas. One had to judge quickly and, without a doubt, we made mistakes. I nearly failed to make the right decision when, without warning or appointment, a man appeared to talk about his project. His manner was diffident and he had his guard up, as if he was expecting rejection. He had made an exhaustive study of Indian rock carvings and petroglyph sites from the American border to Alaska, and had photographs and sketches to back up his interpretations and acute observations.

I could not comment on the value of the work but felt that he deserved more than a brushed-off polite rejection. I decided to consult Wilson Duff, a well-known professor of anthropology and sociology at the University of British Columbia, so I asked the author to leave it with me and took his full name and address. He lived in Campbell River and I carefully wrote down his name, Edward F. Meade; then I looked up. Had he been in the war? He had. By any chance had he written a book called *Remember Me*? Yes, he had, he said almost shyly and I managed to draw out an unusual war anecdote. After I told him I had a copy of his book which I had read in the 1940s, and that it had affected me as much as *All Quiet on the Western Front*, he related the curious circumstances of its survival.

He had been a platoon commander in a tank transporter outfit and had started scribbling an outline of his story between battles, completing it towards the end of the war. Somehow he had it typed and submitted to a publisher in London. Eventually, he received a letter which at first raised his hopes, and then dashed them. Faber and Faber were interested, but they wanted to meet the author in London before proceeding further.

Ed Meade was sitting by himself on a bridge overlooking a river in Normandy during a lull in the advance, feeling utterly dejected, with the letter in his pocket. A jeep rumbled over the bridge, and stopped. Ed didn't look up. It was General Montgomery on reconnaissance and he called out, asking what the matter was. Meade told him about the book and the letter, and how he was going to lose an opportunity. Monty took his name and unit, then drove on. A few days later Ed Meade was yanked from his unit and given a space on a Dakota going to England. He saw his publisher and was back with his unit in a few days. Just like that. Of course, it was in the dying months of the war, but it illustrates that the general who became Field Marshal Viscount Montgomery, K.G., had another side to his military character. *Remember Me* was published by Faber and Faber in 1946, reprinted by the Reprint Society in Canada and published in paperback by McClelland and Stewart.

Wilson Duff heartily endorsed the Meade manuscript on Indian rock carvings and graciously wrote a foreword which stated that the man who had founded the Campbell River Historical Museum, taken a particular interest in the Kwakiutl Indians and travelled up and down the coast collecting artifacts as curator, had some interesting things to say about the subject.

We decided to publish it and handed the job to Gerry Siebert and Evergreen Press in Vancouver whose designer, the late Ed Harrison, recommended a large format to highlight the drawings. Ed Meade was delighted when his book, *Indian Rock Carvings*, appeared in 1971 and he took bus loads of interested students to sites around Cape Mudge. This helped increase respect for the preservation of these ancient records. We were surprised and delighted when a photograph and account appeared in the Campbell River paper, showing the mayor at that time presenting a copy of Ed Meade's book to Queen Elizabeth on one of her visits.

In 1970 Miles and Beryl Smeeton, the internationally known yachting couple, had their famous boat *Tzu Hang* tied to the dock in Deep Cove and were guests of the Barclays. As a result we saw quite a bit of the Smeetons, and Miles often dropped around while John and I were working. One day he suggested that we might be able to work with his publisher in the United Kingdom. After quite a bit of correspondence and many telephone calls the Miles Smeeton epic ... *because the Horn is there...* was published simultaneously with Nautical Publishing Company Limited in England, our edition being run on with theirs to our financial advantage. Thus we were able to take over the American market, adding this successful author to our growing list.

The success of this venture brought us other titles from Nautical which included Smeeton's *The Sea Was Our Village*, Bill Tilman's *Ice With Everything* and Roger Chapman's *No Time On Our Side*.

We continued to be intrigued by letters, manuscripts and publishing ideas often picked up from bookstore owners, teachers and bibliophiles. A letter from Dolores Cline Brown caught our attention. She had ventured into the Yukon from Olympia, Washington, married big-game outfitter and guide Louis Brown and was the first white woman to explore the big-game trails of the Yukon. Living in a remote cabin through long winters, when many suffered cabin fever, she had written and sold articles about her adventures to *Outdoor Life*, *Field & Stream* and *Alaska Sportsman*.

Now we had her first, full-length book, packed with action, breathtaking adventure and original dialogue. She had an ear for colloquialism, good timing and the ability to draw characters and scenery to satisfy the appetite of any armchair adventurer. Charlie Morriss agreed with me and we went to work.

The book was a success but we learned another lesson. By this time we had standing orders with many buyers who accepted a modest shipment of any title we produced. We started this after one large wholesaler in Vancouver said he could sell any book that had our imprint. (It was an embarrassing moment for he said it in front of several reps from Toronto, decent, fair-minded and hard-working chaps. He was trying to pull their legs.) But it gave me the idea to build up a standing order list.

Now it was our turn to have our ears pinned back, with a first-class put-down. We had shipped out the usual standing orders of *Yukon Trophy Trails* by Dolores Cline Brown and several orders were returned so quickly for credit that we wondered what on earth could be wrong with such a promising package. The writing style was bound to captivate the average sportsman so obviously the stores in question had not bothered to read the book.

Our mistake had been the dust jacket; never, ever show a dead animal! The photograph on the front cover displayed the author dismounted, reaching out to make sure the wolf she had shot was properly dispatched. On the back cover she was sitting astride a bull moose with a trophy head and it was quite dead. Dolores had related instances of wolves entering their compound during extremely cold weather and starting to eat the legs of live pack-horses which were huddled rigidly, half-frozen. But we learned the hard way that dead animals on dust jackets were strictly a taboo.

We were by this time battle-hardened, scarred veterans almost ready to face the greatest, nail-biting challenge in our pioneer book-publishing experience. In recalling this stage in our development, like the war years, we mercifully only want to remember the lighter moments. For starters, we would quite likely have had an easier, lazier time to relax and waffle if it had not been for George Pownall, who quite innocently started a chain of events.

Chapter Eleven

WE WOULD never have met George and Terry Pownall if it had not been for Mary Gibbs who had intrigued us with stories of Tofino and Long Beach, convincing us that we would never know the real west coast unless we had visited this lotus land. Mary Gibbs had known Long Beach in the old days, when access was by sailing from Port Alberni in the old Uchuck, and was lyrical in her description. We simply had to make the trip and Mary set about arranging it. Late in March 1964, the old Rover 90 took us to Port Alberni where we paused. The roads past there were unfinished gravel trails with hairpin twists, switchbacks and over-hangs, but we had an option.

If one did not feel up to tackling the drive, there was a bus of sorts that made the run over the trail with mail and supplies. We debated whether we should park the Rover by the hotel in Port Alberni and take the bus, or try the road ourselves. We weren't sure where we were staying. Mary had telephoned ahead for accommodation and Peg Whittington's Singing Sands was fully occupied but we were to stop there and she would direct us on to a friend. So we started out with the Rover, spare tire and a full tank of gas, finding out that if we could handle the mountainous logging roads when the big trucks weren't running, we could reach the coast in three to four hours.

The directions at Singing Sands brought us to the domain of George and Terry Pownall who owned some 170 acres, including all of wild Chesterman's Beach in its pristine state. The main buildings, with a two-room cottage, were inland across the coast road, and a rough trail through the woods led to the beach. It was the perfect setting for an escape; Chesterman's Beach was completely private with no access for vehicles and we had it to ourselves.

George Pownall had roots in our area of North Saanich, having grown up on a farm that is now part of Victoria International Airport. He and Terry had escaped to this wonderful paradise, living in harmony with nature in what George called "Wit's End" which pretty well expressed his original, quirky sense of humour. They made us feel right at home and opened our eyes to all the beauty spots and history of the Long Beach area. George had a scientific, enquiring mind and was a tolerant critic with a voracious appetite for literature but cynical enough to put a curb on my own wild enthusiasms. He enjoyed a wide circle of educated friends who shared his outlook on literature and life; with one psychiatrist buddy he was trying to organize a future in which they could buy a second-hand bookshop that was well stocked where they could lock the door and get some reading done.

At "Wit's End". L. to r.: Cathy, Terry Pownall, Eleanor, Mary Gibbs, George Pownall.

Terry settled us in the little cottage, explained the trails to the beach and then went to the main house to fetch George. I thought the best way to get better acquainted was to ask them if they would like a glass of sherry, standard practice in book publishing, which caused George to confess, later, that he decided to classify me as an amiable lush. It was the start of a growing friendship that soon included our Cathy and the boys and many return visits.

Comfortably settled in our cottage, we turned in early and slept peacefully through the quiet night. It was March 27, 1964, when the earthquake hit Alaska about 5:30 that evening. George, on duty at the Coast Guard station, called Terry from Tofino with the news and told her to stand by in case we should have to evacuate to higher ground in a hurry. The tsunami passed through while we slept, but roared up the Alberni Canal and devastated the lower part of town where we would have parked the car.

When the highway was completed a few years later, it brought in waves of tourists, followed by developers, until Chesterman's Beach began to show signs of wear; the marks of racing rubber, driftwood shelters, beach fires and, unfortunately, garbage. George decided to sell his holdings and move back to our still-unspoiled North Saanich neighbourhood.

In November 1966 we moved into our two acres, while George and Terry left Wit's End and returned to the Sidney area. They decided that they would like to buy the little cottage that we had just vacated, which was a welcome surprise, and helped us over the financial problems of the move. This brought us closer together, for George was an excellent book critic, while Terry often assisted us in the office. They became close friends of the Barclays too and were well versed in all our publishing undertakings.

We were all sitting on the deck of our home overlooking the inlet one summer afternoon, drawing out the Pownall wit and wisdom on the state of the world, when George changed the subject. He thought we would all enjoy meeting an old friend who needed some advice on book publishing, and though his project would not fit our list we might be able to suggest whom he should approach. We were politely curious and learned that Lew Clark, a retired professor of chemistry at the University of Victoria, had spent a lifetime on botanical studies and had completed a work on the wildflowers of British Columbia. My interest in botany has never been awakened, but Eleanor and both Barclays are terribly keen and were curious to see what the professor had done with the subject. So George laid it on and our quiet, rural environment was never quite the same again.

Dr. Lewis J. Clark, a perfectly charming gentleman, came to us for a first visit with an exciting collection of transparencies of flowering plants together with scholarly yet appealing literary descriptions that lifted the work into a new dimension. We learned that he was just as well known as an accomplished photographer, having exhibited and served as judge in international salons. That had been one of his problems, because he had taken the manuscript and photographs to Yale University Press and to Italy, but was never satisfied with the quality of the colour. The longer he talked about the project and his patience and exploration over 45 years, the more he inspired everyone to help him succeed. Not one of us could guess what such a job would amount to, but we had to say something encouraging and I suggested he leave it with us and we would enquire. It was fairly obvious that Lew Clark had something only a person with international connections could advise us on. The only person I knew was Gerry Siebert, our German colleague at Evergreen Press; he had worked with many publishers and regularly attended the Frankfurt International Book Fair to negotiate translations and rights for several large firms.

By this time Gerry was an old friend who came over every month to see how we were doing. I asked him what he remembered of those days. "It was in 1972 when you first talked about the wildflower book project," he wrote. "It was to contain about 250 color plates on 500 pages or so. I was very enthusiastic since the quality of the transparencies was outstanding and there was no book with this subject on the market. I also knew that both Oxford University Press and Macmillan had looked at wildflower books of the Northwest and given up on them since they would have to sell in the $60.00 range, given the retail markup on a short print run of 3,000 copies."

His enthusiasm grew as he studied the quality of the work and he began to believe it "might really fly eventually." He took the manuscript to the plant and started to develop a theoretical production schedule for a 1973 publishing date. Glen Hyatt and Fred Thompson, the colour man, were impressed and Fred started to make some test separations in his spare time. Lew Clark made several trips to Evergreen and was thrilled with the quality of Thompson's work. This created the impression in the plant that they had a real live project. Gerry kept the illusion going by firing off endless memos to the point where he projected a print order of 10,000 copies. One memo went by the desk of Chuck Rittel, the purchasing agent, who felt he should hurry to close a good deal on paper that was available from Holland at the time. We began to worry when Gerry said they had already spent $20,000 on paper in addition to the colour work.

Gerry went on, "Naturally neither you, Eleanor or John had any idea what was happening. One day I closed the door to my little office at Homer Street and tallied what we had spent on the non-existing wildflower book, which came to $37,000 not counting the paper which was on its way to Vancouver via the Panama Canal. It was now time to confess and I went to see Glen Hyatt. Glen told me to be on the next ferry and not to come back unless I had an order! I told Glen it was not that you didn't want to publish the book, it was a question of raising the money. He said to just work it out with you. A sleepless night and the ferry trip made me come up with a battle plan to make sure you would accept the project [so that] Evergreen Press would get paid and you would even make some money the first time around." (I remember Gerry complaining several times that we

Evergreen Press reunion, 1994 . L. to r.: Gerry Siebert, Chuck Rittel, Glen Hyatt, Gray, Roald Dahl.

had to stop Lew from running over to the plant for he was bringing Fred Thompson more transparencies to add to the text.) "The book had now grown into 573 color plates and some 756 pages. The price tag was now $112,000 or so."

Gerry, with his international experience in marketing, had a "battle plan" to use some of the existing separations and turn out a *Reader's Digest* style, book-club promotional brochure implying that the book existed. He would produce a 16-page, full-size booklet with an index and samples of the scholarly text. We could mail this out with a covering letter designed to pre-sell the work in three categories: to industries as Patrons, with a special insert; a specially bound, numbered, limited edition in leather for individuals ($125); and a regular trade edition. The trade book would sell in stores at $24.95.

Gerry's projection meant there would be no huge profit for Gray's, but the book was priced to sell its large run successfully, compared to Oxford and Macmillan's projection of a short run selling at $60 a copy. John and I were very aware of our obligations. We were in a tight corner with little room to manoeuvre and I felt personally responsible for getting us into this situation. Nervously, I signed the order. Gerry packed up and hurried back to Vancouver, able to sleep again as the ball was now in our court. This is what he wrote about the incident: "I guess my career would have ended at that point if the 16-page booklet had not worked and Glen Hyatt had to pay the extra $12,000 or so for that project!"

John and I worked furiously, mailing that brochure out to everyone we could think of and it really was a touch of class. There was no turning back, or aborting the target as we used to say in Bomber Command. We pulled out all the stops and turned desperately in every direction for help, telephoning friends, making up mailing lists and asking everyone for help. *The Daily Colonist* came up with headlines on August 2, 1972, to announce that we were launching the biggest venture of our career, after publishing 30 books in ten years. They said we were printing 10,000 copies and already had orders for about $40,000 but intimated that we were asking for cultural grants so that we could sell the book at $24.95. Gerry estimated that the brochure had pre-sold 3,000 copies and while this was going on, an excited Lew Clark was often in Vancouver, breathing over the shoulder of coordinators like John Houghton, taking some of the pressure off good old Gerry. Back at the barn we were elated by word that

The Canada Council and the University of Victoria were coming
through with financial assistance, our first-ever grants. John
Barclay felt that this was the backing we needed to keep the
retail price firm at $24.95.

On August 24, 1973, Gerry mailed me a package with a short
note, sending the "very first copy . . . with best wishes and
congratulations on this outstanding publishing venture." That
called for a launching party and in the fall there was a great
gathering at the Barclays' waterfront home in Deep Cove. Glen
Hyatt arrived by seaplane, as excited as any of us, and made a
graceful speech pointing out that a breakthrough in book
publishing was happening, right here in Deep Cove. Dr. Clark
made his speech to a crowd of old friends and former colleagues
from an easy chair with his wife, Lorraine, standing by his side.
It was no secret that he had a heart condition. We had discovered it when he often hurried up the hill to tell Eleanor something exciting; before he could talk to her he would pop a nitro
pill in his mouth and catch his breath.

John Barclay had been busy as a beaver, setting up a special
"wildflower" account for the sales that Gerry's brochure would
generate. We had cast a wide net which was bringing in special
orders from patrons like the Province of British Columbia,
MacMillan Bloedel Limited, Finning Tractor & Equipment Co.
Ltd., and B.C. Hydro and Power Authority. We had reasoned
that they owed it to the wildflowers, having destroyed their
share. Among the most satisfactory highlights was the news from
Gerry that it was Bill Duthie's best seller at Christmas. He sold
400 copies, which meant we were starting to repay Bill for his
early faith in us and his unlimited encouragement. Evergreen
Press was expecting that we might be able to pay their account
some time in the middle of 1974, but John and I went over to
Vancouver in January with a cheque in full payment of the
amount owing. Now it was our turn to sleep more easily. Glen
and another executive took us out to lunch but I can only recall
being in a daze, wondering how much of it was real.

Gerry's blood pressure must have improved by then but his
greatest reward came later when he appeared at the Frankfurt
International Book Fair representing several North American
firms on behalf of Evergreen. It is best told in his own words:

The final highpoint of the Wildflower Book project
came when I stood at the Canadian Ambassador's reception

in raindrenched pants in Frankfurt when the Ambassador pronounced your book as the most important Canadian book in the English language. I was in seventh heaven and relished watching all the Toronto bigshots from Prentice Hall, Macmillan, Oxford etc. to Jack McClelland. It was absolutely wonderful and I don't know why I didn't phone ...

The selection had been made by the Canadian Book Publishers Council. Evergreen jumped on the publicity with a special newsletter for the Montreal International Book Fair in 1975 which claimed that the largest publishing venture ever undertaken in western Canada had such a stunning success that 10,000 copies had been sold within 12 months.

Personally, I was too dazed by events to remember much of this but somehow, between Lew Clark, the indefatigable Gerry and ourselves, we came up with the possibility of using the most popular colour plates from the book to create six pocket-sized guidebooks that students could afford and take into the field. They were *Forest and Woodland, Field and Slope, Marsh and Waterway, The Sea Coast, The Arid Flatlands* and *The Mountains*.

Dr. Clark set to work enthusiastically, extending his range to include all of the Pacific Northwest. He had completed the first two, and had outlined the remaining four, when the dear man's heart gave up and the project came to a stop. Then, with Mrs. Clark's encouragement, we decided to complete the series in his memory and turned to a mutual friend in Deep Cove, John Trelawny of the Department of Biology, University of Victoria.

In 1975 the series came out to an eager response from the public. We printed 20,000 copies of each for a total of 120,000. It was our turn to look for a profit that had not been included in the big book. It had paid for the colour separations, the largest part of the cost in this operation. They continue to sell and the last time I looked, 180,000 copies were in print.

Chapter Twelve

WHILE THE miracle of the wildflower book was running its erratic course, another event began to develop with a letter from a chap in the Yukon. Writing from Whitehorse, Allen Wright stated that a group of writers was discussing the possibility of setting up a regional publishing enterprise like ours and asked, if representatives came to Victoria, would it be possible to get together for advice. Our reply was to the effect they'd be welcome, and if we did not have all the answers, perhaps we could point out some of the problems they may have to face. After a few more letters, there was a telephone call from Allen who had arrived in Victoria from Whitehorse, alone.

We were pretty busy at the time and since the cottage where Sarain had stayed was temporarily empty, we put him up as our guest for a few days so he could follow John, Tim and me in our daily round and catch the rhythm of our routine. Eleanor offered to welcome him at our table for he was genial and interesting. By the end of the week he had absorbed all we could tell him. He had also been left alone in the evenings to spend hours studying our files, accounting procedures, contracts and daily trivia. When I suggested that he had completed the course, he asked if he could stay on through the week-end, after which he treated himself to a stay at the Empress Hotel before returning north.

Eventually a manuscript turned up, a surprisingly well-researched, fascinating account of the exploration of the Yukon before the discovery of gold that started the stampede, written by Allen Wright. It seemed that the group who had originally sought to do their own regional publishing had not been able to come to terms with the problem. Allen was relying on us.

With our growing list selling steadily and the wildflower book over its crisis, Eleanor and I felt in need of a little holiday. If we were to take the work of Allen Wright seriously, we felt we should visit the Yukon for a better appreciation of its importance. We wrote to Allen, booked a flight in the fall of 1973 and took off for an exciting ten days. The weather could not have been more perfect and Allen gave us a royal tour of his beloved Yukon, at least within driving distance of Whitehorse.

The fall colours in shimmering sunlight showed that beautiful country at its best. We explored Miles Canyon and Carcross, and drove as far south as Atlin with stops to meet Allen's friends who extended the legendary spirit of the Yukon. At Marsh Lake we met Jim and Flo Whyard; she is a well-known editor and journalist who was also active in local politics. Eleanor surprised the Yukoners by changing in the Whyard cottage and slipping alone into the frigid water for a cool, 45-degree swim. We also explored on our own with picnics on hot, sunny days along rivers and lakes whose sometimes unusual names had caused Allen Wright, as an engineer, to enquire into their sources. From this research he wrote his magnificent work *Prelude to Bonanza* but it took this trip into the country for us to realize its worth.

In Whitehorse Allen took us around to meet bookstore people, newspaper editors and the commissioner. When I mentioned to the latter that the first commissioner, William Ogilvie, was a distant cousin of mine who had died the year I was born, he handed me an antique glass paperweight with Ogilvie's name inscribed. I actually thought he was going to present it to me and handed it back very slowly, hoping that at the last second it might occur to him. Ogilvie had originally surveyed the Yukon-Alaska boundary with primitive instruments set up on tree stumps, working in extremely cold weather in 1887. When his results were checked years later by United States engineers, the error was remarkably small.

The Ogilvie saga was only a part of the broad canvas that Wright had created. A native of Toronto, Allen had completed a year at Queen's University when war broke out in 1939. He served six years overseas with a Canadian field survey company, Royal Canadian Engineers. After the war he resolved to see more of his own country and in the summer of 1946 reached the Yukon Territory where he engaged in survey and construction projects. Eventually he became a consultant involved with highway location and design which took him to remote, unpopulated areas, often with sketchy maps, and these made him curious enough to start his research.

Before returning to Sidney we discussed Allen's valuable government and business connections. On the strength of the experience we had gained from Gerry Siebert over the development of the wildflowers project, we had the author pull out all the stops to pre-sell *Prelude to Bonanza* so that when the book was printed in 1976, there was a special page acknowledging the assistance of The Canada Council, Cassiar Asbestos Mining, Cyprus Anvil Mining, EPEC Consulting Western, General Enterprises, Government of the Yukon Territory, Imperial Oil, the Royal Bank, Trans North Turbo Air, United Keno Hill Mines, White Pass & Yukon Route and the Yukon Electric Company. Before we departed, the Whyards invited us to their home for dinner and an evening of spirited conversation from which I gathered that Flo was an enthusiastic booster of Allen's Yukon history and I suspect she helped line up the list of patrons.

We took the manuscript to Charlie Morriss who decided it deserved a deluxe edition and treated it with the same care and respect that he had given to the Clutesi, Stump and Luxton classics. The design, from dust cover to ink, paper and maps, could be placed beside books produced in London, New York or Toronto so we decided to give it a royal launching. Wednesday, October 13, 1976, we had a reception at the Empress Hotel to introduce the author of *Prelude to Bonanza*, sending out invitations printed by the Morriss firm. In addition to booksellers and the press, quite a few old Yukon friends turned up and to Allen's delight so did Gerald Smedley Andrews, M.C., who had been an officer in his company of engineers overseas, and later the Surveyor General of British Columbia.

Two days later, on October 15, *The Vancouver Sun* featured a superb review by none other than Alan Morley, the respected but crusty critic who had given *The Salmon People* such a bad time. Morley had given the Wright book a startling headline "Tales To Stand Your Hair On End" which set the tone for other papers. Wain King in Ottawa mentioned that the book seemed at times almost contemporary because the author let the history-makers speak out for themselves. Some time later the book got Allen Wright on television's "Front Page Challenge" and we were fascinated to hear Pierre Berton declare it a masterful work. We were well content with the result.

When we returned from the Yukon there were decisions to make. Instead of reprinting the big wildflower book, John Trelawny and Lorraine Clark had been working with the rest of Dr. Clark's material on a plan to bring out *Wild Flowers of the Pacific Northwest*, to include species from Alaska to northern California. Gerry Siebert was giving it an enthusiastic boost and the University of Washington offered to join in the venture. I know he was very disappointed when I failed to respond, letting Evergreen do a print run of 5,000 copies when all the signs indicated another positive success. It was probably the first sign that I was running out of steam.

While I was waffling, wondering how to ease up on the pressure, Eleanor and others continued reacting to ideas like volunteer firemen to a siren. In the spring of 1977 Eleanor was working in the kitchen with the radio on to C.B.C. Vancouver's early morning news, weather and chat. Her attention was drawn to an indignant voice phoning from Duncan because ignorant people were continually calling Matthew Baillie Begbie the "Hanging Judge" when, in fact, he was a brilliant, considerate and caring jurist. The voice belonged to a Duncan lawyer by the name of David Williams who said he had been researching Begbie's life and was prepared to prove it with a book he was writing.

Eleanor reacted by scribbling down the details, handing the note to me and insisting that I telephone Williams immediately before anyone else could, to ask if he had a publisher. I did just that, somewhat surprised at my wife's sudden interest in a radio talk show. Shortly after that we drove to Duncan to meet David Williams and over lunch talked about adding this to our B.C. list. David, Queen's Counsel, a former bencher of the B.C. Law Society and former member of the U.B.C. Board of Governors, was a busy man. We had meetings in Sidney and followed him to a court case in Nanaimo, with extra meetings at Morriss Printing where Charlie and Dick realized the importance of this work. David had spent several years in research, including a sabbatical from his practice to track his evidence about Begbie from Peterhouse College, Cambridge, to the Bancroft Library at Berkeley. The care that everyone took in the design, illustrations and printing at Morriss left me wondering if Charlie had a feeling this might be our last effort together.

"...*The Man For A New Country*": *Sir Matthew Baillie Begbie* appeared in the fall of 1977 and drew both great reviews and tributes to the scholarship of the author. In 1978 it was awarded the University of British Columbia Medal for Canadian Biography. David Williams went on to research other legal subjects, became writer-in-residence at the University of Victoria, and began turning out other interesting titles.

Chapter Thirteen

AFTER THE unexpected successes of the venture into the wild-flower books, followed by Wright's Yukon odyssey and then the definitive biography of Begbie, we began taking a cautious look at the future. Once again we were being forced into growing a mite too big for our britches. The work seemed to be pinning us down.

John, Tim and I had been discussing moves since 1973 when we were desperate for space. We had even made enquiries about leasing land at the airport to build an office and warehouse. Now, in 1977, we had a more serious decision to make. John Barclay deserved more time for his fishing and hunting but it was Tim we were concerned about. He had given us eight hard, loyal years at a minimum wage and we were well aware that he was keen to cut loose and try something on his own. Eleanor was the first to realize it. I think we also felt that the innocent days of pioneering in book publishing had run their course; others were coming on the scene to pick up the action, in particular J.J. Douglas Ltd., later to lead the field as Douglas & McIntyre. Finally I wrote to old friend and mentor Jim Douglas, telling him about our problem and asking for advice before we made any move that might concern bookstore people and the media. Jim Douglas had all the experience to develop his firm beyond regional publishing and I believe today that I secretly felt he was the only one who could keep our list alive.

Jim's quick reply was to the effect that he would discuss it with Scott McIntyre, then come over to see us. I went to Glen Hyatt for his opinion and said I hoped that a British Columbia publisher like Jim Douglas could take over. Before long, letters and enquiries began to trickle in so the moccasin telegraph must have been working while we continued to keep busy.

There was a telephone call from Campbell River and the surprising voice of Jack McClelland who asked if we could meet in Sidney. I think he had been visiting Roderick Haig-Brown. John and I met him in Sidney and after lunch brought him out to see the set-up in the barn and then to meet Eleanor and talk privately at the house. Some time after this I had a telephone call from Robin Farr who said he had had lunch in Toronto with Jack McClelland who had apparently found our little firm so attractive he wanted Farr to move out here and run it. The lid had come off the confidential can, for enquiries began coming in from law firms, larger publishers, and the president of Sterling Newspapers, and Tim received an interesting letter asking for more details from the vice-president of Harlequin Enterprises.

When it boiled down to the bottom line, reality showed us that we had been running on air, as Barry Broadfoot put it, a mixture of sentiment, good will and ideals that suited the period. While we thought our track record made a good start to build upon, the hard nose of business recognized only the value of our inventory, checking on the standards, the best sellers, and the slower books that still had a declining market as remainders. I could not believe that so many of these were considered over the hill or had played out their shelf life. As I write this, in 1994, nine of those old standards have been republished and are selling briskly. Five firms in British Columbia and one in the Yukon have found that another generation is discovering them.

In the meantime Tim was looking after things with the help of friends from his school days while John took time off. Eleanor and I invested in a fifth-wheel trailer and took some tryout trips around the province, fairly itching to explore Canada.

When nothing concrete came up to our expectations for selling, we left the business in the hands of a team consisting of people who had been connected with younger firms and wanted to branch out. While Tim kept an eye on this, Eleanor and I took off with the fifth-wheel and a new vehicle, looking up old friends and spending up to a month in each province, including Prince Edward Island and Newfoundland. On our way back, we telephoned home from a spot on the St. Lawrence near Ogdensburg. Tim advised us to keep going, if we wished, as everything was in order, so we headed south. Avoiding cities and built-up freeways, we drifted aimlessly through rural America in timeless bliss, south to the Mexican border, west to California and lazily home, reaching Deep Cove after ten months or so. During all the miles, provinces and states, we never had a single unpleasant experience, and when we parked in our own driveway we spent the next few nights on board the trailer, nervous about having to cope with a big house again.

After nearly a year of complete freedom from the clock, it took us some time to get back into suburban routine. The firm had carried on and had published a few titles that had suited our list, and a few that had not. They were now employing extra people to do invoicing and shipping, bookkeeping, typing and all the jobs that three of us used to cope with. Sales were keeping up, but the overhead was rising and at our age, after that glorious freedom and travel, we didn't want to get involved again.

The office moved closer to Victoria and the staff kept changing. I don't wish to dwell upon all the details but sadly, gradually, Gray's Publishing ceased to exist. Some books were remaindered and we would see them in discount stores; some went out of print while the steady sellers were picked up by firms such as Douglas & McIntyre and Whitecap Books. By this time there were dozens of regional publishers springing up in British Columbia and Alberta, coming up with some very worthwhile books, so our talented writers were well taken care of.

Before I could start feeling sorry for myself and the little firm we had started, I had a telephone call from the Bank of Montreal in Sidney. Daphne Coney invited us to her waterfront home because, she said, her husband wanted to meet us. It transpired that Mike Coney, an accountant, worked for the British Columbia Forest Service as a financial analyst, but his hobby was science fiction and he had been writing short stories, then novels. When we met him he had had published 14 books, which had been selected for awards and translations into French, German, Spanish, Dutch, Italian, Norwegian and Japanese. He was practically unknown in Canada except for science fiction aficionados.

Now he had written a history of the men of the Forest Service, their wooden ships and their tales of valour, tragedy and humour since the service's inception in 1911. Mike intended to start his own publishing firm to get his book out the way he wanted, and to use it as a hobby for others he might write until he reached retirement. We told him how we had started, the problems he would face and some of the corners he might cut. The rest of the evening was spent hearing how the Coneys had managed an ancient pub in Devon, and a night club in the Caribbean before coming to Canada.

Mike went ahead and registered Porthole Press Ltd., designed a logo and had letterheads printed. Then he invited us around and handed us shares and copies of the official stationery. The letterhead showed that I was now president, Eleanor a director, Mike managing director and Daphne secretary! A handsomely designed, illustrated hardcover *Forest Ranger, Ahoy!* came out in 1983. It was the beginning of an interesting association and a developing friendship that led to projects where I could use Mike's business experience and set-up to continue lending a hand to others without feeling any pressure.

Old associates kept in touch and occasionally we might hear from a veritable stranger whom we had casually encouraged to keep on writing west-coast memoirs. Things began to happen when Bethine Flynn wrote from Seattle. She is the widow of veterinary surgeon Dr. Wallace Flynn, author of *The Flying Flynns*, about his work taking his skills to outlying settlements between Seattle and Alaska. Years after we had exchanged letters about her project, she wrote again to thank me and asked if I could suggest a Canadian publisher, because she had written an account of her experience trying to live alone on the remote west-coast island that she and Wally had loved. The people she had approached in the United States were not interested in the Canadian wilderness or her friends the Indians and missionaries.

I suggested she send it to us so Eleanor and I could read it before recommending anyone. That was the start of a warm association with Bethine who continued her friendship with the natives and missionaries from Nuchatlitz and Ahousat. On her visits she would call on us and we were so charmed with her manuscript we not only had Mike read it, but on the strength of unqualified enthusiasm Mike began to figure out how we could publish it.

Flynn's Cove was the first title by Porthole Press after *Forest Ranger, Ahoy!*, designed, typeset and printed under Mike's management. It was published in 1986 and is still selling to a widening market.

About the same time Nell Horth dropped by to ask for advice with her plan to attempt a memoir of the early families and her young days in North Saanich, where we live. Nell and Brownie Horth had been our first neighbours and while Brownie was a laid-back, comfortable old-timer, Nell was a doer and fixer.

There was no one more suitable to write about the early days in Deep Cove and North Saanich; the only trouble was that Nell was into her eighties, with arthritic hands which prevented her from typing, barely able to scribble with a stubby pencil. Eleanor decided it was a perfect retirement project for me so after a few telephone calls, Nell brought to the house her hand-written pages of notes and I started typing. She had photographs, lists of pioneer families, scrapbook memorabilia and some wonderful personal anecdotes. Eleanor had also been accumulating pioneer notes which helped Nell and whenever I felt frustrated or began to flag in seeing this to completion, it was Eleanor who cranked me up again.

Then we had to convince Mike that it would be good public relations to add this to the Porthole list and he bravely under-took the final editing, layout and an attractive cover for *North Saanich Memories and Pioneers* by Nell Horth. It gave the author a great deal of pleasure and when she died shortly afterward, a sudden victim of cancer, she left the book to Eleanor and me in her will. It is still selling quietly, of interest to the influx of new settlers and visitors fascinated by the history of North Saanich.

Porthole Press was kept throttled down, for while Mike and I both enjoyed designing and publishing the manuscripts that interested us, we did not want it to get out of hand and involve us in the hassle of promoting, warehousing and selling. The basement in Mike's house had limited space for storage.

I continued to have fun helping O.B. Philp develop his history of the Snowbirds, the Royal Canadian Air Force aerobatic squadron, old-time friend and pioneer Bea Bond with her book *Looking Back on James Island* and Jack Watson with *Yukon Memories*. The publishers who revived *The Curve of Time* and R.M. Patterson's titles had me write forewords for the books, and then this assignment came along.

It has taken many drafts, frantic searching for dates and sleep-less nights trying to fill in the memory gaps, for all our files and records were sold to the University of Victoria. When I discov-ered this I also learned they would not be catalogued for some time. Putting this account together under these circumstances has been both fun and hard work, trying to get it right. It leaves me, at 82, still feeling many years younger for the exercise, with much to look forward to and anticipate.

Like the swim in Deep Cove I plan to enjoy with Eleanor when I shut down Ian's computer.

* * *

INDEX